vSphere High Performance Cookbook

Over 60 recipes to help you improve vSphere performance
and solve problems before they arise

Prasenjit Sarkar

[PACKT] enterprise 🏵
PUBLISHING   professional expertise distilled

BIRMINGHAM - MUMBAI

vSphere High Performance Cookbook

First published: July 2013

Production Reference: 1220713

Published by Packt Publishing Ltd.
Livery Place
35 Livery Street
Birmingham B3 2PB, UK.

ISBN 978-1-78217-000-6

www.packtpub.com

Cover Image by Francesco Langiulli (langy86@gmail.com)

Credits

Author
Prasenjit Sarkar

Reviewers
Andy Grant
Craig Risinger
Brian Wuchner

Acquisition Editors
Vinay Agrekar
Andrew Duckworth

Lead Technical Editor
Anila Vincent

Technical Editors
Arvind Koul
Saumya Kunder
Vaibhav Pawar
Larissa Pinto

Project Coordinator
Hardik Patel

Proofreader
Dirk Manuel

Indexer
Tejal Daruwale

Graphics
Disha Haria

Production Coordinator
Aditi Gajjar

Cover Work
Aditi Gajjar

About the Author

Prasenjit Sarkar (@stretchcloud) is a senior member of the technical staff in VMware Service Provider Cloud R&D, where he provides architectural oversight and technical guidance for the design, implementation, and testing of VMware's Cloud datacenters.

He is an author, R&D guy, and a blogger, focusing on Virtualization, Cloud Computing, Storage, Networking, and other enterprise technologies.

He has more than 10 years of expert knowledge in R&D/Professional Services/Alliances/ Solution Engineering/Consulting, and Technical Sales, with expertise in Architecting and Deploying Virtualization Solutions, and rolling out new technology and solution initiatives.

His primary focus is on VMware vSphere Infrastructure and Public Cloud, using VMware vCloud Suite.One of his other focuses is to own the entire life cycle of a VMware based IaaS (SDDC), specially, vSphere, vCloud Director, vShield Manager, and vCenter Operations. He is one of the VMware vExperts in 2012 and 2013 as well, and is well known for his acclaimed Virtualization Blog http://stretch-cloud.info.

He holds certifications from VMware, Cisco, Citrix, RedHat, Microsoft, IBM, HP, and Exin.

Prior to joining VMware, Prasenjit has served in other fine organizations (such as Capgemini, HP, and GE.) as Solution Architect and Infrastructure Architect.

I would like to thank and dedicate this book to my family, my mom, dad, and my lovely wife Lipika. Without their endless and untiring support, this book would not have been possible.

About the Reviewers

Andy Grant is a Technical Consultant for HP Enterprise Services. His primary focus is on datacenter infrastructure and virtualization projects across a number of industries, including government, healthcare, forestry, financial, gas and oil, and international contracting. He currently holds a number of technical certifications including VCAP4/5-DCA/DCD, VCP4/5, MCITP: EA, MCSE, CCNA, Security+, A+ and ASE HP BladeSystem. Outside of work, Andy enjoys hiking, action pistol sports, and spending time adventuring with his son.

Craig Risinger is a consulting architect and VCDX #006, who has been with VMware since 2004. His previous experience includes running help desks and small-shop, all-around, IT system administration. With VMware, he has helped to design virtualization infrastructures and operations for everything from small shops to defense contractors to Fortune 50 financial enterprises. His particular interests include performance management, storage design, and delivering clear and precise technical writing and training. He has had the pleasure of helping to review several books written by his colleagues, including those by Duncan Epping and Frank Denneman, John Arrasjid, and Mostafa Khalil.

Brian Wuchner is a senior systems administrator for a government agency. He has over 10 years of industry experience, with specialties in infrastructure automation, directory services, and data center virtualization. Brian holds the VCP 5 certification, and was awarded the vExpert title from VMware in 2011 and 2012. He can be contacted on LinkedIn (http://www.linkedin.com/in/bwuch), Twitter (@bwuch) or through his blog at http://enterpriseadmins.org.

www.PacktPub.com

Support files, eBooks, discount offers and more

You might want to visit www.PacktPub.com for support files and downloads related to your book.

Did you know that Packt offers eBook versions of every book published, with PDF and ePub files available? You can upgrade to the eBook version at www.PacktPub.com, and as a print book customer you are entitled to a discount on the eBook copy. Get in touch with us at service@packtpub.com for more details.

At www.PacktPub.com, you can also read a collection of free technical articles, sign up for a range of free newsletters and receive exclusive discounts and offers on Packt books and eBooks.

![PACKT LIB logo]

http://PacktLib.PacktPub.com

Do you need instant solutions to your IT questions? PacktLib is Packt's online digital book library. Here, you can access, read, and search across Packt's entire library of books.

Why Subscribe?

- ▶ Fully searchable across every book published by Packt
- ▶ Copy and paste, print, and bookmark content
- ▶ On demand and accessible via a web browser

Free Access for Packt account holders

If you have an account with Packt at www.PacktPub.com, you can use this to access PacktLib today and view nine entirely free books. Simply use your login credentials for immediate access.

Instant Updates on New Packt Books

Get notified! Find out when new books are published by following @PacktEnterprise on Twitter, or the *Packt Enterprise* Facebook page.

I would like to thank and dedicate this book to my mom and dad. Without their endless and untiring support, this book would not have been possible.

Table of Contents

Preface

Welcome to *vSphere High Performance Cookbook*. In this book, we will teach you how to tune and grow a VMware vSphere 5 Infrastructure. This book will provide you with the knowledge, skills, and abilities to build and run a high-performing VMware vSphere virtual infrastructure. Also, we will look at the detailed, step-by-step coverage, with screenshots that are usually not available in product manuals.

You will learn how to configure and manage ESXi CPU, memory, networking, and storage for sophisticated, enterprise-scale environments. Also, you will learn how to manage changes to the vSphere environment, and optimize the performance of all vSphere components.

This book focuses on high value and often overlooked performance-related topics, such as NUMA Aware CPU Scheduler, VMM Scheduler, Core Sharing, the Virtual Memory Reclamation technique, Checksum offloading, VM DirectPath I/O, queuing on storage array, command queuing, vCenter Server design, and virtual machine and application tuning.

What this book covers

Chapter 1, *CPU Performance Design*, covers VMM Scheduler, Cache aware CPU Scheduler, Hyperthreaded Core Sharing, Ready Time (%RDY), and so on.

Chapter 2, *Memory Performance Design*, covers virtual memory reclamation technique, how to rightly size a VM's memory, monitoring host ballooning, swapping activity, and so on.

Chapter 3, *Networking Performance Design*, covers different vSwitch load balancing, options consideration for checksum offloading, VMDirectPath I/O, NetQueue, SplitRx mode for multicast traffic, Multi NIC vMotion, NIOC, and so on.

Chapter 4, *DRS, SDRS, and Resource Control Design*, covers the DRS algorithm, resource pool guidelines, SIOC threshold considerations, profile driven storage, SDRS and its affinity/anti-affinity rules, and so on.

Chapter 5, vSphere Cluster Design, covers considerations for scale
up and scale out cluster design, FT and its caveats, application monitoring, DPM, Host affinity/
anti-affinity rules, and so on.

Chapter 6, Storage Performance Design, covers how to design vSphere storage based on
various workloads, how you design iSCSI, FC storage for best performance, considerations
for VAAI, and so on.

Chapter 7, Designing vCenter and vCenter Database for Best Performance, covers what
platform to choose when designing your vCenter Server, redundant vCenter design, vCenter
design for highly-available Auto Deploy, vCenter SSO and its deployment, and so on.

Chapter 8, Virtual Machine and Application Performance Design, covers how to select the
best time synchronization in virtual machines, considerations for Virtual NUMA, VM swapfile
placement best practices and its impact, and so on.

What you need for this book

You need VMware vSphere 5.1, which includes, VMware vSphere ESXi, vCenter Server, any
SSH Client (Putty), and vSphere Client.

Who this book is for

This book is a valuable addition for technical professionals with system administration skills
and some VMware experience who wish to learn about advanced optimization and the
configuration features and functions of vSphere 5.1.

Conventions

In this book, you will find a number of styles of text that distinguish between different kinds
of information.

New terms and **important words** are shown in bold. Words that you see on the screen, in
menus or dialog boxes for example, appear in the text like this: "clicking the **Next** button
moves you to the next screen".

> Warnings or important notes appear in a box like this.

> Tips and tricks appear like this.

Reader feedback

Feedback from our readers is always welcome. Let us know what you think about this book—what you liked or may have disliked. Reader feedback is important for us to develop titles that you really get the most out of.

To send us general feedback, simply send an e-mail to `feedback@packtpub.com`, and mention the book title via the subject of your message.

If there is a topic that you have expertise in and you are interested in either writing or contributing to a book, see our author guide on `www.packtpub.com/authors`.

Customer support

Now that you are the proud owner of a Packt book, we have a number of things to help you to get the most from your purchase.

Errata

Although we have taken every care to ensure the accuracy of our content, mistakes do happen. If you find a mistake in one of our books—maybe a mistake in the text or the code—we would be grateful if you would report this to us. By doing so, you can save other readers from frustration and help us improve subsequent versions of this book. If you find any errata, please report them by visiting `http://www.packtpub.com/submit-errata`, selecting your book, clicking on the **errata submission form** link, and entering the details of your errata. Once your errata are verified, your submission will be accepted and the errata will be uploaded on our website, or added to any list of existing errata, under the Errata section of that title. Any existing errata can be viewed by selecting your title from `http://www.packtpub.com/support`.

Piracy

Piracy of copyright material on the Internet is an ongoing problem across all media. At Packt, we take the protection of our copyright and licenses very seriously. If you come across any illegal copies of our works, in any form, on the Internet, please provide us with the location address or website name immediately so that we can pursue a remedy.

Please contact us at `copyright@packtpub.com` with a link to the suspected pirated material.

We appreciate your help in protecting our authors, and our ability to bring you valuable content.

Questions

You can contact us at `questions@packtpub.com` if you are having a problem with any aspect of the book, and we will do our best to address it.

1
CPU Performance Design

In this chapter, we will cover the tasks related with CPU performance design. You will learn the following aspects of CPU performance design:

- ▸ Critical performance consideration – VMM scheduler
- ▸ CPU scheduler – processor topology/cache aware
- ▸ Ready time – warning sign
- ▸ Hyperthreaded core sharing
- ▸ Spotting CPU overcommitment
- ▸ Fighting guest CPU saturation in SMP VMs
- ▸ Controlling CPU resources using resource settings
- ▸ What is most important to monitor in CPU performance
- ▸ CPU performance best practices

Introduction

Ideally, a performance problem should be defined within the context of an ongoing performance management process. Performance management refers to the process of establishing performance requirements for applications, in the form of a **service-level agreement** (**SLA**), and then tracking and analyzing the achieved performance to ensure that those requirements are met. A complete performance management methodology includes collecting and maintaining baseline performance data for applications, systems, and subsystems, for example, storage and network.

In the context of performance management, a performance problem exists when an application fails to meet its predetermined SLA. Depending on the specific SLA, the failure might be in the form of excessively long response times or throughput below some defined threshold.

ESX/ESXi and virtual machine performance tuning is complicated because virtual machines share underlying physical resources, and in particular the CPU.

Finally, configuration issues or inadvertent user errors might lead to poor performance. For example, a user might use a **symmetric multiprocessing** (**SMP**) virtual machine when a single processor virtual machine would work well. You might also see a situation where a user sets shares but then forgets about resetting them, resulting in poor performance because of the changing characteristics of other virtual machines in the system.

If you overcommit any of these resources, you might see performance bottlenecks. For example, if too many virtual machines are CPU intensive, you might see slow performance because all of the virtual machines need to share the underlying physical CPU.

Critical performance consideration – VMM scheduler

The **virtual machine monitor** (**VMM**) is a thin layer that provides a virtual x86 hardware environment to the guest operating system on a virtual machine. This hardware includes a virtual CPU, virtual I/O devices, and timers. The VMM leverages key technologies in the **VMkernel**, such as scheduling, memory management, and the network and storage stacks.

Each VMM is devoted to one virtual machine. To run multiple virtual machines, the VMkernel starts multiple VMM instances, also known as worlds. Each VMM instance partitions and shares the CPU, memory, and I/O devices to successfully virtualize the system. The VMM can be implemented by using hardware virtualization, software virtualization (binary translation), or paravirtualization (which is deprecated) techniques.

Paravirtualization refers to the communication between the guest operating system and the hypervisor to improve performance and efficiency. The value proposition of paravirtualization is in the lower virtualization overhead, but the performance advantage of paravirtualization over hardware or software virtualization can vary greatly depending on the workload. Because paravirtualization cannot support unmodified operating systems (for example, Windows 2000/XP), its compatibility and portability is poor.

Paravirtualization can also introduce significant support and maintainability issues in production environments because it requires deep modifications to the operating system kernel and for this reason it was most widely deployed on Linux-based operating systems.

Getting ready

To step through this recipe, you need a running ESXi Server, a Virtual Machine, vCenter Server, and a working installation of the vSphere Client. No other prerequisites are required.

How to do it...

Let's get started:

1. Open up VMware vSphere Client.

2. Log in to the vCenter Server.

3. In the virtual machine inventory, right-click on the **virtual machine**, and then click on **Edit Settings**. The **Virtual Machine Properties** dialog box appears.

4. Click on the **Options** tab.

5. Change the **CPU/MMU Virtualization** option under **Advanced** to one of the following options:

   ❑ **Automatic**

   ❑ **Use software for instruction set and MMU virtualization**

   ❑ **Use Intel VT-X/AMD-V for instruction set virtualization and software for MMU virtualization**

   ❑ **Use Intel VT-X/AMD-V for instruction set virtualization and Intel EPT/AMD RVI for MMU virtualization**

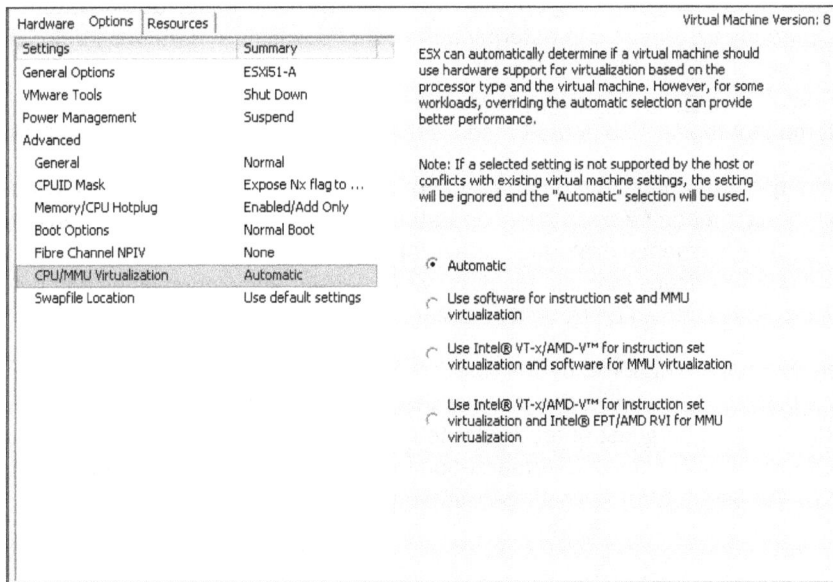

Hardware Options Resources		Virtual Machine Version: 8
Settings	**Summary**	ESX can automatically determine if a virtual machine should use hardware support for virtualization based on the processor type and the virtual machine. However, for some workloads, overriding the automatic selection can provide better performance.
General Options	ESXi51-A	
VMware Tools	Shut Down	
Power Management	Suspend	
Advanced		
General	Normal	Note: If a selected setting is not supported by the host or conflicts with existing virtual machine settings, the setting will be ignored and the "Automatic" selection will be used.
CPUID Mask	Expose Nx flag to ...	
Memory/CPU Hotplug	Enabled/Add Only	
Boot Options	Normal Boot	
Fibre Channel NPIV	None	
CPU/MMU Virtualization	Automatic	⦿ Automatic
Swapfile Location	Use default settings	⚪ Use software for instruction set and MMU virtualization
		⚪ Use Intel® VT-x/AMD-V™ for instruction set virtualization and software for MMU virtualization
		⚪ Use Intel® VT-x/AMD-V™ for instruction set virtualization and Intel® EPT/AMD RVI for MMU virtualization

6. Click on **OK** to save your changes.

7. For the change to take effect, perform one of these actions:

    ❏   Reset the virtual machine

    ❏   Suspend and then resume the virtual machine

    ❏   vMotion the virtual machine

How it works...

The VMM determines a set of possible monitor modes to use, and then picks one to use as the default monitor mode, unless something other than **Automatic** has been specified. The decision is based on:

▸   The physical CPU's features and guest operating system type

▸   Configuration file settings

There are three valid combinations for the monitor mode, as follows:

▸   BT: Binary translation and shadow page tables

▸   HV: AMD-V or Intel VT-x and shadow page tables

▸   HWMMU: AMD-V with RVI, or Intel VT-x with EPT (RVI is inseparable from AMD-V, and EPT is inseparable from Intel VT-x)

BT, HV, and HWMMU are abbreviations used by ESXi to identify each combination.

When a virtual machine is powering on, the VMM inspects the physical CPU's features and the guest operating system type to determine the set of possible execution modes. The VMM first finds the set of modes allowed. Then it restricts the allowed modes by configuration file settings. Finally, among the remaining candidates, it chooses the preferred mode, which is the default monitor mode. This default mode is then used if you have left **Automatic** selected.

For the majority of workloads, the default monitor mode chosen by the VMM works best. The default monitor mode for each guest operating system on each CPU has been carefully selected after a performance evaluation of available choices. However, some applications have special characteristics that can result in better performance when using a non-default monitor mode. These should be treated as exceptions, not the rule.

The chosen settings are honored by the VMM only if the settings are supported on the intended hardware. For example, if you select **Use software instruction set and MMU virtualization** for a 64-bit guest operating system running on a 64-bit Intel processor, the VMM will choose Intel VT-x for CPU virtualization instead of BT. This is because BT is not supported by the 64-bit guest operating system on this processor.

There's more...

The virtual CPU consists of the virtual instruction set and the virtual **memory management unit** (**MMU**). An instruction set is a list of instructions that a CPU executes. The MMU is the hardware that maintains the mapping between the virtual addresses and the physical addresses in the memory.

The combination of techniques used to virtualize the instruction set and memory determines the monitor execution mode (also called the monitor mode). The VMM identifies the VMware ESXi hardware platform and its available CPU features, and then chooses a monitor mode for a particular guest operating system on that hardware platform. The VMM might choose a monitor mode that uses hardware virtualization techniques, software virtualization techniques, or a combination of hardware and software techniques.

We always had a challenge in hardware virtualization. x86 operating systems are designed to run directly on the bare metal hardware, so they assume that they have full control on the computer hardware. The x86 architecture offers four levels of privilege to operating systems and applications to manage access to the computer hardware: ring 0, ring 1, ring 2, and ring 3. User-level applications typically run in ring 3, the operating system needs to have direct access to the memory and hardware, and must execute its privileged instructions in ring 0.

Binary translation allows the VMM to run in ring 0 for isolation and performance, while moving the guest operating system to ring 1. Ring 1 is a higher privilege level than ring 3 and a lower privilege level than ring 0.

VMware can virtualize any x86 operating systems by using a combination of binary translation and direct execution techniques. With binary translation, the VMM dynamically translates all guest operating system instructions and caches the results for future use. The translator in the VMM does not perform a mapping from one architecture to another; that would be emulation not translation. Instead, it translates from the full unrestricted x86 instruction set issued by the guest operating system to a subset that is safe to execute inside the VMM. In particular, the binary translator replaces privileged instructions with sequences of instructions that perform the privileged operations in the virtual machine rather than on the physical machine. This translation enforces encapsulation of the virtual machine while preserving the x86 semantics as seen from the perspective of the virtual machine.

Meanwhile, user-level code is directly executed on the processor for high-performance virtualization. Each VMM provides each virtual machine with all of the services of the physical system, including a virtual BIOS, virtual devices, and virtualized memory management.

In addition to software virtualization, there is support for hardware virtualization. This allows some of the work of running virtual CPU instructions to be offloaded onto the physical hardware. Intel has the **Intel Virtualization Technology** (**Intel VT-x**) feature. AMD has the **AMD Virtualization** (**AMD-V**) feature. Intel VT-x and AMD-V are similar in aim but different in detail. Both designs aim to simplify virtualization techniques.

CPU scheduler – processor topology/cache aware

ESXi Server has an advanced CPU scheduler geared towards providing high performance, fairness, and isolation of virtual machines running on Intel/AMD x86 architectures.

The ESXi CPU scheduler is designed with the following objectives:

- ▸ Performance isolation: Multi-VM fairness.
- ▸ Co-scheduling: illusion that all vCPUs are concurrently online.
- ▸ Performance: high throughput, low latency, high scalability, and low overhead.
- ▸ Power efficiency: saving power without losing performance.
- ▸ Wide Adoption: enabling all the optimizations on diverse processor architecture.

There can be only one active process per CPU at any given instant, for example, multiple vCPUs can run on the same pCPU, just not at one instant, but there are often more processes than CPUs. Therefore, queuing will occur, and the scheduler is responsible for controlling the queue, handling priorities, and preempting the use of the CPU.

The main tasks of the CPU scheduler are to choose which world is to be scheduled to a processor. In order to give each world a chance to run, the scheduler dedicates a time slice (also known as the duration a world can be executed (usually 10-20 ms, 50 for VMkernel by default)) for each process and then migrates the state of the world between run, wait, costop, and ready.

ESXi implements the proportional share-based algorithm. It associates each world with a share of CPU resource across all virtual machines. This is called entitlement and is calculated from the user-provided resource specifications, such as shares, reservations, and limits.

Getting ready

To step through this recipe, you need a running ESXi Server, a Virtual Machine, and a working installation of vSphere Client. No other prerequisites are required.

How to do it...

Let's get started:

1. Log in to the VMware vSphere Client.

2. In the virtual machine inventory, right-click on the virtual machine, and click on **Edit Settings**. The **Virtual Machine Properties** dialog box appears.

3. Click on the **Options** tab.

4. Under the **Advanced** section, click on **General Row**.

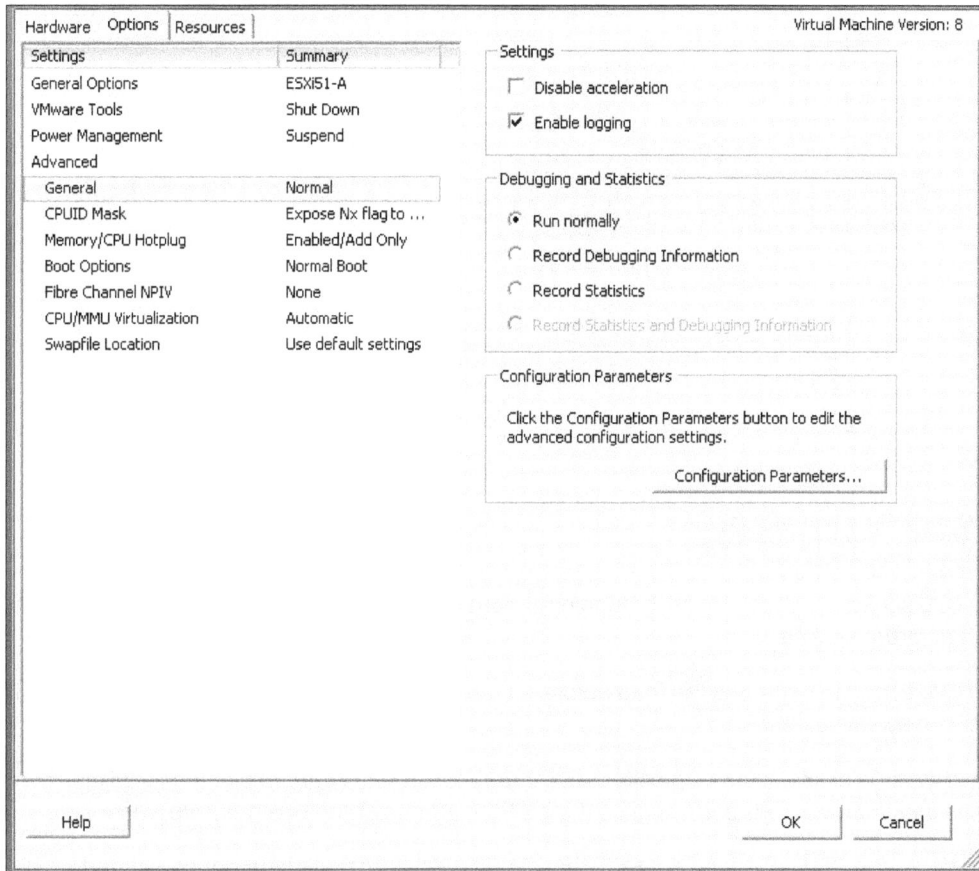

5. Now on the right-hand side click on the **Configuration Parameters** button.

6. Now click on the **Add Row** button at the bottom and add the parameter **sched.cpu. vsmpConsolidate** and on the **Value** section type TRUE.

7. The final screen should like the following screenshot and then click on **OK** to save the setting.

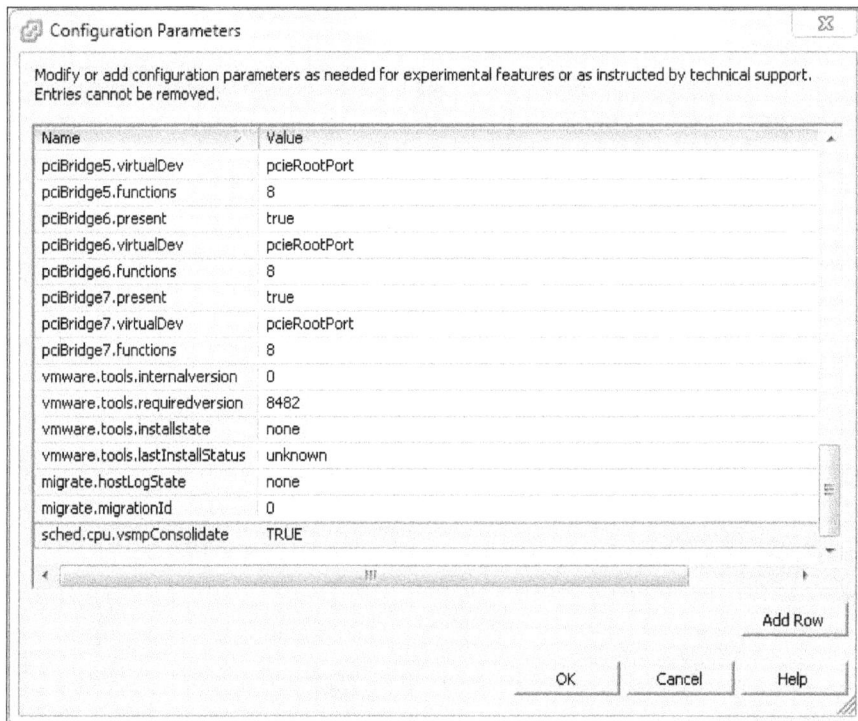

Name	Value
pciBridge5.virtualDev	pcieRootPort
pciBridge5.functions	8
pciBridge6.present	true
pciBridge6.virtualDev	pcieRootPort
pciBridge6.functions	8
pciBridge7.present	true
pciBridge7.virtualDev	pcieRootPort
pciBridge7.functions	8
vmware.tools.internalversion	0
vmware.tools.requiredversion	8482
vmware.tools.installstate	none
vmware.tools.lastInstallStatus	unknown
migrate.hostLogState	none
migrate.migrationId	0
sched.cpu.vsmpConsolidate	TRUE

Configuration Parameters

Modify or add configuration parameters as needed for experimental features or as instructed by technical support. Entries cannot be removed.

Add Row

OK   Cancel   Help

How it works...

The CPU scheduler uses processor topology information to optimize the placement of vCPUs onto different sockets.

The CPU scheduler spreads the load across all the sockets to maximize the aggregate amount of cache available.

Cores within a single socket typically use a shared last-level cache. Use of a shared last-level cache can improve vCPU performance if the CPU is running memory-intensive workloads.

By default, the CPU scheduler spreads the load across all sockets in under-committed systems. This improves performance by maximizing the aggregate amount of cache available to the running vCPUs. For such workloads, it can be beneficial to schedule all of the vCPUs on the same socket, with a shared last-level cache, even when the ESXi host is under committed. In such scenarios, you can override the default behavior of the spreading vCPUs across packages by including the following configuration option in the virtual machine's VMX configuration file, **sched.cpu.vsmpConsolidate=TRUE**. However, it is usually better to stick with the default behavior.

Ready time – warning sign

To achieve the best performance in a consolidated environment, you must consider a ready time.

Ready time is the time that the vCPU waits, in the queue, for the pCPU (or physical Core) to be ready to execute its instruction. The scheduler handles the queue and when there is contention, and the processing resources are stressed, the queue might become long.

The ready time describes how much of the last observation period a specific world spent waiting in the queue. The ready time for a particular world (for example, a vCPU) is how much time during that interval was spent waiting in the queue to get access to a pCPU. The ready time can be expressed in percentage per vCPU over the observation time and statistically it can't be zero on average.

The value of the ready time, therefore, is an indicator of how long the VM was denied access to the pCPU resources which it wanted to use. This makes it a good indicator of performance.

When multiple processes are trying to use the same physical CPU, that CPU might not be immediately available, and a process must wait before the ESXi host can allocate a CPU to it.

The CPU scheduler manages access to the physical CPUs on the host system. A short spike in CPU used or CPU ready indicates that you are making the best use of the host resources. However, if both values are constantly high, the hosts are probably overloaded and performance is likely poor.

Generally, if the CPU used value for a virtual machine is above 90 percent and the CPU ready value is above 20 percent per vCPU (high number of vCPUs), performance is negatively affected.

This latency may impact the performance of the guest operating system and the running applications within a virtual machine.

Getting ready

To step through this recipe, you need a running ESXi Server, a couple of CPU-hungry virtual machines, VMware vCenter Server, and a working installation of vSphere Client. No other prerequisites are required.

How to do it...

Let's get started:

1. Open up vSphere Client.
2. Log in to the VMware vCenter Server.
3. On the home screen, navigate to **Hosts and Clusters.**
4. Expand the left-hand navigation list.
5. Navigate to one of the CPU-hungry virtual machines.
6. Navigate to the **Performance** screen.
7. Navigate to the **Advanced** view.
8. Click on **Chart Options**.
9. Navigate to **CPU** from the **Chart metrics**.
10. Navigate to the VM object.

    1. Select only **Demand**, **Ready**, and **Usage in MHz**.

       The key metrics when investigating a potential CPU issue are:

       ❑ **Demand**: Amount of CPU that the virtual machine is trying to use.

       ❑ **Usage**: Amount of CPU that the virtual machine is actually being allowed to use.

       ❑ **Ready**: Amount of time for which the virtual machine is ready to run but (has work it wants to do) but was unable to because vSphere could not find physical resources to run the virtual machine on.

11. Click on **Ok**.

In the following screenshot you will see the high ready time for the virtual machine:

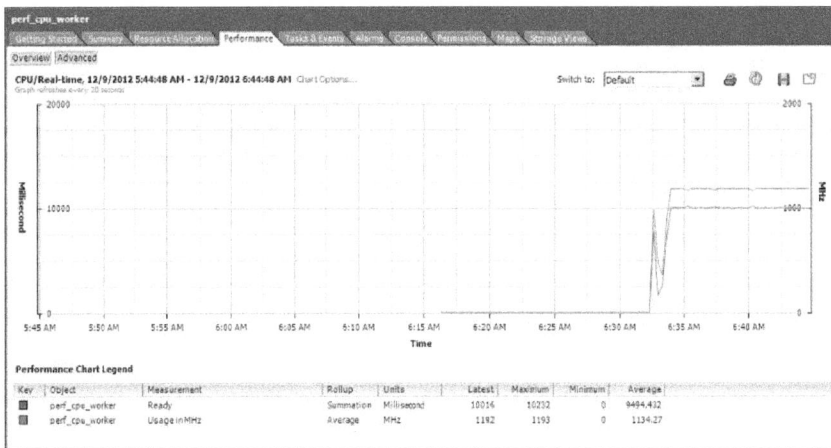

Notice the amount of CPU this virtual machine is demanding and compare that to the amount of CPU usage the virtual machine is actually being able to get (usage in MHz). The virtual machine is demanding more than it is currently being allowed to use.

Notice that the virtual machine is also seeing a large amount of ready time.

> Ready time greater than 10 percent could be a performance concern. However, some less CPU-sensitive applications and virtual machines can have much higher values of ready time and still perform satisfactorily.

How it works...

Bad performance is when the users are unhappy. But that's subjective and hard to measure. We can measure other metrics easily, but they don't correlate perfectly with whether user's expectations are met. We want to find metrics that correlate well (though never perfectly) with user satisfaction. It's always the case that the final answer to "Is there a performance problem?" is subjective, but we can use objective metrics to make reasonable bets, and decide when it's worth asking the users if they're satisfied with the performance.

A vCPU is in ready state when the vCPU is ready to run (that is, it has a task it wants to execute) but is unable to run because the vSphere scheduler is unable to find physical host CPU resources to run the virtual machine on. One potential reason for elevated ready time is that the virtual machine is constrained by a user-set CPU limit or resource pool limit, reported as **max limited** (**MLMTD**). The amount of CPU denied because of a limit is measured as the metric max limited (MLMTD).

Ready time is reported in two different values between resxtop/esxtop and vCenter Server. In resxtop/esxtop, it is reported in an easily-understood percentage format. A figure of 5 percent means that the virtual machine spent 5 percent of its last sample period waiting for available CPU resources (only true for 1-vCPU VMs). In vCenter Server, ready time is reported as a time measurement. For example, in vCenter Server's real-time data, which produces sample values every 20,000 milliseconds, a figure of 1,000 milliseconds is reported for a 5 percent ready time. A figure of 2,000 milliseconds is reported for a 10 percent ready time.

> As you may know that vCenter reports ready time in milliseconds (ms), use the following formula to convert the ms value to a percentage:
>
> $$\text{Metric Value (In Percent)} = \frac{\text{Metric Value (In Millisecond)}}{\text{Total Time of Sample Period}} \times 100$$
>
> (By default 20000 ms in vCenter for real-time graphs)

Although high ready time typically signifies CPU contention, the condition does not always warrant corrective action. If the value for ready time is close in value to the amount of time used on the CPU, and if the increased ready time occurs with occasional spikes in CPU activity but does not persist for extended periods of time, this might not indicate a performance problem. The brief performance hit is often within the accepted performance variance and does not require any action on the part of the administrator.

Hyperthreaded core sharing

The **Hyperthreaded** (**HT**) core sharing option enables us to define the different types of physical core sharing techniques with the virtual machines.

A Hyperthreaded processor (or lCPU) has the same number of function units as an older, non-Hyperthreaded processor. HT offers two execution contexts, so that it can achieve better function unit utilization by letting more than one thread execute concurrently. On the other hand, if you're running two programs which compete for the same function units, there is no advantage at all on having both running concurrently. When one is running, the other is necessarily waiting on the same function units.

A dual core processor has two times as many function units as a single-core processor, and can really run two programs concurrently with no competition for function units. A CPU socket can contain multiple cores. Each core can do CPU-type work. Twice as many cores will be able to do (roughly) twice as much work. If a core also has Hyperthreading enabled, then each core has two logical processors. However, two lCPUs cannot do twice as much work as one.

Getting ready

To step through this recipe, you need a running ESXi Server, a running virtual machine, VMware vCenter Server, and a working installation of vSphere Client. No other prerequisites are required.

How to do it...

Let's get started:

1. Open up VMware vSphere Client.
2. Log in to the vCenter Server.
3. From the home screen, navigate to **Hosts and Clusters**.
4. Expand the left-hand navigation list.
5. Navigate to any one of the virtual machine.

6. Right-click on the virtual machine and select Edit Settings.

7. Click on the **Resources** tab.

8. Click on **Advanced CPU**.

9. Under **Hyperthreaded Core Sharing**, use the drop-down list to select any one of the available options.

There are three different HT sharing methods, as follows:

- ▶ Any
- ▶ None
- ▶ Internal

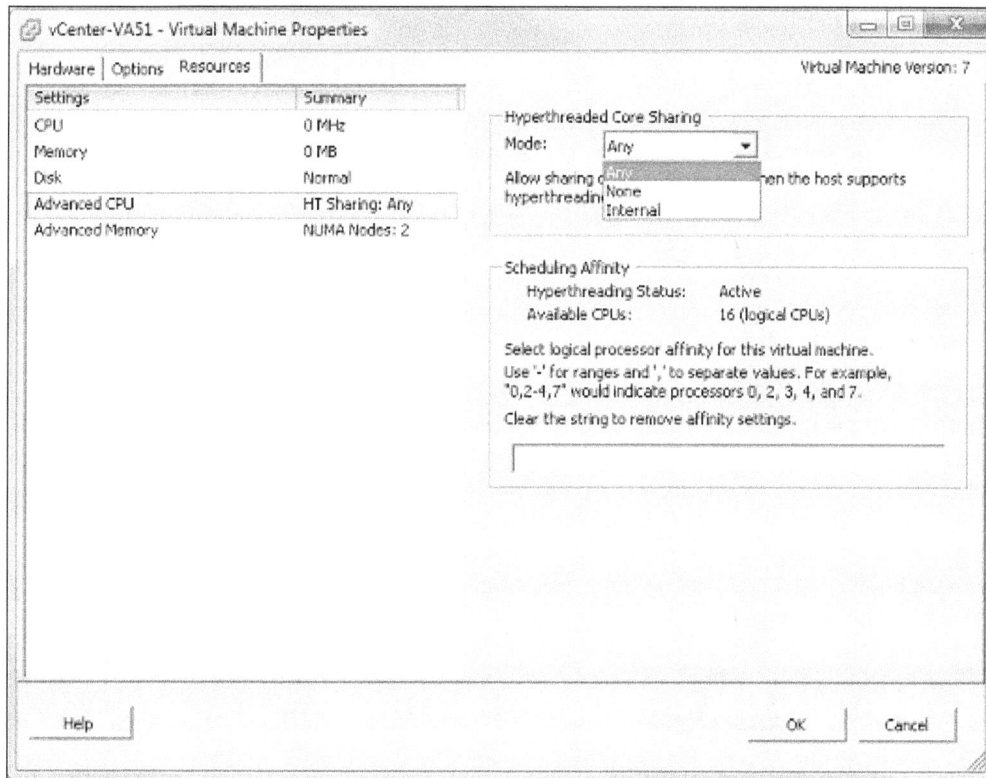

How it works...

The following table elaborates the three methods of core sharing:

Option	Description
Any	The default for all virtual machines on a Hyperthreaded system. The virtual CPUs of a virtual machine with this setting can freely share cores with other virtual CPUs from this or any other virtual machine at any time.
None	Virtual CPUs of a virtual machine should not share cores with each other or with virtual CPUs from other virtual machines. That is, each virtual CPU from this virtual machine should always get a whole core to itself, with the other logical CPUs on that core being placed into the halted state.
Internal	This option is similar to none. Virtual CPUs from this virtual machine cannot share cores with virtual CPUs from other virtual machines. They can share cores with the other virtual CPUs from the same virtual machine. You can select this option only for SMP virtual machines. If applied to a uniprocessor virtual machine, the system changes this option to none.

These options have no effect on the fairness or CPU time allocation. Regardless of a virtual machine's hyperthreading settings, it still receives CPU time proportional to its CPU shares, and constrained by its CPU reservation and CPU limit values.

There's more...

If there are running VMs on the same virtual infrastructure cluster with different numbers of vCPU (for example, one vCPU and two vCPUs) then there is a good chance that one vCPU of your dual vCPU VM can work alone on one physical CPU and the other vCPU has to share a physical CPU with another VM. This causes tremendous synchronization overhead between the two vCPUs (you don't have this in physical multi-CPU machines because this sync is hardware based) which can cause the system process within the VM to go up from 50 percent to 100 percent CPU load.

Spotting CPU overcommitment

When we provision the CPU resources, which is the number of vCPUs allocated to running the virtual machines and that is greater than the number of physical cores on a host, is called CPU overcommitment.

CPU overcommitment is a normal practice in many situations; however, you need to monitor it closely. It increases the consolidation ratio.

CPU overcommitment is not recommended in order to satisfy or guarantee the workload of a tier-1 application with a tight SLA. CPU overcommitment may be successfully leveraged to highly consolidate and reduce the power consumption of light workloads on modern, multi-core systems.

Getting ready

To step through this recipe, you need a running ESXi Server, a couple of running CPU-hungry virtual machines, a SSH client (Putty), vCenter Server, and a working installation of vSphere Client. No other prerequisites are required.

The following table elaborates on Esxtop CPU Performance Metrics:

Esxtop Metric	Description	Implication
%RDY	Percentage of time a vCPU in a run queue is waiting for the CPU scheduler to let it run on a physical CPU.	A high **%RDY** time (use 20 percent as a starting point) may indicate the virtual machine is under resource contention. Monitor this; if the application speed is ok, a higher threshold may be tolerated.
%USED	Percentage of possible CPU processing cycles which were actually used for work during this time interval.	The **%USED** value alone does not necessarily indicate that the CPUs are overcommitted. However high **%RDY** values, plus high **%USED** values, are a sure indicator that your CPU resources are overcommitted.

How to do it...

To spot CPU overcommitment there are a few CPU resource parameters which you should monitor closely. Those are:

1. Log in to the ESXi Server through the SSH client.
2. Type `esxtop` and hit enter.

3. Monitor the preceding values to understand CPU overcommitment.

```
8:27:05am up 22:23, 401 worlds, 12 VMs, 24 vCPUs: CPU load average: 0.68, 0.58, 0.44
PCPU USED(%):  52   52 1.5 1.2 2.0 1.1 1.4 1.2 2.1 1.2 3.1 1.0 2.0 1.3 1.7 1.1 AVG: 8.0
PCPU UTIL(%): 100  100 1.9 1.6 2.1 1.3 1.7 1.4 2.6 1.7 3.8 1.5 2.5 1.7 2.2 1.6 AVG: 14
CORE UTIL(%): 100      2.8      3.2      2.7      4.0      5.0      4.0      3.5     AVG: 15

   ID    GID NAME            NWLD  %USED    %RUN    %SYS   %WAIT %VMWAIT    %RDY  %IDLE  %OVRLP  %CSTP %MLMTD %SWPWT
    1      1 idle              16 681.25 1600.00    0.00    0.00       - 1600.00   0.00    1.72   0.00   0.00   0.00
96067  96067 Res-Hungry-4       8  44.60   67.64    0.03  619.52    0.90   98.34  33.69    0.08  15.67   0.00   0.00
95554  95554 Res-Hungry-3       8  43.80   66.18    0.01  634.87    2.11   84.09  39.86    0.08  16.01   0.00   0.00
94278  94278 Res-Hungry-2       7  21.96   33.42    0.00  592.44    0.00   75.14   0.00    0.09   0.00   0.00   0.00
91336  91336 Res-Hungry-1       7  21.76   33.17    0.00  589.64    0.00   78.21   0.00    0.06   0.00   0.00   0.00
83604  83604 vCenter-VA51       8   3.78    4.21    0.05  796.85    0.19    0.10 196.06    0.02   0.00   0.00   0.00
83528  83528 ESX151-B           9   3.75    3.96    0.17  897.08    1.68    0.26 394.83    0.04   0.00   0.00   0.00
83520  83520 ESX151-A           9   3.37    4.28    0.10  896.87    1.22    0.16 395.10    0.03   0.00   0.00   0.00
93942  93942 esxtop.61739       1   2.14    2.13    0.00   98.01       -    0.00   0.00    0.00   0.00   0.00   0.00
83620  83620 Analytics VM       8   2.06    2.44    0.06  798.66    0.45    0.07 197.60    0.01   0.00   0.00   0.00
83586  83586 vCloud Director    6   1.57    1.53    0.05  599.28    0.02    0.06  98.66    0.00   0.00   0.00   0.00
83627  83627 UI VM              8   1.11    1.12    0.04  799.96    0.91    0.09 198.32    0.00   0.00   0.00   0.00
83611  83611 vShieldManager     7   1.01    0.96    0.04  699.98    0.00    0.07 199.83    0.01   0.00   0.00   0.00
 1743   1743 hostd.2978        20   1.00    1.02    0.01 2000.00       -    0.07   0.00    0.00   0.00   0.00   0.00
 2643   2643 vpxa.3454         19   0.53    0.55    0.02 1900.00       -    0.04   0.00    0.00   0.00   0.00   0.00
83535  83535 OpenFiler          8   0.50    0.64    0.01  800.00    0.15    0.03  99.42    0.00   0.00   0.00   0.00
```

This example uses `esxtop` to detect CPU overcommitment. Looking at the pCPU line near the top of the screen, you can determine that this host's two CPUs are 100 percent utilized. Four active virtual machines are shown, **Res-Hungry-1** to **Res-Hungry-4**. These virtual machines are active because they have relatively high values in the **%USED** column. The values in the **%USED** column alone do not necessarily indicate that the CPUs are overcommitted. In the **%RDY** column, you see that the three active virtual machines have relatively high values. High **%RDY** values, plus high **%USED** values, are a sure indicator that your CPU resources are overcommitted.

From the CPU view, navigate to a VM and press the *E* key to expand the view. It will give a detailed vCPU view for the VM. This is important because at a quick level, CPU ready as a metric is best referenced when looking at performance concerns more broadly than a specific VM. If there is high ready percentage noted, contention could be an issue, particularly if other VMs show high utilization when more vCPUs than physical cores are present. In that case, other VMs could be leading to high ready time on a low idle VM. So, long story short, if the CPU ready time is high on VMs on a host, it's time to verify that no other VMs are seeing performance issues.

You can also use vCenter performance chart to spot the CPU overcommitment, as follows:

1. Log in to the vCenter Server using vSphere Client.

2. On the home screen, navigate to **Hosts and Clusters**.

3. Go to the ESXi host.

4. Click on the **Performance** tab.

5. Navigate to the CPU from the **Switch To** drop-down menu on the right-hand side.

6. Navigate to the **Advanced** tab and click on the **Chart Options**.

7. Navigate to the ESXi host in the **Objects** section.

8. Select only **Used** and **Ready** in the **Counters** section and click on **OK**.

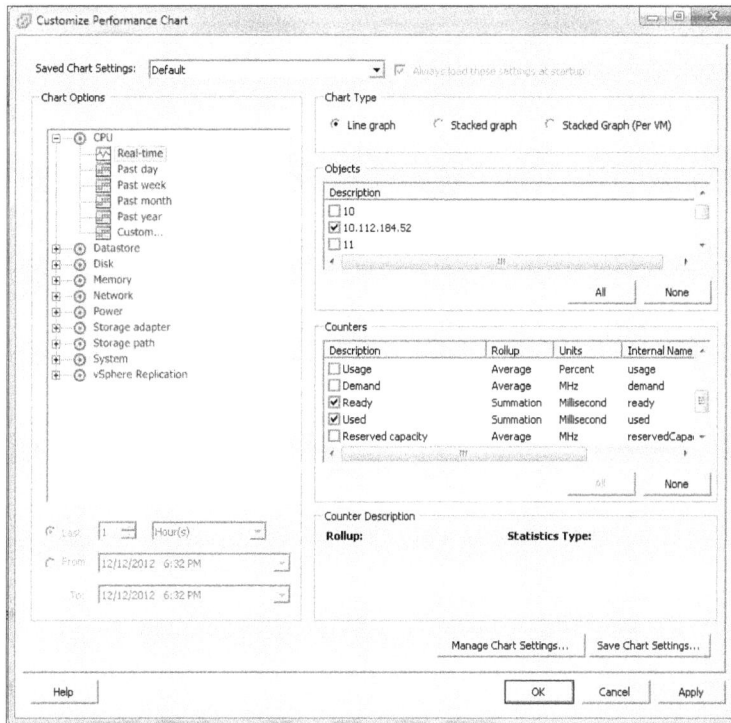

Now you will see the ready time and the used time in the graph and you can spot the overcommitment. The following screenshot is an example output:

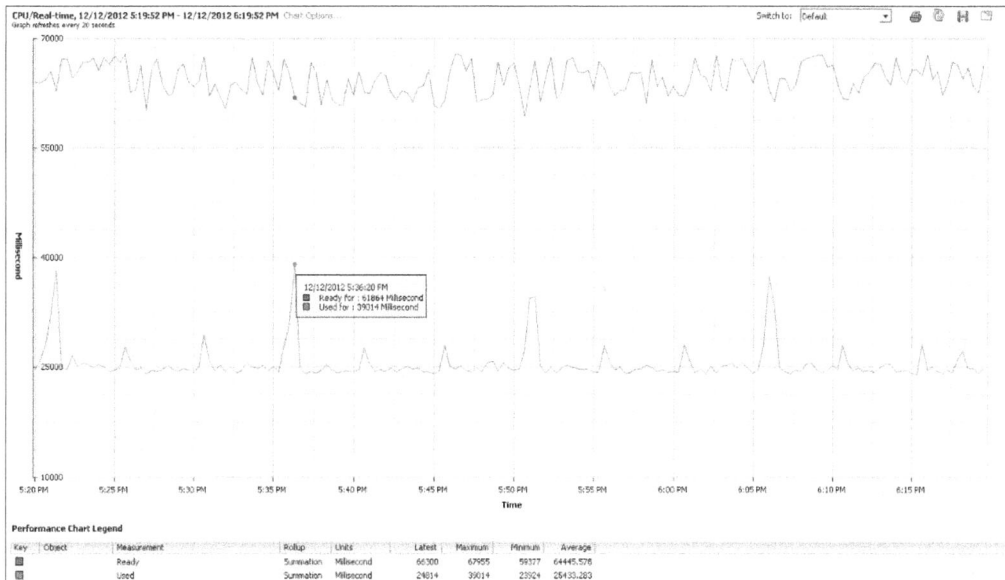

The following example shows that the host has high used time.

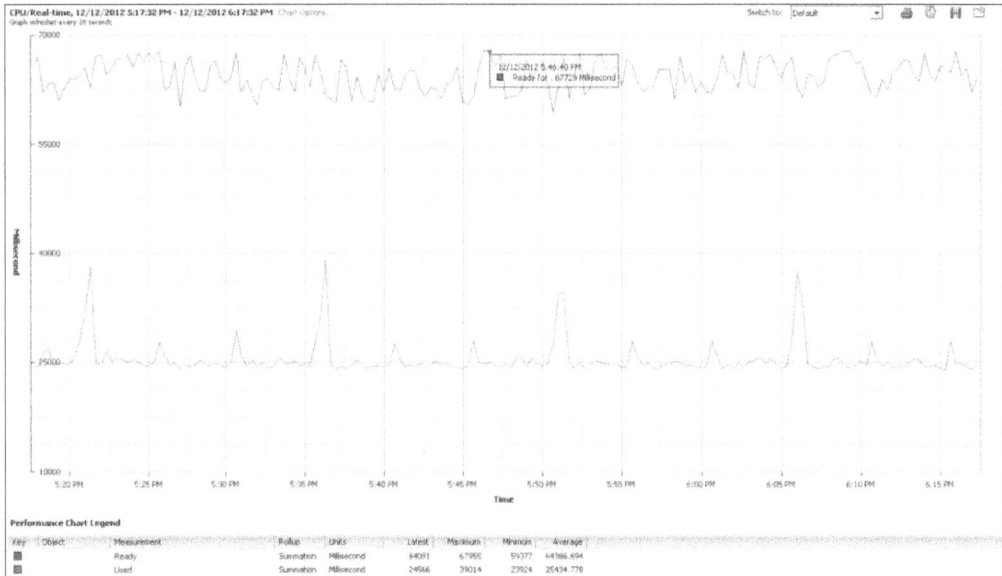

How it works...

Although high ready time typically signifies a CPU contention, the condition does not always warrant corrective action. If the value for ready time is also accompanied by high used time then it might signify that the host is overcommitted.

So used time and ready time for an host might signal contention. However, the host might not be over-committed, due to workload availability.

There might be periods of activity and periods that are idle. So the CPU is not over-committed all the time. Another very common source of high ready time for VMs, even when pCPU utilization is low, is due to storage being slow. A vCPU, which occupies a pCPU, can issue a storage I/O and then sits in the WAIT state on the pCPU blocking other vCPUs. Other vCPUs accumulate ready time; this vCPU and this pCPU accumulate wait time (which is not a part of the used or utilized time).

Fighting guest CPU saturation in SMP VMs

Guest CPU saturation happens when the application and operating system running in a virtual machine use all of the CPU resources that the ESXi host is providing for that virtual machine. However, this guest CPU saturation does not necessarily indicate that a performance problem exists.

Compute-intensive applications commonly use all of the available CPU resources, but this is expected and might be acceptable (as long as the end user thinks that the job is completing quickly enough). Even less-intensive applications might experience periods of high CPU demand without experiencing performance problems. However, if a performance problem exists when guest CPU saturation is occurring, steps should be taken to eliminate the condition.

When a virtual machine is configured with more than one vCPU but actively uses only one of those vCPUs, resources that could be used to perform useful work are being wasted. At this time you may see a potential performance problem—at least from the most active vCPU perspective.

Getting ready

To step through this recipe, you need a running ESXi Server, a couple of running CPU-hungry virtual machines, vCenter Server, and a working installation of vSphere Client. No other prerequisites are required.

How to do it...

To spot CPU overcommitment in the guest OS there are two CPU resource parameters which you should monitor closely as follows:

- The ready time
- The usage percentage

1. Log in to the vCenter Server using vSphere Client.
2. From the home screen, navigate to **Hosts and Clusters**.
3. Expand the ESXi host and go to the CPU hungry VM.
4. Click on the **Performance** tab.
5. Navigate to the CPU from the **Switch To** drop-down menu on the right-hand side.
6. Navigate to the **Advanced** tab and click on the **Chart Options**.

7. Select only **Usage Average in Percentage**, **Ready**, and **Used** in the **Counters** section and click on **OK**

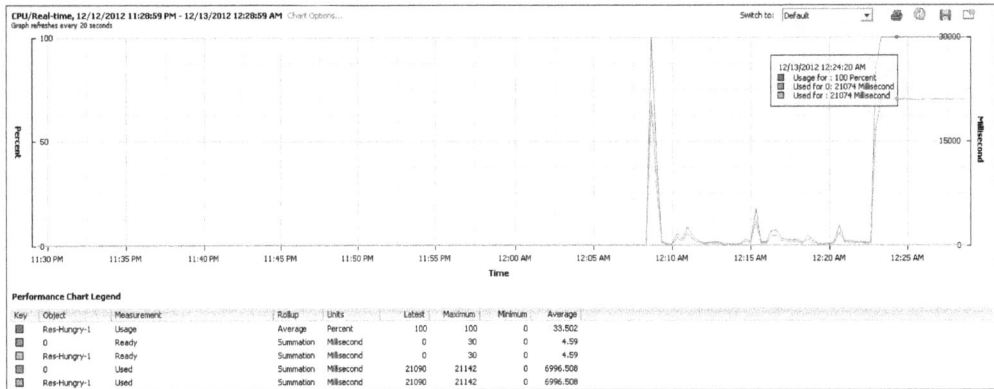

The preceding example shows the high usage and used value. We can see it is 100 percent.

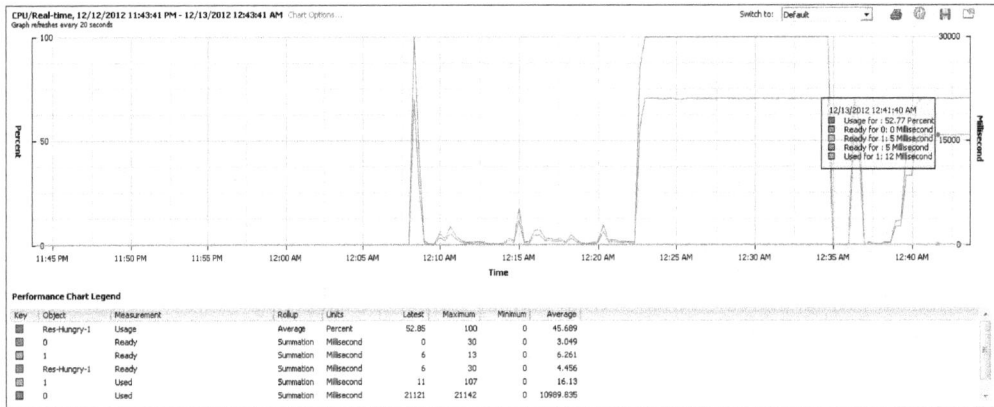

The preceding example shows that after the CPU increase in the VM, the percentage of CPU usage dropped down to 52 percent.

How it works...

So for a SMP VM if you see it is the high CPU resources demanding, it may happen that either the application is single threaded or the guest operating system is configured with **uniprocessor HAL**.

Many applications are written with only a single thread of control. These applications cannot take advantage of more than one processor core.

In order for a virtual machine to take advantage of multiple vCPUs, the guest operating system running on the virtual machine must be able to recognize and use multiple processor cores. If the virtual machine is doing all of its work on vCPU0, the guest operating system might be configured with a kernel or a HAL that can recognize only a single processor core.

You have two possible approaches to solving performance problems related to guest CPU saturation:

▸ Increase the CPU resources provided to the application.

▸ Increase the efficiency with which the virtual machine uses CPU resources.

Adding CPU resources is often the easiest choice, particularly in a virtualized environment. If a virtual machine continues to experience CPU saturation even after adding CPU resources, the tuning and behavior of the application and operating system should be investigated.

Controlling CPU resources using resource settings

If you cannot rebalance the CPU load or increase the processor efficiency even after all of the recipes discussed earlier, then it might be something else which keeps the host CPU still saturated.

Now that could be a resource pool and its allocation of resources towards the virtual machine.

Many applications, such as batch jobs, respond to a lack of CPU resources by taking longer to complete but still produce correct and useful results. Other applications might experience failure or might be unable to meet the critical business requirements when denied sufficient CPU resources.

The resource controls available in vSphere can be used to ensure that the resource-sensitive applications always get sufficient CPU resources, even when host CPU saturation exists. You need to make sure that you understand how shares, reservations, and limits work when applied to resource pools or to individual VMs. The default values ensure that ESXi will be efficient and fair to all VMs. Change from the default settings only when you understand the consequences.

Getting ready

To step through this recipe, you need a running ESXi Server, a couple of running CPU hungry virtual machines, vCenter Server, and a working installation of vSphere Client. No other prerequisites are required.

How to do it...

Let's get started:

1. Log in to the vCenter Server using vSphere Client.

2. From the home screen, navigate to **Hosts and Clusters**.

3. Expand the ESXi host and navigate to the CPU hungry virtual machine.

4. Click on the **Performance** tab.

5. Go to CPU from the **Switch To** drop-down menu on the right-hand side.

6. Go to **Advanced** tab and click on the **Chart Options**.

7. Select only **Ready** and **Used** in the **Counters** section and click on **OK**.

Now if there is a lower limit configured on the VM and at the same time if it is craving for a resource, then you will see a high ready time and a low used metric. An example of what it may look like is given in the following image:

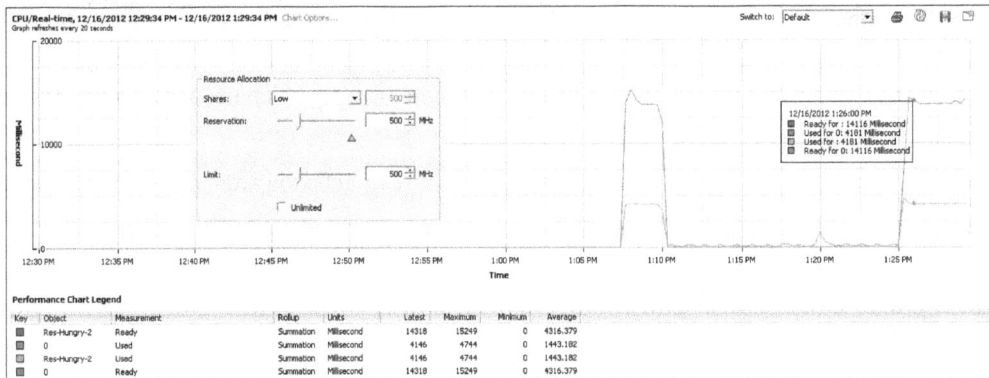

Look at the preceding example and see when the VM is craving for more CPU resource, if you put a limit on top of it, then it will experience a high ready time and a low used time. Here in the above example this VM is set with a limit of 500MHz.

Now to rectify this, we can change the limit value and the VM should perform better with a low ready time and a high used value.

1. Right-click on the CPU-hungry virtual machine and select **Edit** Settings.

2. Click on the **Resources** tab.

3. Click on **CPU**.

4. Change the **Share Value** to **High** (2000 Shares).

5. Change the **Limit** value to **2000MHz** and **Reservation** to **2000MHz**.

6. Click on **OK**.

Now the VM should look and perform as shown in the following screenshot:

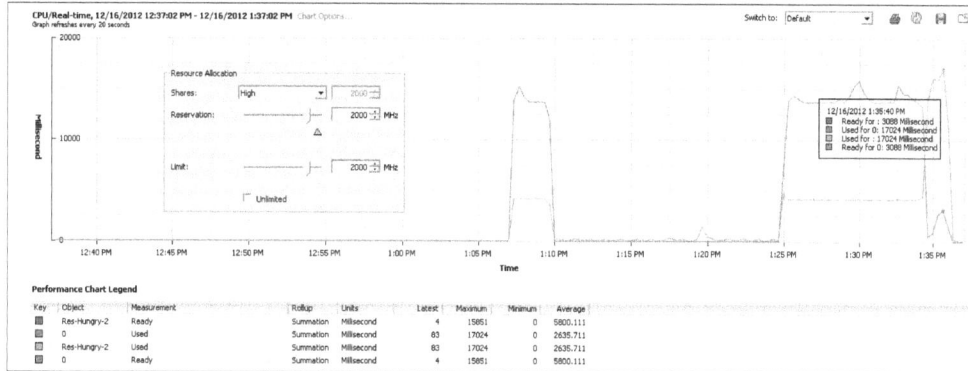

What is most important to monitor in CPU performance

Before you jump onto conclusion as to what to monitor for the CPU performance, you need to make sure that you know what affects the CPU performance. Things that can affect the CPU performance include:

- ▶ CPU affinity: When you pin down a virtual CPU to a physical CPU, it may happen that your resource gets imbalanced. So, this is not advised until you have a strong reason to do that.

- ▶ CPU prioritization: When CPU contention happens, the CPU scheduler will be forced to prioritize VMs based on entitlement and queue requests.

- ▶ SMP VMs: If your application is not multithreaded then there is no benefit adding more CPU resources in VMs. In fact, the extra idle vCPUs add overhead that prevent some more useful work from being done.

- ▶ Idle VMs: You may have too many idle VMs, which you think should not eat up resources. However, in reality CPU interrupt, shares, reservations, and specially limit settings can still be created for those VMs if they were changed from their default settings.

So, now you know what affects the CPU performance. You can now look at what it takes to monitor the CPU performance.

You can categorize the factors that should be monitored for the CPU performance into three main sections:

- ▶ Host CPU usage
- ▶ VM CPU usage
- ▶ VM CPU ready time

To monitor these sections you need to know the esxtop counters and those are:

- ► **PCPU Used (%)**
- ► Per group statistics

  - ❏ **%Used**
  - ❏ **%Sys**
  - ❏ **%RDY**
  - ❏ **%Wait**
  - ❏ **%CSTP**
  - ❏ **%MLMTD**

Getting ready

To step through this recipe, you need a running ESXi Server, a couple of running CPU-hungry virtual machines, and a SSH Client (for example, Putty). No other prerequisites are required.

How to do it...

Let's get started:

1. Log in to the ESXi host using SSH client (Putty).

2. Run `esxtop` and monitor the statistics. The following screenshot is an example output:

```
11:10:59am up 10 days  1:07, 392 worlds, 12 VMs, 25 vCPUs: CPU load average: 0.64, 0.54, 0.24
PCPU USED(%):  67  38  30  18   48 0.0 8.8 0.0 4.4 1.5 1.8 1.1 2.3 1.2 2.6 1.2 AVG:   14
PCPU UTIL(%): 100  72  29  17   45 0.0 8.4 0.1 6.0 2.7 3.0 2.0 3.8 2.0 4.1 2.1 AVG:   18
CORE UTIL(%): 100      46       45   8.4     8.1     4.6     5.4     5.7     AVG:   28

      ID       GID NAME               NWLD   %USED    %RUN    %SYS   %WAIT %VMWAIT    %RDY   %IDLE  %OVRLP   %CSTP  %MLMTD  %SWPWT
       1         1 idle                 16  596.41 1600.00    0.00    0.00       -  1600.00    0.00    1.87    0.00    0.00    0.00
  994040    994040 Res-Hungry-4          7  105.94  100.68    0.01  600.63    0.00     0.05   99.86    0.09    0.00    0.00    0.00
  487530    487530 Res-Hungry-2          7   54.73   68.44    0.01  590.39    0.00    41.82    0.00    0.15    0.00    0.00    0.00
  994024    994024 Res-Hungry-1          8   37.66   57.13    0.01  623.12    0.00    94.60   34.41    0.05   26.59    0.00    0.00
  994032    994032 Res-Hungry-3          8   31.80   46.68    0.01  645.39    0.03    94.84   49.27    0.08   14.58    0.00    0.00
   83528     83528 ESXi51-B              9    3.41    5.07    0.17  897.45    0.07     0.43  395.87    0.02    0.00    0.00    0.00
   83604     83604 vCenter-VA51          8    2.72    3.88    0.07  798.88    0.00     0.13  196.87    0.01    0.00    0.00    0.00
   83520     83520 ESXi51-A              9    2.70    3.95    0.17  898.65    0.36     0.28  396.78    0.04    0.00    0.00    0.00
  995022    995022 esxtop.661028         1    1.76    2.56    0.00   97.83       -     0.00    0.00    0.00    0.00    0.00    0.00
   83620     83620 Analytics VM          8    1.38    1.98    0.06  800.00    0.00     0.10  198.88    0.01    0.00    0.00    0.00
   83586     83586 vCloud Director       6    1.11    1.63    0.04  600.00    0.00     0.09   98.82    0.00    0.00    0.00    0.00
   83627     83627 UI VM                 8    0.76    1.08    0.02  800.00    0.00     0.10  200.83    0.01    0.00    0.00    0.00
   83611     83611 vShieldManager        7    0.48    0.69    0.03  700.00    0.00     0.07  201.16    0.01    0.00    0.00    0.00
   83535     83535 OpenFiler             8    0.33    0.48    0.03  800.00    0.30     0.04   99.62    0.00    0.00    0.00    0.00
```

3. Now look at the performance counters as mentioned previously. In the following example output, look at the different metrics.

```
11:19:32am up 10 days  1:16, 391 worlds, 12 VMs, 25 vCPUs; CPU load average: 0.62, 0.62, 0.56
PCPU USED(%):  66  38  28 0.3  39  24  15 0.1 2.5 1.3 3.7 1.1 2.0 1.0 1.5 1.7 AVG:  14
PCPU UTIL(%): 100  73  27 0.4  37  22  15 0.2 4.3 2.2 6.0 2.1 3.5 1.8 2.7 2.9 AVG:  18
CORE UTIL(%): 100      27      60      15     6.2     7.6     4.8     5.1  AVG:  28
```

In the preceding example, you can see our pCPU 0 and pCPU 1 are heavily being used (100 percent and 73 percent **UTIL** respectively) and it shows the following figure:

```
11:10:59am up 10 days  1:07, 392 worlds, 12 VMs, 25 vCPUs; CPU load average: 0.64, 0.54, 0.24
PCPU USED(%):  67  38  30  18  48 0.0 8.8 0.0 4.4 1.5 1.8 1.1 2.3 1.2 2.6 1.2 AVG:  14
PCPU UTIL(%): 100  72  29  17  45 0.0 8.4 0.1 6.0 2.7 3.0 2.0 3.8 2.0 4.1 2.1 AVG:  18
CORE UTIL(%): 100      46      45      8.4     8.1     4.6     5.4     5.7  AVG:  28
```

ID	GID	NAME	NWLD	%USED	%RUN	%SYS	%WAIT	%VMWAIT	%RDY	%IDLE	%OVRLP	%CSTP	%MLMTD	%SWPWT
1	1	idle	16	596.41	1600.00	0.00	0.00	-	1600.00	0.00	1.87	0.00	0.00	0.00
994040	994040	Res-Hungry-4	7	105.94	100.68	0.01	600.63	0.00	0.05	99.86	0.09	0.00	0.00	0.00
487530	487530	Res-Hungry-2	7	54.73	68.44	0.01	590.39	0.00	41.82	0.00	0.15	0.00	0.00	0.00
994024	994024	Res-Hungry-1	8	37.66	57.13	0.01	623.12	0.00	94.60	34.41	0.05	26.59	0.00	0.00
994032	994032	Res-Hungry-3	8	31.80	46.68	0.01	645.39	0.03	94.84	49.27	0.08	14.58	0.00	0.00
83528	83528	ESXi51-B	9	3.41	5.07	0.17	897.45	0.07	0.43	395.87	0.02	0.00	0.00	0.00
83604	83604	vCenter-VA51	8	2.72	3.88	0.07	798.88	0.00	0.13	196.87	0.01	0.00	0.00	0.00
83520	83520	ESXi51-A	9	2.70	3.95	0.17	898.65	0.36	0.28	396.78	0.04	0.00	0.00	0.00
995022	995022	esxtop.661028	1	1.76	2.56	0.00	97.83	-	0.00	0.00	0.00	0.00	0.00	0.00
83620	83620	Analytics VM	8	1.38	1.98	0.06	800.00	0.00	0.10	198.88	0.01	0.00	0.00	0.00
83586	83586	vCloud Director	6	1.11	1.63	0.04	600.00	0.00	0.09	98.82	0.00	0.00	0.00	0.00
83627	83627	UI VM	8	0.76	1.08	0.02	800.00	0.00	0.10	200.83	0.01	0.00	0.00	0.00
83611	83611	vShieldManager	7	0.48	0.69	0.03	700.00	0.00	0.07	201.16	0.01	0.00	0.00	0.00
83535	83535	OpenFiler	8	0.33	0.48	0.03	800.00	0.30	0.04	99.62	0.00	0.00	0.00	0.00

Now in the preceding example, you see that the %**Used** value for the four CPU-hungry virtual machines are pretty high.

Also look at the %**RDY** screen, and you will see a high ready time, which indicates a performance problem.

The following list is a quick explanation for each of these metrics:

- **PCPU USED (%)**: This is the CPU utilization per physical CPU.
- %**USED**: This is the physical CPU usage by per group.
- %**SYS**: This is the VMkernel system activity time.
- %**RDY**: This is the ready time. This is referred as the amount of time that the group spent ready to run, but waiting for the CPU to be available. Note that this is not adjusted for the number of vCPUs. You should expand the group to see %**Ready** for each vCPU, or at least divide this by the number of vCPUs to use an average per vCPU.
- %**WAIT**: This is the percentage of time spent in blocked or busy state. This includes idle time and also the time waiting for I/O from the disk or network.
- %**CSTP**: This is referred as the percentage of time spent in the VMkernel, on behalf of the group for processing interrupts. %**CSTP** for a vCPU is how much time the vCPU spent not running in order to allow the extra vCPUs in the same VM to catch up. High values suggest that this VM has more vCPUs than it needs and the performance might be suffering.
- %**MLMTD**: This is the amount of time spent ready to run, but not scheduled because of a CPU limit.

CPU performance best practices

CPU virtualization adds varying amount of overhead, because of this you may need to fine tune the CPU performance and need to know what are the standard best practices.

Following are the standard CPU performance best practices:

- ▶ You need to avoid using SMP VMs unless it is required by the application running inside the guest OS. That means if the application is not multithreaded then there is no benefit of using SMP VM.

- ▶ You should prioritize the VM CPU usage with proportional share algorithm.

- ▶ Use **DRS** (**Distributed Resource Scheduler**) and vMotion to redistribute VMs and reduce contention.

- ▶ Use the latest available virtual hardware for the VMs.

- ▶ Reduce the number of VMs running inside a single host. This way, you can not only reduce the contention, but also reduce the fault domain configuration.

- ▶ You should leverage the application tuning guide from the vendor to tune your VMs for best performance.

Getting ready

To step through this recipe, you need a running ESXi Server, a couple of running virtual machines, and a working installation of vSphere Client. No other prerequisites are required.

How to do it...

Let's get started:

1. For the first best practice, you need to check whether the application is single threaded or multi-threaded. If it is single threaded, then avoid running SMP VM.

2. You need to log in to vCenter using vSphere Client, then go to the **Home** tab. Once there, go to the VM and look at the **Summary** tab.

3. Now you can see whether the VM has one vCPU or multiple vCPUs. You see whether it's using them by looking at **%Utilization** or similar metric for each vCPU. This **Summary** tab doesn't tell us whether the app is single threaded or multi-threaded.

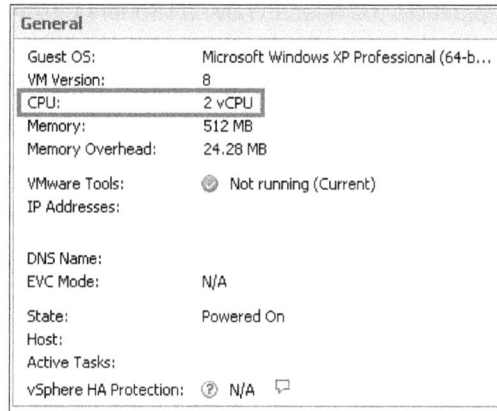

4. For the second best practice, you need to prioritize the VM CPU using shares and reservation. Depending on the customer SLA, this has to be defined.

5. You need to log in to the vCenter using vSphere Client, then go to the **Home** tab. Once there, go to the VM, right-click on it, and then select **Edit Settings**.

6. Now go to the **Resources** tab and select **CPU**. Here, you need to define the **Shares** and **Reservation** values depending on your SLA and the performance factors. By default, ESXi is efficient and fair. It does not waste physical resources. If all the demands can be met, all will. If not all demands can be satisfied, the deprivation is shared equitably among VMs, by default.

   VMs can use, and then adjust the shares, reservations, or limits settings. But be sure that you know how they work first.

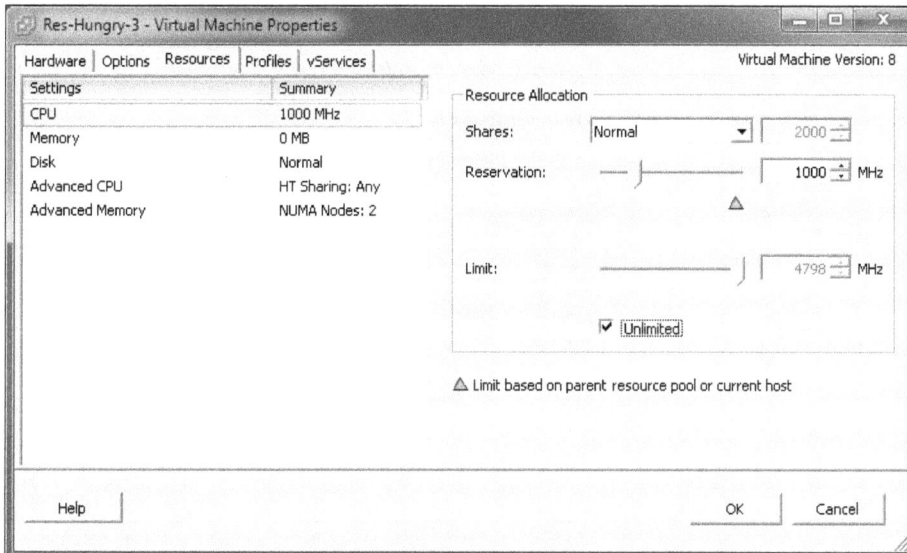

7. For the third best practice, you need to have a vSphere Cluster and have DRS enabled for this. DRS would load balance the VMs across the ESXi hosts using vMotion.

The first screenshot shows that the DRS is enabled on this vSphere Cluster:

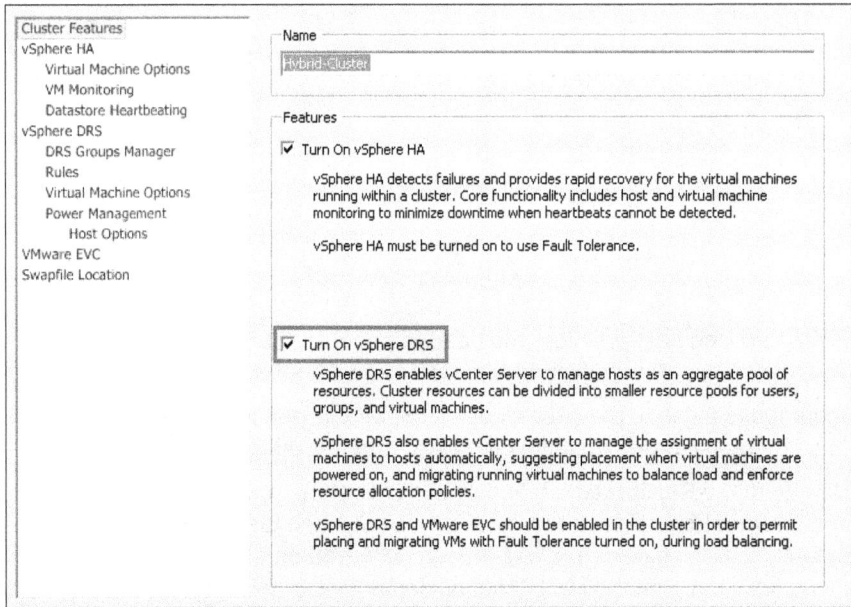

The second screenshot shows the automation level and migration threshold.

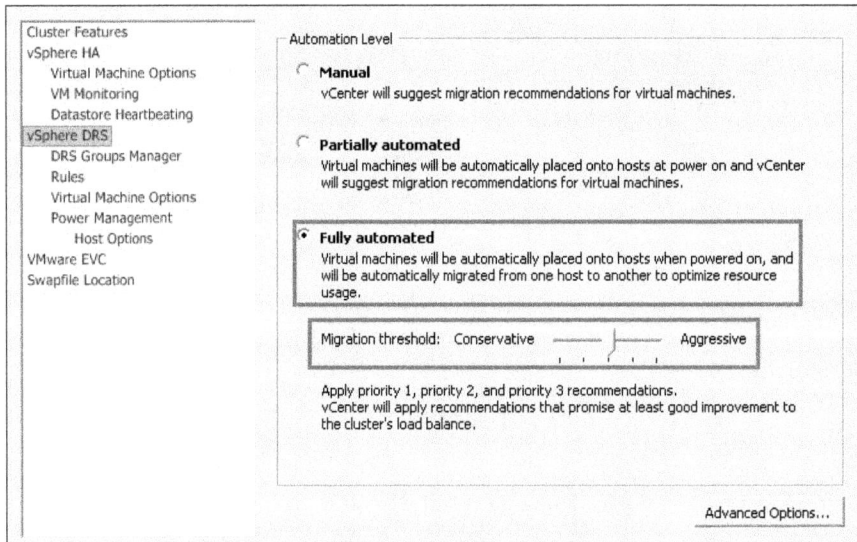

8. For the fourth best practice, you first need to see what virtual hardware the VM is running on, and if it is not current then you need to upgrade that. Virtual hardware version can limit the number of vCPUs.

9. You need to log in to the vCenter using vSphere Client, then go to the **Home** tab. Once there, go to VM and look at the **Summary** tab.

10. In the following example it is hardware Version 8, which is old and we can upgrade it to hardware Version 9.

> For further information, refer to the following article:
>
> ```
> http://blogs.vmware.com/vsphere/2013/02/managing-
> virtual-hardware-versions-during-a-vsphere-upgrade.
> html
> ```

11. Now to upgrade the virtual hardware of a VM, it has to be powered off and then right-click on the VM and go to **Upgrade Virtual Hardware**. It should give you a warning.

> Take a snapshot prior to upgrading in order to mitigate the rare occurrence of a failure to boot the **Guest Operating System** after upgrading.

Confirm Virtual Machine Upgrade

⚠ This operation will cause the virtual hardware your guest operating
system runs on to change. It is an irreversible operation that will make
your virtual machine incompatible with earlier versions of VMware
software products. It is strongly recommended that you make a backup
copy of your disks before proceeding.

Are you sure you want to upgrade your configuration?

| Yes | No |

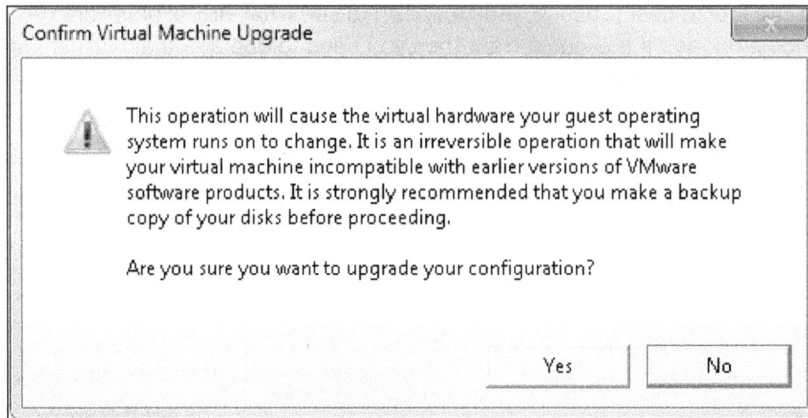

12. Once you click on **OK**, the virtual hardware version will be upgraded.

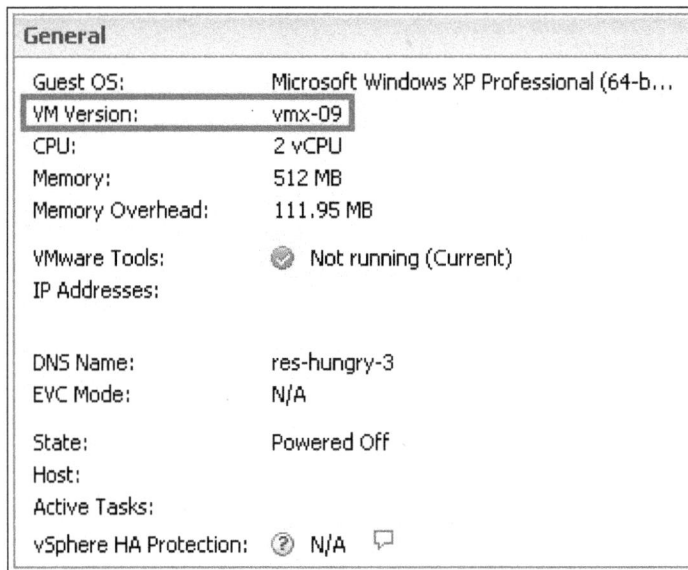

General

Guest OS:	Microsoft Windows XP Professional (64-b...
VM Version:	vmx-09
CPU:	2 vCPU
Memory:	512 MB
Memory Overhead:	111.95 MB
VMware Tools:	⊘ Not running (Current)
IP Addresses:	
DNS Name:	res-hungry-3
EVC Mode:	N/A
State:	Powered Off
Host:	
Active Tasks:	
vSphere HA Protection:	⑦ N/A

13. For the fifth recommendation, you need to limit the number of vCPUs required by the
VMs that would run on the host and the number of sockets/cores available in each
physical host. Remember the golden rule of "Don't keep all your eggs in one basket"
can be retrieved based on fault domain tolerance and customer SLA. There is no
simple answer to this. Monitor the VMs for performance and adjust as necessary.

14. For the last recommendation, you need to get the vendor application tuning guide
and follow that to tune your virtual environment. A typical example is *Exchange 2010
Best Practices guide on VMware*.

2
Memory Performance Design

In this chapter, we will cover the tasks related to memory performance design. You will learn the following aspects of memory performance design:

- ▶ Virtual memory reclamation techniques
- ▶ Monitoring host-swapping activity
- ▶ Monitoring host-ballooning activity
- ▶ Keeping memory free for VMkernel
- ▶ Key memory performance metrics to monitor
- ▶ What metrics not to use
- ▶ Identifying when memory is the problem
- ▶ Analyzing host and VM memory
- ▶ Memory performance best practices

Introduction

Although VMware vSphere uses various mechanisms to efficiently allocate memory, you might still encounter a situation where virtual machines are allocated insufficient physical memory.

You should know how to monitor memory usage of both the host and virtual machines. You should also know how to troubleshoot common memory performance problems, such as those involving an excessive demand for memory.

Virtual memory reclamation techniques

Virtual machines perform memory allocation in the same way, as an operating system handles memory allocation and deallocation. The guest operating system frees itself from a piece of physical memory by adding the memory page numbers to the guest free list.

The guest operating system free list is not accessible to the hypervisor and thus it is difficult for the hypervisor to know when to free host physical memory and when the guest physical memory is freed. The hypervisor is completely unaware of which pages are free or allocated in the guest operating system, and because of this the hypervisor cannot reclaim host physical memory when the guest operating system frees guest physical memory.

So VMware hypervisor relies on memory reclamation techniques to reclaim the host physical memory that is freed by the guest operating system. The memory reclamation techniques are:

- ► Transparent page sharing
- ► Memory ballooning
- ► Host-level (or hypervisor) swapping

Getting ready

To step through this recipe, you will need a running ESXi Server, a couple of running virtual machines, and a working installation of vSphere Client. No other prerequisites are required.

How to do it...

Perhaps you don't need to do anything to enable Transparent Memory Page Sharing, as it is by default enabled on your ESXi Hypervisor.

Memory ballooning is driven by the VMware tools. So you need to install the latest version of VMware tools on all of your virtual machines. It will load the `vmmemctl` driver, which is responsible for memory ballooning.

Perform the following steps:

1. Log in to the VMware vSphere Client.
2. In the virtual machine inventory, right-click on the virtual machine and click on **Install** or **Upgrade VMware Tools**.
3. Go to the VM Console and follow the on-screen instruction to install it.

Similarly, Host-level or Hypervisor Swapping is also enabled by default. You don't need to perform any additional steps to enable it.

How it works...

Let us now look at how these techniques work.

Transparent page sharing

When there are multiple virtual machines running on the same hypervisor, most of the time some of them might have identical sets of memory content (known as memory pages). This creates opportunities for sharing memory across virtual machines. ESXi Hypervisor can reclaim the redundant copies and keep only one copy using transparent page sharing. You can think of it as Memory De-duplication.

Traditionally in x86 systems, memory is split into 4 kilobytes pages and that happens only if you are using small pages with shadow pages tables. The TPS process runs every 60 minutes. It scans all memory pages and calculates a hash value for each of them. Those hashes are saved in a separate table and compared to each other by the kernel. Every time the ESXi kernel finds two identical hashes it starts a bit-by-bit comparison of the corresponding memory pages. If these pages are absolutely the same, the kernel leaves only one copy of page in memory and removes the second one. When one of your VM requests to write to this page, the kernel creates a new page because the change made by one VM must not affect the memory contents of another VM.

VMware ESXi scans the guest physical pages randomly, with a base scan rate specified by `Mem.ShareScanTime`. The maximum number of scanned pages per second in the host and the maximum number of per-virtual machine scanned pages, (that is, `Mem.ShareScanGHz` and `Mem.ShareRateMax` respectively) can also be specified in ESXi advanced settings.

Memory ballooning

Memory ballooning makes the guest operating system aware that it does not have enough memory from the host, so that the guest operating system frees some of its memory. When there is a memory crisis, hypervisor tells the balloon driver to request some amount of megabytes from the guest operating system. The hypervisor knows that pages occupied by the balloon driver will never store data, so the pages of pRAM backing the balloon driver can then be reallocated safely to other VMs. It is the guest operating system's call to decide which pages of vRAM it should allocate to the balloon driver, and it will start with free pages. If it has a plenty of free or idle guest physical memory, inflating the balloon will induce no guest-level paging and thus it will not affect guest performance. However, in a case of memory contention within the guest, the VM guest decides which guest physical pages are to be paged out to the virtual swap device in order to satisfy the balloon driver's allocation requests.

The balloon driver reclaims guest operating systems allocated memory using the **Idle Memory Tax** (**IMT**). IMT may reclaim up to 75 percent of idle memory. A guest operating system page file is necessary in order to prevent guest operating system kernel starvation. The `memctl` should aggressively reclaim memory due to severe host contention (make sure that the guest operating system page file is at least 65 percent of the configured vRAM). Even here, the guest operating system can make intelligent guesses about which pages of data are least likely to be requested in the future. (You'll see this in contrast with hypervisor-level swapping, which is discussed next.) Look at the following pictorial representation of memory page mapping to host memory:

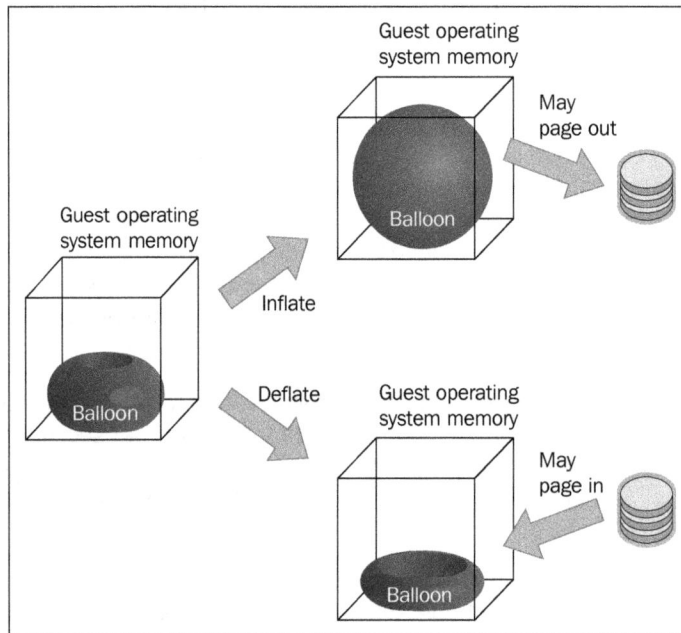

Host-level swapping stars in ESXi are not sufficient to reclaim memory during transparent page sharing and ballooning. To support this, when starting a virtual machine, the hypervisor creates a separate swap file for the virtual machine. This is primarily because if it frees pRAM for other virtual machines, the hypervisor can directly swap out vRAM to the swap file.

Swapping is a guaranteed technique to reclaim a specific amount of memory within a specific amount of time. However, you should be concerned about host-level swapping because it can severely penalize guest performance. This occurs when the hypervisor has no knowledge about which guest physical pages should be swapped, and the swapping might cause unintended interactions with the native memory management policies in the guest operating system. The following is a pictorial representation of host-level memory page swapping:

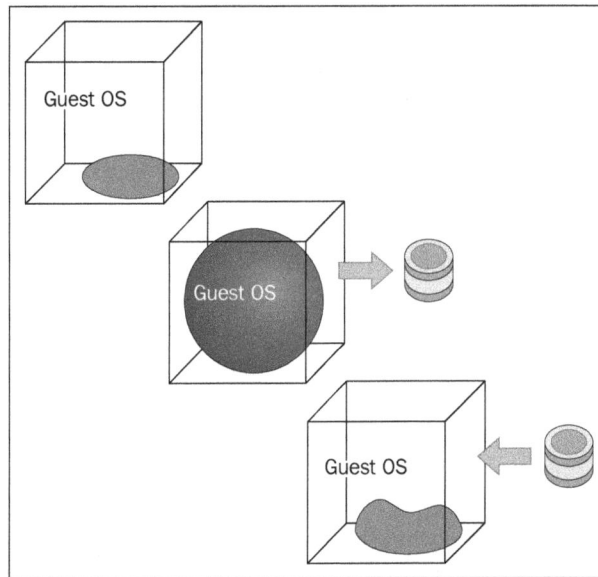

Monitoring host-swapping activity

Excessive memory demand can cause severe performance problems for one or more virtual machines on an ESXi host. When ESXi is actively swapping from the memory of a virtual machine to disk, the performance of that virtual machine will degrade. The overhead of swapping a virtual machine's memory to disk can also degrade the performance of other virtual machines, because the virtual machine expects to be writing to RAM (speeds measured in nanoseconds) but it is unknowingly writing to disk (speeds measured in milliseconds).

The metrics in the vSphere Client for monitoring swapping activity are the following:

- **Memory Swap In rate**: The rate at which memory is being swapped in from disk.

- **Memory Swap Out rate**: The rate at which memory is being swapped out to disk.

- **Swapped**: The total amount of data that is sitting inside the .vswp hypervisor-level swap file. However, this doesn't tell you anything about the current state of performance, nor about the current state of free pRAM. It just tells you that at some point in the past, there was low free pRAM. The only use of this metric is to see if there was a memory shortage in the past, and to see if there's a risk of Swap In (and bad performance) in the future. But it's hard to estimate how likely the Swap In will be, because sometimes there's "junk data" that will be rarely requested again (for example, pages holding rarely-accessed data, like an overly aggressive filesystem caching, or zeroed-out pages that were actually deemed free by the guest operating system).

High values for metric indicate a lack of memory and that performance is suffering as a result.

However, a high Swap Out rate means that the host is low on free pRAM, but essentially it does not indicate a current performance problem. A high Swap In rate indicates a current performance problem but not necessarily that the host is currently low on free pRAM (Swap In happens only on demand, which could be a week after the data was swapped out, and maybe the free-host-memory shortage has long since been resolved).

Getting ready

To step through this recipe, you will need a running ESXi Server, a couple of memory-hungry Virtual Machines, a vCenter Server, and a working installation of vSphere Client. No other prerequisites are required.

How to do it...

To monitor a host's swapping activity in vSphere Client, view the **Memory** screen. A couple of useful metrics are Swapped, Swap In, and Swap Out. This metric represents total swapping for a virtual machine on the host.

To monitor host-level swapping activity for all virtual machines, you need to select one single ESXi Host and then go to the **Performance** tab. There, you need to go to the **Memory** tab, which will show the entire VMs. After this is done, perform the following steps:

1. Open **vSphere Client**.
2. Log in to the **vCenter Server**.
3. On your **Home** screen, select **VMs and Templates**.
4. Choose the memory-hungry.
5. Go to the **Performance** tab, and switch to the **Memory** screen.
6. Click on the **Advanced** tab, and select **Chart Options**.
7. Select the three values there, that is, **Swapped, Swap in Rate in KBps**, and **Swap Out Rate in KBps**.
8. Click on **OK**. Now you should see something similar to the following image, if there are swapping activities on your VM:

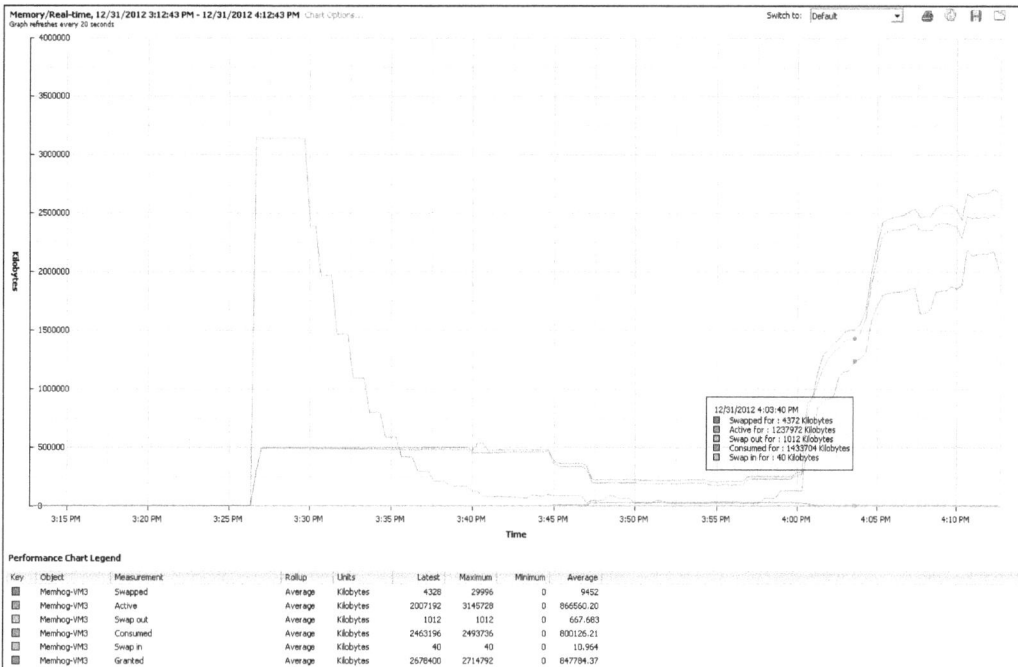

Memory/Real-time, 12/31/2012 3:12:43 PM - 12/31/2012 4:12:43 PM   Chart Options...

Performance Chart Legend

Key	Object	Measurement	Rollup	Units	Latest	Maximum	Minimum	Average
	Memhog-VM3	Swapped	Average	Kilobytes	4328	29996	0	9452
	Memhog-VM3	Active	Average	Kilobytes	2007192	3145728	0	866560.20
	Memhog-VM3	Swap out	Average	Kilobytes	1012	1012	0	667.683
	Memhog-VM3	Consumed	Average	Kilobytes	2463196	2493736	0	800126.21
	Memhog-VM3	Swap in	Average	Kilobytes	40	40	0	10.964
	Memhog-VM3	Granted	Average	Kilobytes	2678400	2714792	0	847784.37

In the preceding example, you can see that this VM has swapped **4372 Kilobytes**, Swap out for **1012 Kilobytes**, and Swap in for **40 Kilobytes**.

Now to see the overall swapped situation for all VMs in a single ESXi server, you should perform the following steps:

1. Open **vSphere Client**.

2. Log in to the **vCenter Server**.

3. On your **Home** screen, select **Hosts and Clusters**.

4. Choose the poorly-performing ESXi host.

5. Go to the **Performance** tab, and switch to the **Memory** screen.

6. Click on the **Advanced** tab, and select **Chart Options**.

7. Select the three values there, that is, **Swap Used**, **Swap In**, and **Swap Out** rate in KBps.

8. Click on **OK**. Now you should see something similar to the following image if there are swapping activities on your ESXi host:

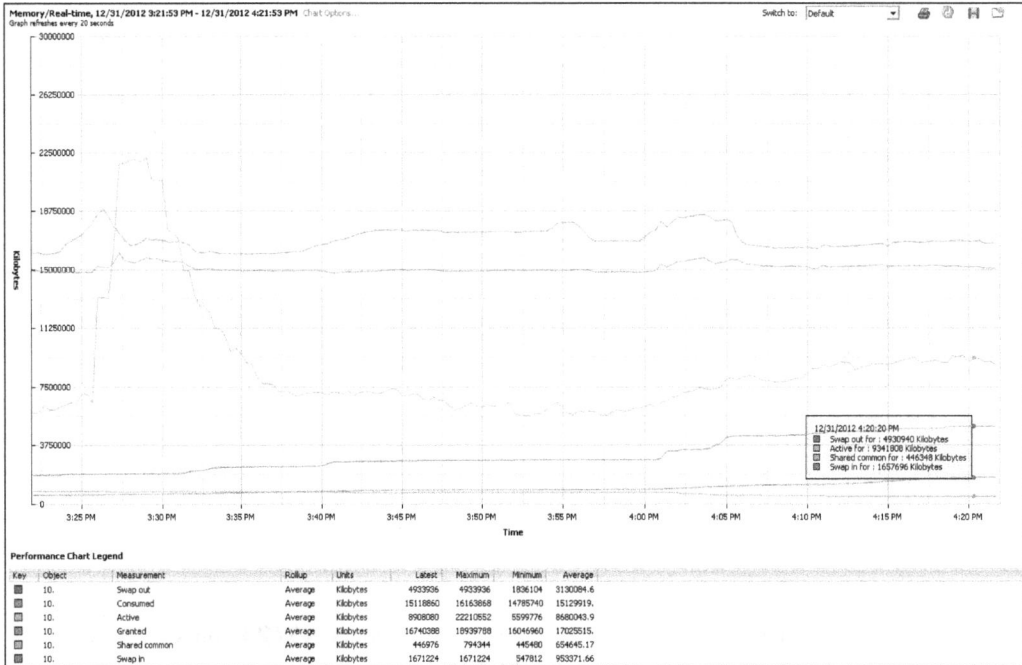

In this example, you can see that this ESXi host Swap in for **1657976 Kilobytes** and Swap out for **4930940 Kilobytes**.

How it works...

We talked about how it works in the previous recipe. Please refer to the *Virtual memory reclamation technique* recipe.

There's more...

The basic cause of host-level swapping is memory overcommitment from using memory intensive virtual machines whose combined configured memory is greater than the amount of host physical memory available.

To resolve this problem, you should consider the following factors:

- Reduce the level of memory overcommitment (for example, reduce oversized VM's, and add more memory where necessary, add more hosts to the cluster if necessary, and so on)

- Enable the balloon driver in all virtual machines by installing VMware tools

- Reduce memory Reservations. This is covered in *Chapter 5, vSphere Cluster Design*

- Use resource controls (Shares, Reservations, and Limits) with careful understanding and planning, to reduce memory contention on the most critical virtual machines

Note that this will not reduce the total memory contention on this host, but it allows you to mitigate the risk to the performance of your most important VMs.

Monitoring host-ballooning activity

Ballooning is a part of normal operations when memory is overcommitted. The fact that ballooning occurrence is not necessarily an indication of a performance problem. The use of the balloon driver enables the guest to give up physical memory pages that are not being used. In fact, ballooning can be a sign that you're getting extra value out of the memory you have in the host.

However, if ballooning causes the guest to give up memory that it actually needs, performance problems can occur due to guest operating system paging.

Note, however, that this is fairly uncommon because the guest operating system will always assign already-free memory to the balloon driver whenever possible, thereby avoiding any guest operating system swapping.

In the vSphere Client, use the Memory Balloon metric to monitor a host's ballooning activity. This metric represents the total amount of memory claimed by the balloon drivers of the virtual machines on the host. The memory claimed by the balloon drivers can be used by other virtual machines. Again, this is not a performance problem, but it represents that the host starts to take memory from less needful virtual machines for those with large amounts of active memory. If the host is ballooning, check the swap rate counters (Memory Swap In Rate and Memory Swap Out Rate), which might indicate performance problems, but it does not mean that you have a performance problem presently. It means that the unallocated pRAM on the host has dropped below a predefined threshold.

In a world where a vast majority of VMs have oversized vRAM, much of the vRAM -> pRAM mapping is just holding zeroed-out free pages, and these will be freed up by ballooning, without displacing real data and not risking poor performance in the future.

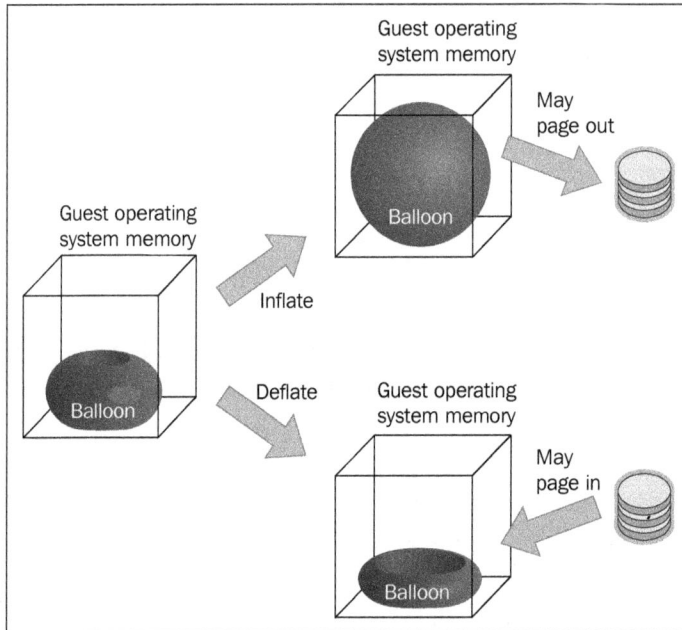

Getting ready

To step through this recipe, you will need a running ESXi Server, a couple of memory-hungry Virtual Machines, a vCenter Server, and a working installation of vSphere Client. No other prerequisites are required.

How to do it...

Balloon activity can also be monitored in Performance Chart through vSphere Client. The metric that you should follow in this case is Balloon Average in kilobytes.

You should select the same metric when you monitor the Ballooning activity for ESXi as well.

To monitor the Ballooning activity using vSphere client for individual VM, follow these steps:

1. Open **vSphere Client**.
2. Log in to the **vCenter Server**.
3. On your **Home** Screen, select **VMs and Templates**.

4. Choose the memory-hungry VM.

5. Go to the **Performance** tab, and switch to the **Memory** screen.

6. Click on the **Advanced** tab, and select **Chart Options**.

7. Select **Balloon** as the metric.

8. Click on **OK**. Now you should see something similar to the following image if there is Ballooning activity on your VM:

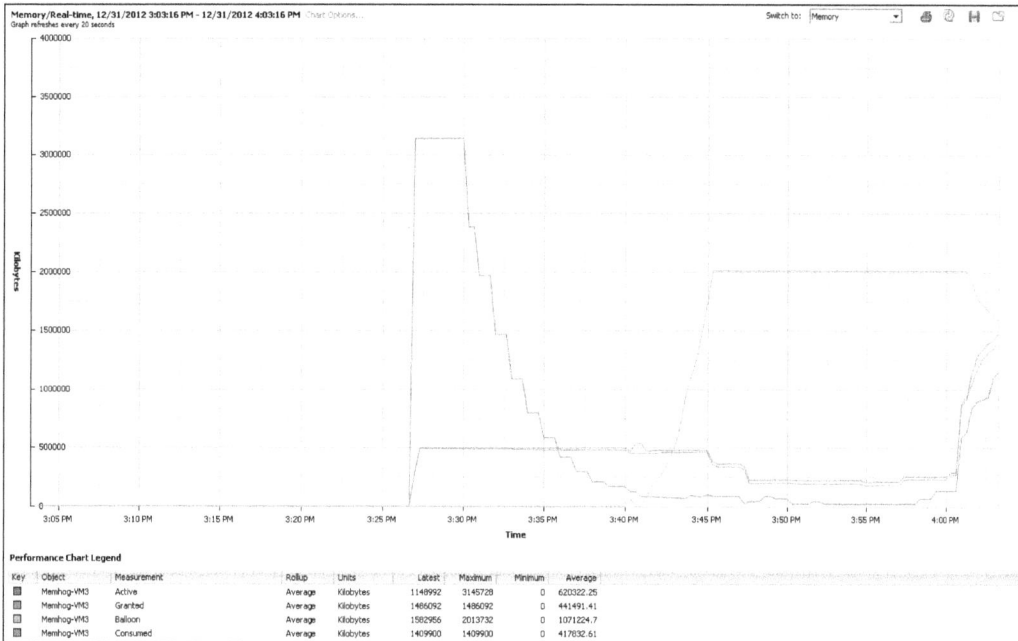

In this example you can see that this VM (Memhog-VM3) is releasing its inactive memory pages to Host memory. Here it is **1582956 Kilobytes**.

To monitor the Ballooning activity using vSphere client for your ESXi, you should follow these steps:

1. Open **vSphere Client**.

2. Log in to the **vCenter Server**.

3. On your **Home** Screen, select **Hosts and Clusters**.

4. Choose the poorly performing ESXi host.

5. Go to the **Performance** tab and switch to the **Memory** screen.

6. Click on the **Advanced** tab and select **Chart Options**.

7. Select **Balloon** as the metric.

8. Click on **OK**. Now you should see something similar to this if there is ballooning activity on your ESXi host:

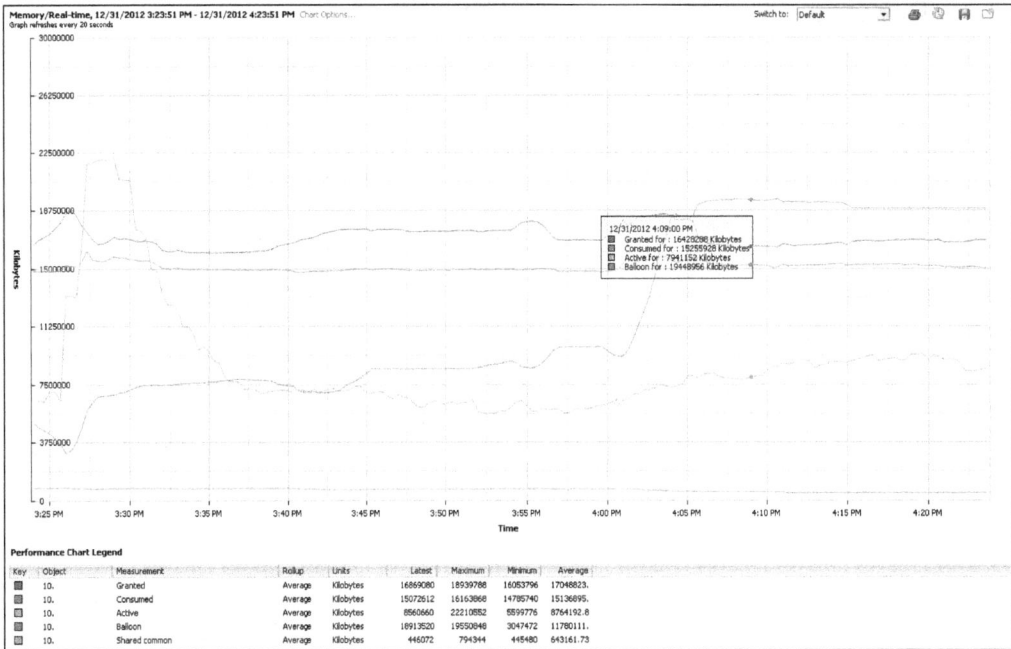

In this example you can see that this ESXi host is involved in ballooning and its VMs are actively releasing inactive memory pages.

How it works...

In our previous recipe, we talked about how it works. Refer to the *Virtual memory reclamation technique* recipe.

There's more...

The basic cause of memory that ballooning is again memory overcommitment from using memory-intensive virtual machines. However, this is just indicative, which means that the presence of ballooning does not always say it's a performance problem. Ballooning is an effective way to use pRAM more efficiently, usually with no negative performance impact.

In order to maximize the ability of ESXi to recover idle memory from virtual machines, the balloon driver should be enabled on all virtual machines. The balloon driver should never be deliberately disabled on a virtual machine. Disabling the balloon driver might cause unintended performance problems.

Keeping memory free for VMkernel

The amount of memory the VMkernel will try to keep free can be achieved through the `Mem.MemMinFreePct` parameter. `MemMinFreePct` determines the amount of memory that the VMkernel should keep free. vSphere 4.1 introduced a dynamic threshold of the Soft, Hard, and Low state to set appropriate thresholds and prevent virtual machine performance issues, while protecting VMkernel. The different states, based on **%pRAM** which is still free, determines what type of memory reclamation techniques are being used.

For `MemMinFreePct`, using a default value of 6 percent can be inefficient when 256 gigabyte or 512 gigabyte systems are becoming more and more mainstream. A 6 percent threshold on a 512 gigabyte results in 30 gigabyte idling most of the time. However, not all customers use large systems; some prefer to scale out rather than to scale up. In this scenario, a 6 percent `MemMinFreePct` might be suitable. To have the best of both worlds, VMkernel uses a sliding scale to determine the `Mem.MemMinFreePct` threshold based on the amount of RAM installed in vSphere 5 hosts. Sliding scale is not applicable to vSphere 4.

Getting ready

To step through this recipe, you will need a running ESXi Server and a working installation of vSphere Client. No other prerequisites are required.

How to do it...

1. VMkernel uses a sliding scale to determine the `Mem.MinFreePct` threshold based on the amount of RAM installed in the host and it is automatic. However, if you need to change this behavior and set something on your own, then follow these steps:

2. Open **vSphere Client.**

3. Log in to the **vCenter Server**.

4. On your **Home** Screen, select **Hosts and Clusters**.

5. Choose the ESXi host where you want to perform this activity.

6. Go to the **Configuration** tab, and click on **Advanced Settings**.

7. In the **Memory** section, scroll down and locate `Mem.MemMinFreePct`.

8. Choose a value between 0 to 50, where 0 indicates automatic.

So here you can set the percentage of host memory to reserve for accelerating memory allocations when free memory is low, which means this percentage determines when memory reclamation techniques (besides TPS) will start to be used.

The following is a sample screenshot when you configure this parameter:

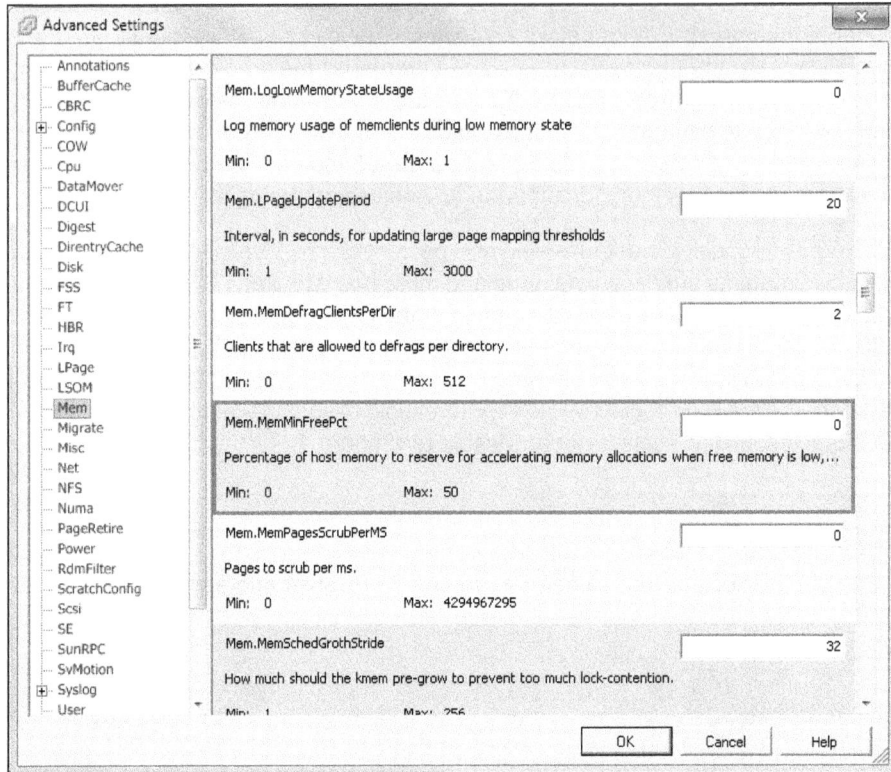

How it works...

MemMinFreePct is used to calculate the minimum free memory which we want to keep by reclaiming memory. For systems with smaller memory (0 to 4 gigabytes), we want to keep 6 percent free, otherwise memory requests from VMkernel or VMs might not be fulfilled.

Now for the systems having relatively more memory than previously mentioned (4 to 12 gigabyte), we want to keep 4 percent free. For systems having memory ranging from (12 to 28 gigabyte), we want to keep the Free State threshold at 2 percent.

The thresholds for the "high", "soft", and "hard" states are about performance and each state corresponds to a successively lower amount of free pRAM. The main intention is to kick off ballooning and other reclamation mechanisms before hitting the low state.

So, in a nutshell, the MemMinFreePct parameter defines the minimal desired amount of free memory in the system. Falling below this level causes the system to reclaim memory through ballooning or swapping.

So, the amount of memory the VMkernel keeps free is controlled by the value of `MemMinFreePct`, which is now determined using a sliding scale. This means that when free memory is greater than or equal to the derived value, the host is not under memory pressure. Check out the following points. Note that these are based on vSphere 4.x.

- 6 percent free (High): Split small pages for TPS (if applicable); begin ballooning.

- 4 percent free (Soft): Ballooning in full swing; in vSphere 4.1 begin compressing virtual memory.

- 2 percent free (Hard): VM swap; break large pages for TPS in full swing.

- 1 percent free (Low): No new pages provided to VMs.

> Even if a host is under memory pressure, it just means that less free pRAM is available than is preferred. It does not mean that a performance problem is present, currently. Because VMs often have extra vRAM, and because the hypervisor doesn't know how much vRAM is considered free by the guest operating system, there is often pRAM allocated to back vRAM, which is holding junk data and which could be freed for use elsewhere without any negative performance impact.

Key memory performance metrics to monitor

To troubleshoot memory performance in a VMware vSphere environment, you should monitor the memory performance very carefully. In this aspect you should monitor the following metrics:

- **Average memory active**: Memory estimated to be used based on recently touched memory pages.

- **Average memory swapped in or out**: Virtual memory swapped to or from disk.

- **Average memory swapped**: Total amount of memory swapped out. This indicates a possibility (with an unknown likelihood) of poor performance in the future.

Getting ready

To step through this recipe, you will need a running ESXi Server, a couple of running memory-hungry Virtual Machines, and a working installation of vSphere Client. No other prerequisites are required.

How to do it...

To spot the average Active Memory, you should check both the VM level and Host level. To monitor at the VM level, you should perform the following steps:

1. Open up **vSphere Client**.

2. Log in to the **vCenter Server**.

3. On the **Home** screen, select **VMs and Templates**.

4. Choose the VM where you want to monitor **Active Memory**.

5. Go to the **Performance** tab on the right-hand side.

6. Select **Memory** from the drop-down list.

7. Click on the **Advanced** tab, and select **Chart Options**.

8. Select **Active** metric from there and click on **OK** to continue. Active is usually the one that estimates how much the VM would actually need.

One of the biggest myths is that when a host is low on memory, performance problems are likely, or that a VM needs more memory than it has installed, because you're looking at a Granted or Consumed type of metric instead of Active-type metrics.

The following is a sample screenshot, which you see once you select the Active metric to monitor memory performance:

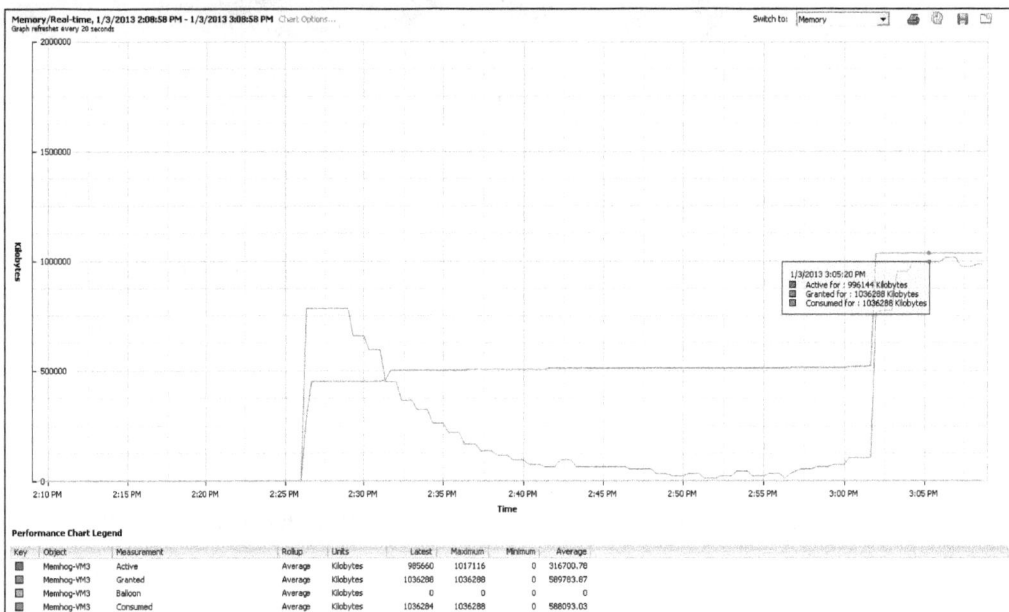

Memory/Real-time, 1/3/2013 2:08:58 PM - 1/3/2013 3:08:58 PM   Chart Options...   Switch to: Memory

1/3/2013 3:05:20 PM
Active for : 996144 Kilobytes
Granted for : 1036288 Kilobytes
Consumed for : 1036288 Kilobytes

Performance Chart Legend

Key	Object	Measurement	Rollup	Units	Latest	Maximum	Minimum	Average
	Memhog-VM3	Active	Average	Kilobytes	985660	1017116	0	316700.78
	Memhog-VM3	Granted	Average	Kilobytes	1036288	1036288	0	589783.87
	Memhog-VM3	Balloon	Average	Kilobytes	0	0	0	0
	Memhog-VM3	Consumed	Average	Kilobytes	1036284	1036288	0	588093.03

In the preceding example, you can see that **Memhog-VM3** is using close to 1 gigabyte of memory, which means the Active memory is 1 gigabyte, whereas the configured memory for this VM is also 1 gigabyte.

If you want to monitor this metric for the ESXi Host level then perform the following steps:

1. Open up **vSphere Client**.
2. Log in to the **vCenter Server**.
3. On the **Home** screen, select **Hosts and Clusters**.
4. Choose the ESXi host where you want to monitor the **Active Memory**.
5. Go to the **Performance** tab at the right-hand side.
6. Select **Memory** from the drop-down list.
7. Click on the **Advanced** tab, and select **Chart Options**.
8. Select **Active** metric from there and click on **OK** to continue.

The following is a sample screenshot, which you see once you select the **Active** metric to monitor memory performance:

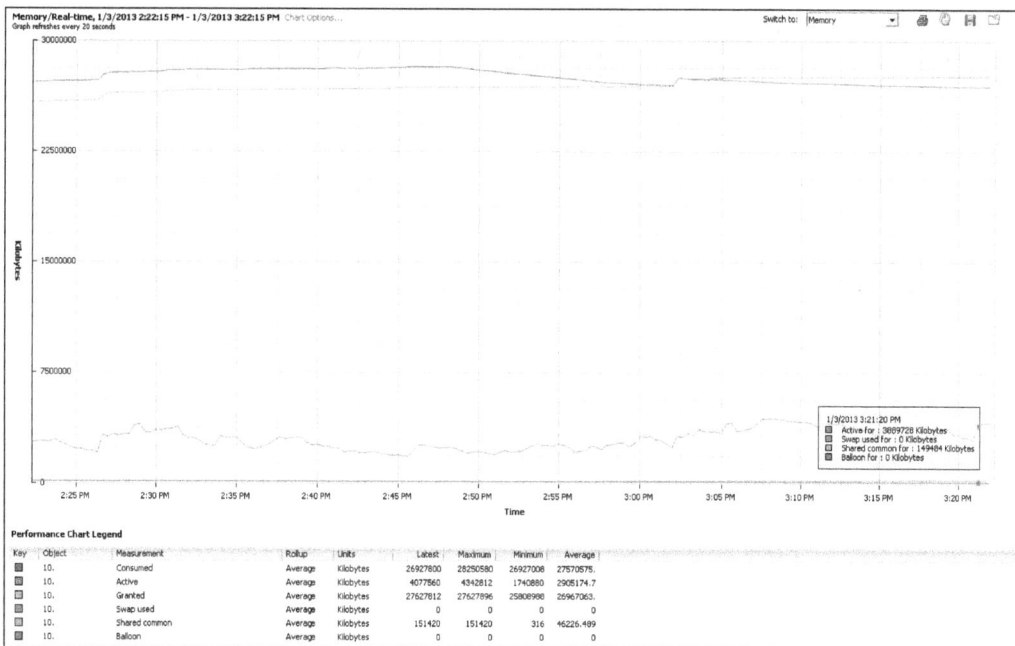

In this example, you can see that ESXi host is using **4077560 Kilobytes** of **Active** memory.

You may notice another **Shared common** metric here. This is a measure of savings due to TPS. Having TPS run does not have any downside and does not provide any reason to monitor it either. You could get into most shared pages being zeroed pages, and the VDI is more likely to share memory if all of the guest operating systems are the same. TPS doesn't work with large pages, which are standard now, until you hit a threshold, where the large pages are broken down and then TPS starts.

Now to monitor Swapped, Swap in, and Swap out, you should follow the *Monitoring host swapping activity* recipe.

How it works...

To understand how swapping happens, you should check the *Monitoring host swapping activity* recipe.

The average active memory refers to the average amount of memory that is actively used in kilobytes.

What metrics not to use

A lot of the time, we assume that some very popular metric would be better to monitor memory performance. However, many a times, it leads to something else. This means that these are not an indication of a memory performance issue. If this metric is combined with something else then it may indicate performance degradation.

In this aspect you should not use two of the most popular metrics just to understand whether memory is under pressure or not:

▶   `Mem.consumed` (Consumed Memory)

▶   `Mem.vmmemctl` (Ballooned Memory)

Let me show you what they essentially indicate.

`Mem.consumed` is the amount of memory consumed by one or all virtual machines. This is calculated as memory granted minus memory saved by sharing. Now the question is why we should not use this. The reason is that memory allocation will vary dynamically based on the VM's entitlement. It is important that a VM should get whatever it actually demands.

Similarly, `Mem.vmmemctl` is the amount of ballooned memory. This does not indicate a performance problem as well. However, when it gets combined with Host Swapping then it indicates a performance problem.

Getting ready

To step through this recipe, you will need a running ESXi Server, a couple of running Memory Hungry Virtual Machines, and a working installation of vSphere Client. No other prerequisites are required.

How to do it...

To spot the Consumed Memory metric value within the vSphere infrastructure, this is what you should do:

1. Open up **vSphere Client**.
2. Log in to the **vCenter Server**.
3. In the **Home** screen, select **VMs and Templates**.
4. Choose the VM where you want to monitor the **Consumed Memory**.
5. Go to the **Performance** tab on the right-hand side.
6. Select **Memory** from the drop-down list.
7. Click on the **Advanced** tab, and select **Chart Options**.
8. Select the **Consumed** metric, and then click on **OK** to continue.

Now you should see something similar to the following screenshot:

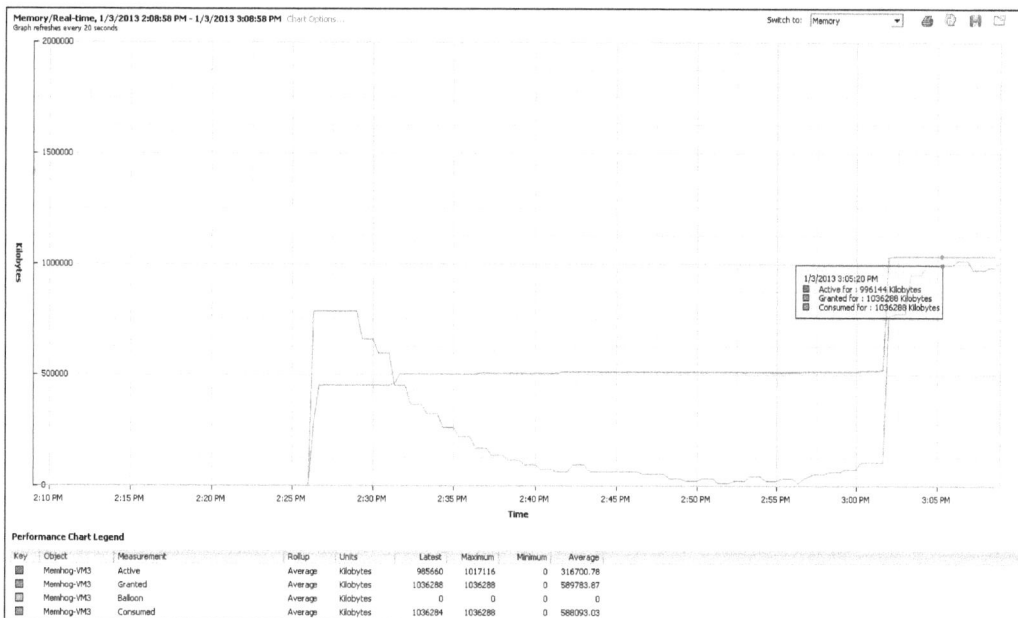

In this example you can see that the Consumed value of the **Memhog-VM3** VM is **1409900 Kilobyte**.

To understand the `Mem.vmmemctl` metric you should follow the *Monitoring host ballooning* recipe.

Identifying when memory is the problem

Both your host memory and VM memory can indicate that it is under pressure. But the main challenge to a VMware admin is how to determine that there is a memory performance issue.

There are a few things which a VMware admin should understand is that there could be a memory performance issue and those are:

- Your host memory consumption is approaching your total host memory
- Active memory in your host is approaching your total memory
- Ballooning is occurring
- Host swapping is occurring

Now, if you wonder what is Active memory here in relation to Consumed memory, let me tell you that Active Memory is the amount of memory that is actively used, as estimated by VMkernel based on recently touched memory pages. For a VM this is referred to the amount of guest "physical" memory actively used.

An ESXi host calculates Active memory by using the sum of all active metrics for all powered-on virtual machines plus vSphere services on the host.

There could be another side to it, which can depict that VM is under memory pressure and to determine that you could combine the factors described previously. You should check whether VM memory has high percent utilization.

Getting ready

To step through this recipe, you will need a running ESXi Server, a couple of running memory-hungry Virtual Machines, and a working installation of vSphere Client. No other prerequisites are required.

How to do it...

To check the Memory Utilization of VM, you should follow the following steps:

1. Open up **vSphere Client**.

2. Log in to the **vCenter Server**.

3. On the **Home** screen, select **VMs and Templates**.

4. Choose the VM, where you want to monitor the **Utilization** of memory.

5. Go to the **Performance** tab on the right-hand side.

6. Select **Memory** from the drop-down list.

7. Click on the **Advanced** tab and select **Chart Options**.

8. Select the **Usage** metric from there and click on **OK** to continue.

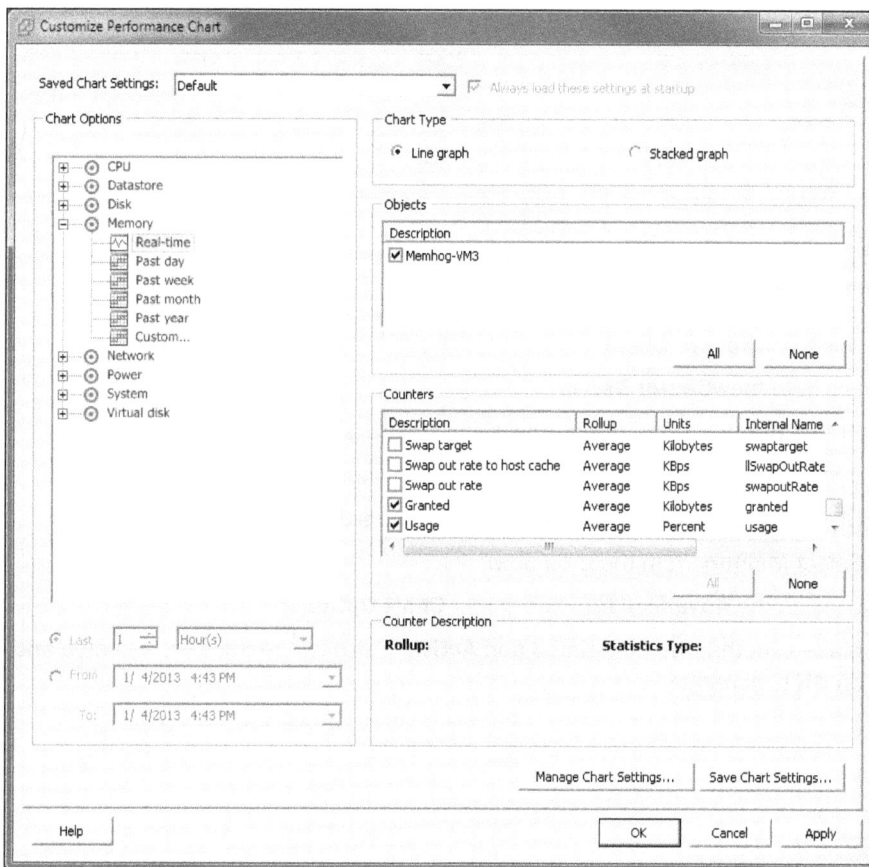

The following is an example where you can see the utilization of this VM is almost 97 percent.

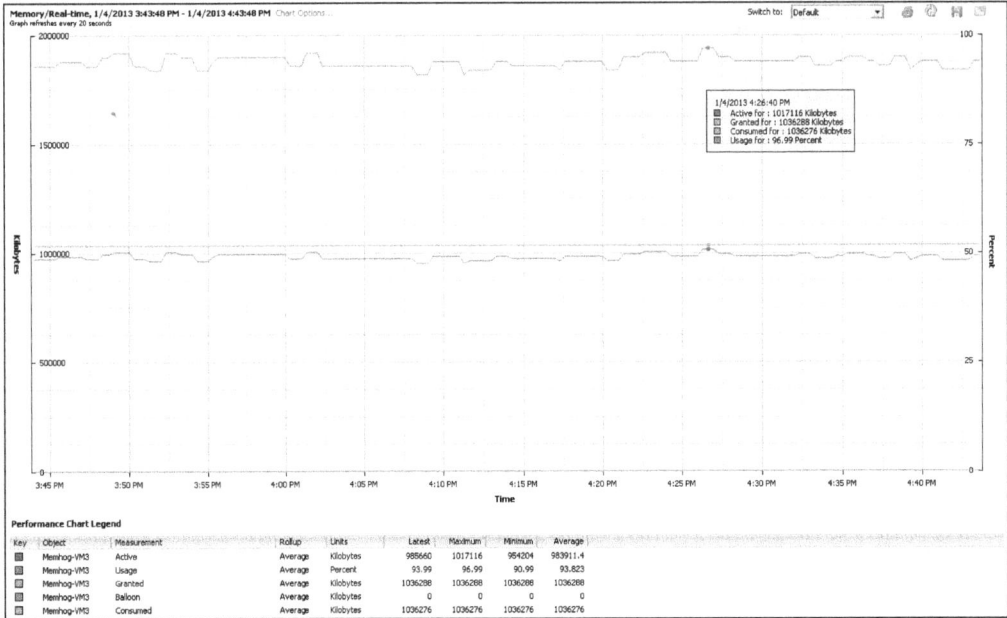

Now to check the overall host memory consumption and active host memory consumption, you need to perform the following steps:

1. Open up **vSphere Client**.

2. Log in to the **vCenter Server**.

3. On the **Home** screen, select **Hosts and Clusters**.

4. Choose the ESXi host where you want to monitor the **Memory Consumption**.

5. Go to the **Performance** tab on the right-hand side.

6. Select **Memory** from the drop-down list.

7. Click on the **Advanced** tab, and select **Chart Options**.

8. Make sure that the **Consumed** and **Active**, these two metrics are selected and click on **OK** to continue.

Now let us look at a sample screenshot and see what it looks like:

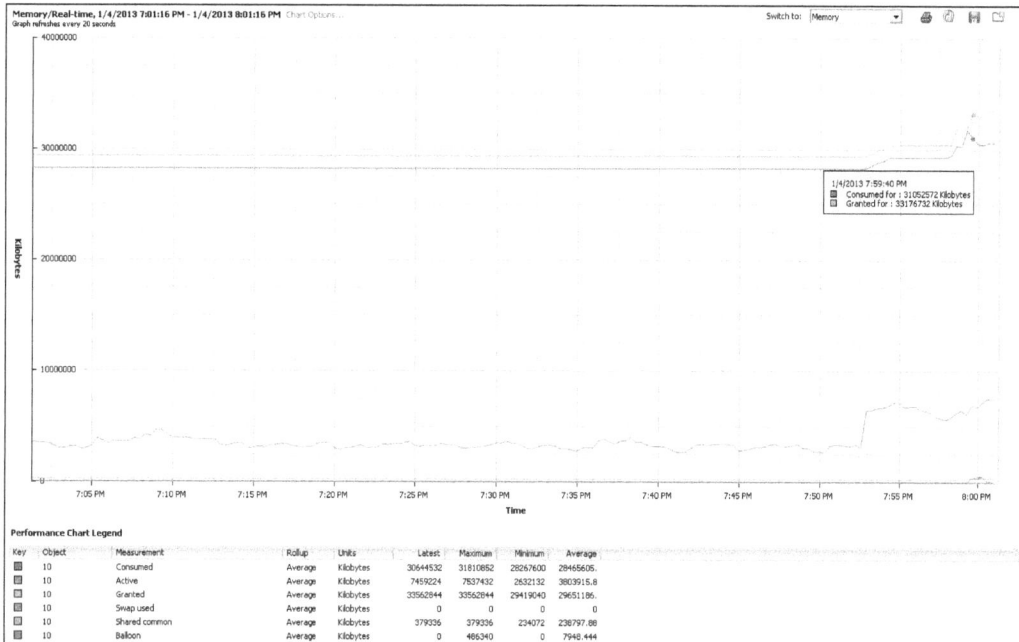

You can see in this example, that we have an ESXi host that has 32 gigabytes of physical memory, and we are consuming almost every bit of it.

However, if you look at the Active memory here, we are using little more than 7 gigabytes. So that means that although we have more than 30 gigabytes of consumed memory, we only have 7 gigabytes of Active memory. It should not create many issues. This could indicate overprovisioning of resources; if applicable, VMs should be right-sized by removing allocated RAM that is not required.

Analyzing host and VM memory

Often you need to monitor virtual machine and host memory usage; the good part about this is that VMware vSphere Client exposes two memory statistics in the **Summary** tab of a virtual machine. These are consumed host memory and active guest memory.

Consumed host memory is the amount of host physical memory that is allocated to the virtual machine. Please note that this value includes the virtualization overhead also.

Also note that many VMs have oversized vRAM, and the guest operating system is likely to opportunistically fill up its vRAM with unnecessary things (for example, caching everything read from disk, no matter how unlikely it will be requested again). Consumed memory only means that the VM used this memory at some point, not that it's likely to use it again.

Active guest memory is defined as the amount of guest physical memory that is currently being used by the guest operating system and its applications.

These two statistics are quite useful for analyzing the memory status of the virtual machine and providing hints to address potential performance issues.

For host memory usage, you may want to look at the **Resources** section of the **Summary** tab for an ESXi Host and to understand how much is the actual usage by VM, you need to check the **Memory** section of the **Configuration** page.

Getting ready

To step through this recipe, you will need a running ESXi Server, a couple of running Virtual Machines, and a working installation of vSphere Client. No other prerequisites are required.

How to do it...

1. Open up **vSphere Client**.

2. Log in to the **vCenter Server**.

3. On the **Home** screen, select **VMs and Templates**.

4. Choose the VM where you want to monitor the **Utilization of Memory**.

5. Go to the **Summary** page of the VM and locate **Consumed Host Memory** and **Active Guest Memory** under the **Resources** section:

Memhog-VM1		

| Getting Started | Summary | Resource Allocation | Performance | Tasks & Events | Alarms | Console | Permissions | Maps | Storage Views | vShield |

General		Resources	
Guest OS:	Other 2.6.x Linux (32-bit)	Consumed Host CPU:	407 MHz
VM Version:	8	Consumed Host Memory:	2034.00 MB
CPU:	2 vCPU	Active Guest Memory:	1966.00 MB
Memory:	2048 MB		Refresh Storage Usage
Memory Overhead:	34.18 MB	Provisioned Storage:	12.09 GB
VMware Tools:	Running (Current)	Not-shared Storage:	6.40 GB
IP Addresses:	View all	Used Storage:	6.40 GB

Storage	Status	Drive Type
NFS-Local (1)	Normal	Non-SSD

DNS Name:	lin32-tools
EVC Mode:	N/A

Network	Type	Sta
VM Network	Standard port group	

State:	Powered On
Host:	
Active Tasks:	
vSphere HA Protection:	N/A

You can see in the previous example that the **Consumed Host Memory** of VM is **2034.00 MB**, and its **Active Guest Memory** is **1966.00 MB**.

You can also check this through performance graph of the VM. Here is what you need to do to get to this:

1. Open up **vSphere Client**.

2. Log in to the **vCenter Server**.

3. On the **Home** screen, select **VMs and Templates**.

4. Choose the VM where you want to monitor the **Utilization of Memory**.

5. Go to the **Performance** tab on the right-hand side.

6. Select **Memory** from the drop-down list.

7. Click on the **Advanced** tab and select **Chart Options**.

8. Make sure that the **Active** and **Consumed** metrics are selected, and click on **OK** to see the result:

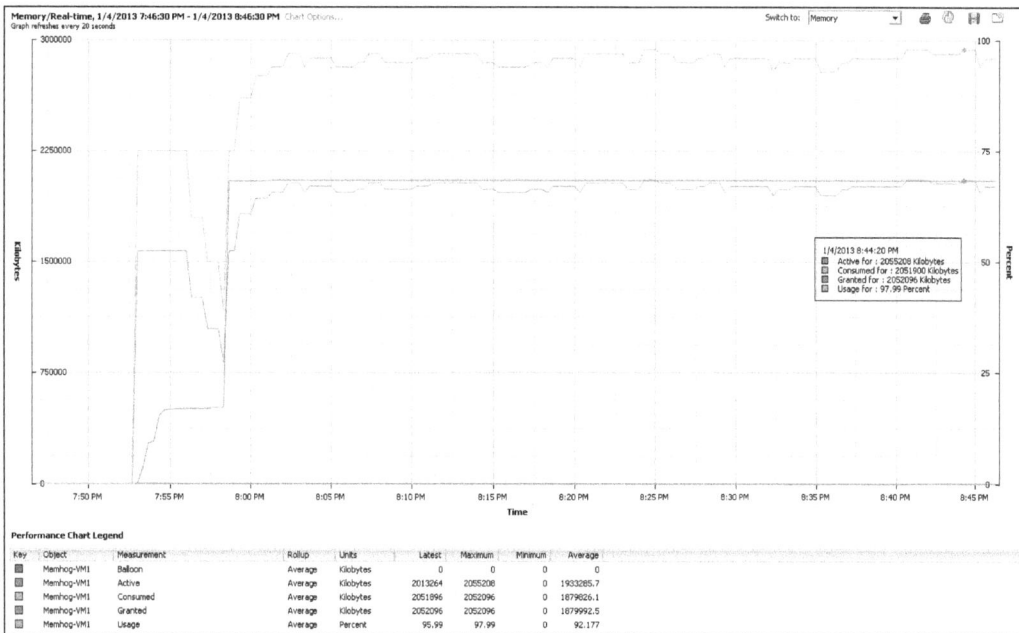

You can see in this example that the memory usage of this VM is 95 percent. Guest Active memory and Consumed Host memory are also quite high.

Now to check the Host memory you need to follow these steps:

1. Open up **vSphere Client**.

2. Log in to the **vCenter Server**.

3. On the **Home** screen, select **Hosts and Clusters**.

4. Choose the ESXi Host where you want to monitor the **Utilization of Memory**.

5. Go to the **Summary** tab on the right-hand side, and check the **Resources** section:

Resources	
CPU usage: **4304 MHz**	Capacity
	8 x 2.399 GHz
Memory usage: **29761.00 MB**	Capacity
	32757.67 MB

6. Click on the **Configuration** tab, and go to the **Memory** section to see the **VM Memory Usage**:

VMware ESXi, 5.1.0, 700125

Getting Started | Summary | Virtual Machines | Resource Allocation | Performance | Configuration | Tasks & Events | Alarms | Permissions | Maps | Storage Views | Hardware Status | vShield

Hardware

- Processors
- ▸ Memory
- Storage
- Networking
- Storage Adapters
- Network Adapters
- Advanced Settings
- Power Management

Memory

Physical

Total	32757.7 MB
System	160.7 MB
Virtual Machines	32597.0 MB

How it works...

Sometimes you may see that consumed host memory is greater than active guest memory. The reason for this is that for physical hosts that are not overcommitted on memory, consumed host memory represents the highest amount of memory usage by a virtual machine. It is possible that in the past this virtual machine was actively using a very large amount of memory.

Because the host physical memory is not overcommitted, there is no reason for the hypervisor to invoke ballooning or host-level swapping to reclaim memory. Therefore, you can find the virtual machine in a situation where its active guest memory use is low but the amount of host physical memory assigned to it is high. This is a perfectly normal situation, so there is nothing to be concerned about.

Please note that consumed memory on the host being close to 100 percent does not indicate reliably that a performance problem is likely to happen.

If consumed host memory is less than or equal to active guest memory, this might be because the active guest memory of a virtual machine might not completely reside in the host physical memory. This might occur if a guest's active memory has been reclaimed by the balloon driver, or if the virtual machine has been swapped out by the hypervisor. In both cases, this is probably due to high memory overcommitment.

Memory performance best practices

Virtualization causes an increase in the amount of physical memory required, due to the extra memory needed by ESXi for its own code and data structures, and you need to know what are the best practice standards you have.

There are four basic principles, which you should keep in mind:

- ▶ Allocate enough memory to hold the working set of applications that you will run on the virtual machine, thus minimizing swapping. You can estimate the working set by monitoring the Active memory metric.
- ▶ Do not disable the balloon driver
- ▶ Keep transparent page sharing enabled. It's free!
- ▶ Avoid overcommitting memory to the point that it results in heavy memory reclamation, especially non-trivial Swap In rates (KBps).

How to do it...

So you may ask how we can determine the total required datacenter memory.

Well, there are several methods to determine the total memory capacity requirement:

- ▶ Use the information gathered during the current-state analysis to determine the current memory capacity requirements.
- ▶ Use application vendor documentation to estimate memory capacity requirements.
- ▶ Actual datacenter usage analysis is typically more accurate.

Do not plan on fully utilizing host memory resources, plan only for 70–90 percent usage. Leave some headroom for such things as:

- ▶ Increases in short-term utilization as part of the normal business cycle
- ▶ Hardware maintenance and host patching
- ▶ Failover in a VMware HA cluster
- ▶ Failover from other datacenters during disaster recovery
- ▶ VMkernel overhead
- ▶ Virtual machine overhead
- ▶ Future growth

3
Networking Performance Design

In this chapter, we will cover the tasks related with networking performance design. You will learn the following aspects of networking performance design:

- ▶ Designing a network for load balancing and failover for vSphere Standard Switch
- ▶ Designing a network for load balancing and failover for vSphere Distributed Switch
- ▶ What to know when offloading checksum
- ▶ Selecting the correct virtual network adapter
- ▶ Improving performance through VMDirectPath I/O
- ▶ Improving performance through NetQueue
- ▶ Improving network performance using the SplitRx mode for multicast traffic
- ▶ Designing a multi-NIC vMotion
- ▶ Improving network performance using network I/O control
- ▶ Monitoring network capacity and performance matrix

Introduction

Device and I/O virtualization involves managing the routing of I/O requests between virtual devices and the shared physical hardware. Software-based I/O virtualization and management, in contrast to a direct pass through to the hardware, enables a rich set of features and simplified management. With networking, virtual NICs and virtual switches create virtual networks between virtual machines which are running on the same host without the network traffic consuming bandwidth on the physical network.

NIC teaming consists of multiple, physical NICs and provides failover and load balancing for virtual machines. Virtual machines can be seamlessly relocated to different systems by using VMware vMotion, while keeping their existing MAC addresses and the running state of the VM. The key to effective I/O virtualization is to preserve these virtualization benefits while keeping the added CPU overhead to a minimum.

The hypervisor virtualizes the physical hardware and presents each virtual machine with a standardized set of virtual devices. These virtual devices effectively emulate well-known hardware and translate the virtual machine requests to the system hardware. This standardization on consistent device drivers also helps with virtual machine standardization and portability across platforms, because all virtual machines are configured to run on the same virtual hardware, regardless of the physical hardware in the system. In this chapter we will discuss the following:

▸ Describe various network performance problems

▸ Discuss the causes of network performance problems

▸ Propose solutions to correct network performance problems

Designing a network for load balancing and failover for vSphere Standard Switch

The load balancing and failover policies that are chosen for the infrastructure can have an impact on the overall design. Using NIC teaming we can group several physical network adapters attached to a vSwitch. This grouping enables load balancing between the different physical NICs and provides fault tolerance if a card or link failure occurs.

Network adapter teaming offers a number of available load balancing and load distribution options. Load balancing is load distribution based on the number of connections, not on network traffic. In most cases, load is managed only for the outgoing traffic and balancing is based on three different policies:

▸ Route based on the originating virtual switch port ID (default)

▸ Route based on the source MAC hash

▸ Route based on IP hash

Also, we have two network failure detection options and those are:

▸ Link status only

▸ Beacon probing

Getting ready

To step through this recipe, you will need one or more running ESXi hosts, a vCenter Server, and a working installation of vSphere Client. No other prerequisites are required.

How to do it...

To change the load balancing policy and to select the right one for your environment, and also select the appropriate failover policy, you need to follow the proceeding steps:

1. Open up your VMware vSphere Client.

2. Log in to the vCenter Server.

3. On the left hand side, choose any ESXi Server and choose configuration from the right hand pane.

4. Click on the **Networking** section and select the vSwitch for which you want to change the load balancing and failover settings.

> You may wish to override this per port group level as well.

5. Click on **Properties**.

6. Select the vSwitch and click on **Edit**.

7. Go to the **NIC Teaming** tab.

8. Select one of the available policies from the **Load Balancing** drop-down menu.

9. Select one of the available policies on the **Network Failover Detection** drop-down menu.

10. Click on **OK** to make it effective.

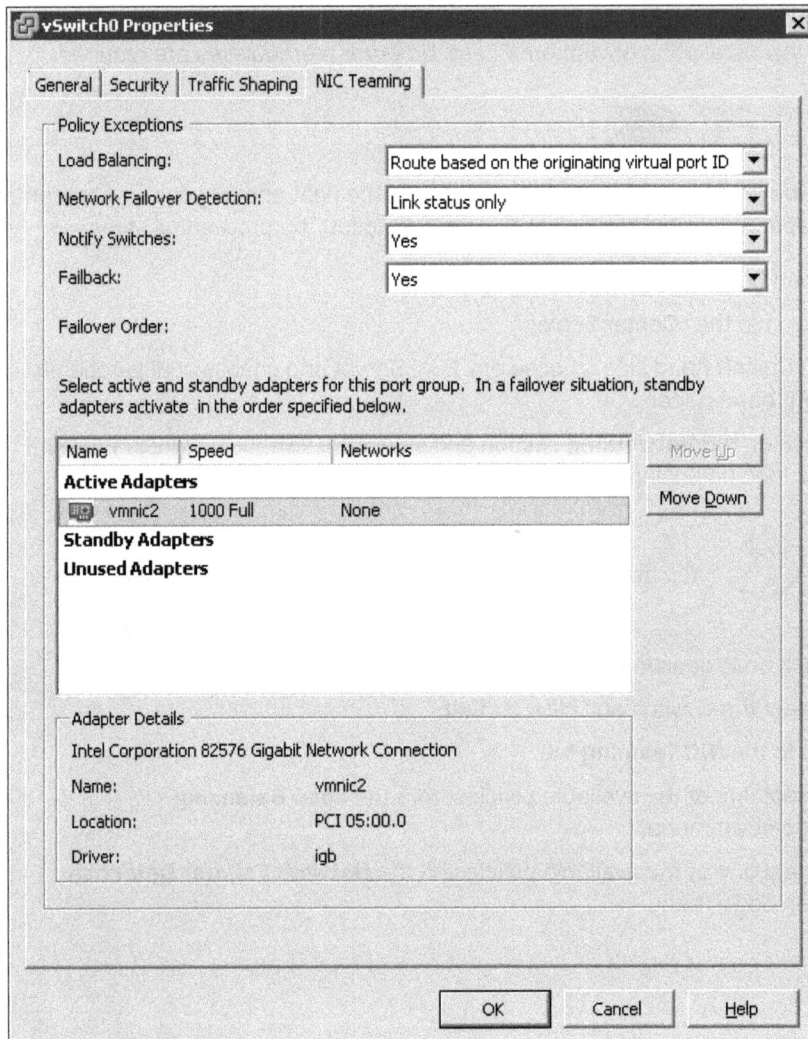

How it works...

Route based on the originating virtual switch port ID (default)

In this configuration, load balancing is based on the number of physical network cards and the number of virtual ports used. With this configuration policy, a virtual network card connected to a vSwitch port will always use the same physical network card. If a physical network card fails, the virtual network card is redirected to another physical network card.

You typically do not see the individual ports on a vSwitch. However, each vNIC that gets connected to a vSwitch is implicitly using a particular port on the vSwitch. (It's just that there's no reason to ever configure which port, because that is always done automatically.)

It does a reasonable job of balancing your egress uplinks for the traffic leaving an ESXi host as long as all the virtual machines using these uplinks have similar usage patterns.

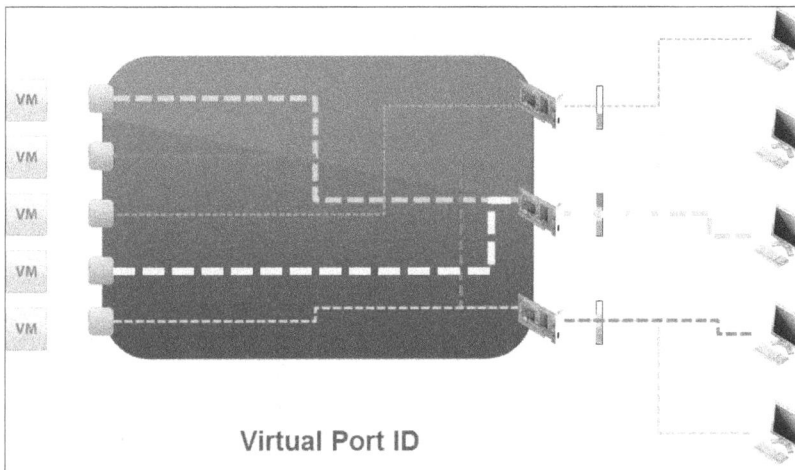

Virtual Port ID

It is important to note that port allocation occurs only when a VM is started or when a failover occurs. Balancing is done based on a port's occupation rate at the time the VM starts up. This means that which pNIC is selected for use by this VM is determined at the time the VM powers on based on which ports in the vSwitch are occupied at the time. For example, if you started 20 VMs in a row on a vSwitch with two pNICs, the odd-numbered VMs would use the left pNIC and the even-numbered VMs would use the right pNIC and that would persist even if you shut down all the even-numbered VMs; the left pNIC, would have all the VMs and the right pNIC would have none. It might happen that two heavily-loaded VMs are connected to the same pNIC, thus load is not balanced.

This policy is the easiest one and we always call for the simplest one to map it to a best operational simplification.

Now when speaking of this policy, it is important to understand that if, for example, teaming is created with two 1 GB cards, and if one VM consumes more than one card's capacity, a performance problem will arise because traffic greater than 1 Gbps will not go through the other card, and there will be an impact on the VMs sharing the same port as the VM consuming all resources. Likewise, if two VMs each wish to use 600 Mbps and they happen to go to the first pNIC, the first pNIC cannot meet the 1.2 Gbps demand no matter how idle the second pNIC is.

Route based on source MAC hash

This principle is the same as the default policy but is based on the number of MAC addresses. This policy may put those VM vNICs on the same physical uplink depending on how the MAC hash is resolved.

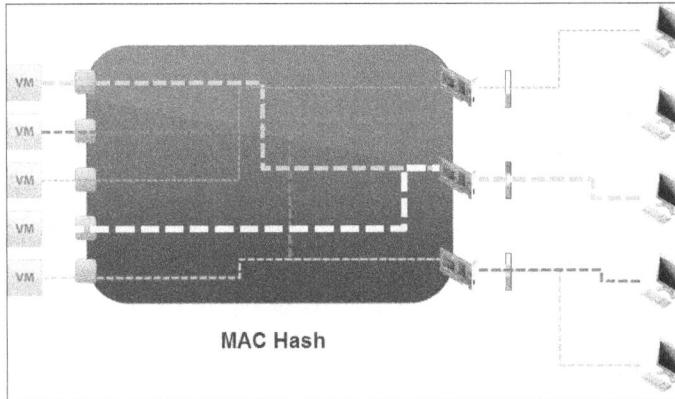

MAC Hash

For MAC hash, VMware has a different way of assigning ports. It's not based on the dynamically changing port (after a power off and power on the VM usually gets a different vSwitch port assigned), but is instead based on fixed MAC address. As a result one VM is always assigned to the same physical NIC unless the configuration is not changed. With the port ID, the VM could get different pNICs after a reboot or VMotion.

If you have two ESXi Servers with the same configuration, the VM will stay on the same pNIC number even after a vMotion. But again, one pNIC may be congested while others are bored. So there is no real load balancing.

Route based on IP hash

The limitation of the two previously-discussed policies is that a given virtual NIC will always use the same physical network card for all its traffic. IP hash-based load balancing uses the source and destination of the IP address to determine which physical network card to use. Using this algorithm, a VM can communicate through several different physical network cards based on its destination. This option requires configuration of the physical switch's ports to EtherChannel. Because the physical switch is configured similarly, this option is the only one that also provides inbound load distribution, where the distribution is not necessarily balanced.

There are some limitations and reasons why this policy is not commonly used. These reasons are described as follows:

> ▶ The route based on IP hash load balancing option involves added complexity and configuration support from upstream switches. Link **Aggregation Control Protocol (LACP)** or EtherChannel is required for this algorithm to be used. However, this does not apply for a vSphere Standard Switch.

▶ For IP hash to be an effective algorithm for load balancing there must be many IP sources and destinations. This is not a common practice for IP storage networks, where a single VMkernel port is used to access a single IP address on a storage device.

> The same NIC will always send all its traffic to the same destination (for example, Google.com) through the same pNIC, though another destination (for example, bing.com) might go through another pNIC.

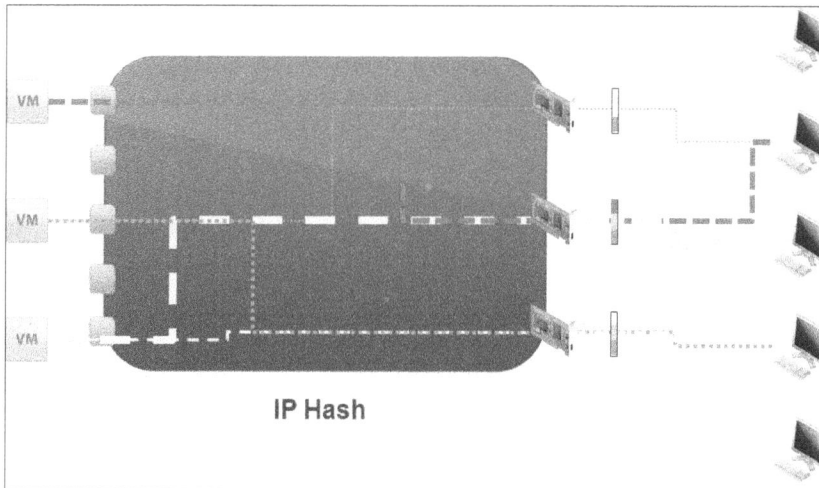

IP Hash

So, in a nutshell, due to the added complexity, the upstream dependency on the advanced switch configuration and the management overhead, this configuration is rarely used in production environments. The main reason is that if you use IP hash, the pSwitch must be configured with LACP or EtherChannel. Also, if you use LACP or EtherChannel, the load balancing algorithm *must* be IP hash. This is because with LACP, inbound traffic to the VM could come through either of the pNICs, and the vSwitch must be ready to deliver that to the VM and only IP Hash will do that (the other policies will drop the inbound traffic to this VM that comes in on a pNIC that the VM doesn't use).

We have only two failover detection options and those are:

Link status only

The link status option enables the detection of failures related to the physical network's cables and switch. However, be aware that configuration issues are not detected. This option also cannot detect the link state problems with upstream switches; it works only with the first hop switch from the host.

Beacon probing

The beacon probing option allows the detection of failures unseen by the link status option, by sending the Ethernet broadcast frames through all the network cards. These network frames authorize the vSwitch to detect faulty configurations or upstream switch failures and force the failover if the ports are blocked. When using an inverted U physical network topology in conjunction with a dual-NIC server, it is recommended to enable link state tracking or a similar network feature in order to avoid traffic black holes. According to VMware's best practices, it is recommended to have at least three cards before activating this functionality. However, if IP hash is going to be used, beacon probing should not be used as a network failure detection, in order to avoid an ambiguous state due to the limitation that a packet cannot hairpin on the port it is received. Beacon probing works by sending out and listening to beacon probes from the NICs in a team. If there are two NICs, then each NIC will send out a probe and the other NICs will receive that probe. Because EtherChannel is considered one link, this will not function properly as the NIC uplinks are not logically separate uplinks. If beacon probing is used, this can result in MAC address flapping errors, and the network connectivity may be interrupted.

Designing a network for load balancing and failover for vSphere Distributed Switch

The load balancing and failover policies that are chosen for the infrastructure can have an impact on the overall design. Using NIC teaming, we can group several physical network switches attached to a vSwitch. This grouping enables load balancing between the different Physical NICs, and provides fault tolerance if a card failure occurs.

The vSphere distributed vSwitch offers a load balancing option that actually takes the network workload into account when choosing the physical uplink. This is route based on a physical NIC load. This is also called **Load Based Teaming** (**LBT**). We recommend this load balancing option over the others when using a distributed vSwitch. Benefits of using this load balancing policy are as follows:

- ▶ It is the only load balancing option that actually considers NIC load when choosing uplinks.

- ▶ It does not require upstream switch configuration dependencies like the route based on IP hash algorithm does.

- ▶ When the route based on physical NIC load is combined with the network I/O control, a truly dynamic traffic distribution is achieved.

Getting ready

To step through this recipe, you will need one or more running ESXi Servers, a vCenter Server, and a working installation of vSphere Client. No other prerequisites are required.

How to do it...

To change the load balancing policy and select the right one for your environment, and also select the appropriate failover policy you need to follow the proceeding steps:

1. Open up your VMware vSphere Client.

2. Log in to the vCenter Server.

3. Navigate to **Networking** on the home screen.

4. Navigate to a **Distributed Port group** and right click and select **Edit Settings**.

5. Click on the **Teaming and Failover** section.

6. From the **Load Balancing** drop-down menu, select **Route Based on physical NIC load** as the load balancing policy.

7. Choose the appropriate network failover detection policy from the drop-down menu.

8. Click on **OK** and your settings will be effective.

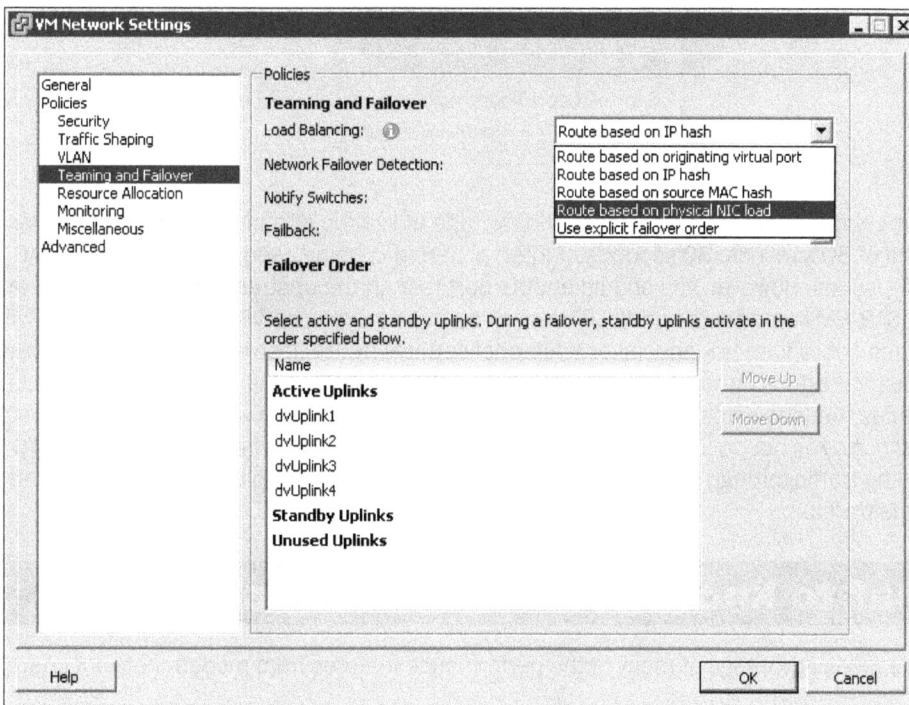

How it works...

Load based teaming, also known as route based on physical NIC load, maps vNICs to pNICs and remaps the vNIC to pNIC affiliation if the load exceeds specific thresholds on a pNIC. LBT uses the originating port ID load balancing algorithm for the initial port assignment, which results in the first vNIC being affiliated to the first pNIC, the second vNIC to the second pNIC, and so on. Once the initial placement is over after the VM being powered on, LBT will examine both the inbound and outbound traffic on each of the pNICs and then distribute the load across if there is congestion.

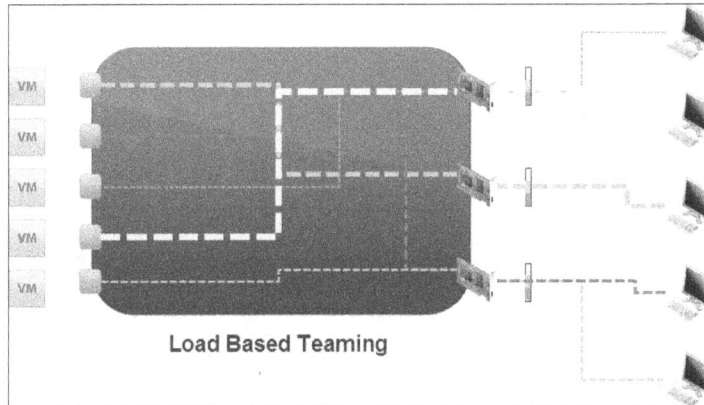

Load Based Teaming

LBT will send a congestion alert when the average utilization of a pNIC is 75 percent over a period of 30 seconds. 30 seconds of interval period is being used for avoiding the MAC flapping issues. However, you should enable port fast on the upstream switches if you plan to use STP. VMware recommends LBT over IP hash when you use vSphere Distributed Switch, as it does not require any special or additional settings in the upstream switch layer. In this way you can reduce unnecessary operational complexity. LBT maps vNIC to pNIC and then distributes the load across all the available uplinks, unlike IP hash which just maps the vNIC to pNIC but does not do load distribution. So it may happen that when a high network I/O VM is sending traffic through pNIC0, your other VM will also get to map to the same pNIC and send the traffic.

What to know when offloading checksum

VMware takes advantage of many of the performance features from modern network adaptors.

In this section we are going to talk about two of them and those are:

  ▸ TCP checksum offload
  ▸ TCP segmentation offload

Getting ready

To step through this recipe, you will need a running ESXi Server and a SSH Client (Putty). No other prerequisites are required.

How to do it...

The list of network adapter features that are enabled on your NIC can be found in the file **/etc/vmware/esx.conf** on your ESXi Server. Look for the lines that start with /net/vswitch.

However, do not change the default NIC's driver settings unless you have a valid reason to do so. A good practice is to follow any configuration recommendations that are specified by the hardware vendor. Carry out the following steps in order to check the settings:

1. Open up your SSH Client and connect to your ESXi host.
2. Open the file etc/vmware/esx.conf
3. Look for the line that starts with /net/vswitch
4. Your output should look like the following screenshot:

```
/net/vswitch/child[0000]/uplinks/child[0000]/pnic = "vmnic2"
/net/vswitch/child[0000]/name = "vSwitch0"
/net/vswitch/child[0000]/teamPolicy/maxActive = "1"
/net/vswitch/child[0000]/teamPolicy/uplinks[0000]/pnic = "vmnic2"
/net/vswitch/child[0000]/teamPolicy/linkCriteria/beacon = "ignore"
/net/vswitch/child[0000]/teamPolicy/team = "lb_srcid"
/net/vswitch/child[0000]/teamPolicy/notifySwitch = "true"
/net/vswitch/child[0000]/teamPolicy/rollingRestoration = "false"
/net/vswitch/child[0000]/teamPolicy/hasUplinkOrder = "true"
/net/vswitch/child[0000]/shapingPolicy/enabled = "false"
/net/vswitch/child[0000]/cdp/status = "listen"
/net/vswitch/child[0000]/capabilities/HighDMA = "true"
/net/vswitch/child[0000]/capabilities/ChecksumOffloadIPv6ExtHdrs = "true"
/net/vswitch/child[0000]/capabilities/ChecksumOffload = "true"
/net/vswitch/child[0000]/capabilities/VlanUntag = "true"
/net/vswitch/child[0000]/capabilities/VlanTag = "true"
/net/vswitch/child[0000]/capabilities/Offload8Offset = "true"
/net/vswitch/child[0000]/capabilities/TcpSegmentationOffloadIPv6ExtHdrs = "true"
/net/vswitch/child[0000]/capabilities/UplinkReadOnlyInetHeaders = "true"
/net/vswitch/child[0000]/capabilities/ScatterGatherTx = "true"
/net/vswitch/child[0000]/capabilities/TcpSegmentationOffload256k = "true"
/net/vswitch/child[0000]/capabilities/TcpSegmentationOffload = "true"
/net/vswitch/child[0000]/capabilities/TcpSegmentationOffloadIPv6 = "true"
/net/vswitch/child[0000]/capabilities/ScatterGatherSpanPagesTx = "true"
/net/vswitch/child[0000]/capabilities/Offload16Offset = "true"
/net/vswitch/child[0000]/capabilities/ChecksumOffloadIPv6 = "true"
/net/vswitch/child[0000]/securityPolicy/macChange = "true"
/net/vswitch/child[0000]/securityPolicy/promiscuous = "false"
/net/vswitch/child[0000]/securityPolicy/forgedTx = "true"
/net/vswitch/child[0000]/portgroup/child[0000]/vlanId = "0"
/net/vswitch/child[0000]/portgroup/child[0000]/name = "VM Network"
```

How it works...

A TCP message must be broken down into Ethernet frames. The size of each frame is the **maximum transmission unit (MUT)**. The default maximum transmission unit is 1500 bytes. The process of breaking messages into frames is called segmentation.

Modern NIC adapters have the ability to perform checksum calculations natively. TCP checksums are used to determine the validity of transmitted or received network packets based on error correcting code. These calculations are traditionally performed by the host's CPU. By offloading these calculations to the network adapters, the CPU is freed up to perform other tasks. As a result, the system as a whole runs better. **TCP segmentation offload** (**TSO**) allows a TCP/IP stack from the guest OS inside the VM to emit large frames (up to 64KB) even though the MTU of the interface is smaller.

Earlier operating system used the CPU to perform segmentation. Modern NICs try to optimize this TCP segmentation by using a larger segment size as well as offloading work from the CPU to the NIC hardware. ESXi utilizes this concept to provide a virtual NIC with TSO support, without requiring specialized network hardware.

▸ With TSO, instead of processing many small MTU frames during transmission, the system can send fewer, larger virtual MTU frames.

▸ TSO improves performance for the TCP network traffic coming from a virtual machine and for network traffic sent out of the server.

▸ TSO is supported at the virtual machine level and in the VMkernel TCP/IP stack.

▸ TSO is enabled on the VMkernel interface by default. If TSO becomes disabled for a particular VMkernel interface, the only way to enable TSO is to delete that VMkernel interface and recreate it with TSO enabled.

▸ TSO is used in the guest when the VMXNET 2 (or later) network adapter is installed. To enable TSO at the virtual machine level, you must replace the existing VMXNET or flexible virtual network adapter with a VMXNET 2 (or later) adapter. This replacement might result in a change in the MAC address of the virtual network adapter.

Selecting the correct virtual network adapter

When you configure a virtual machine, you can add NICs and specify the adapter type. The types of network adapters that are available depend on the following factors:

▸ The version of the virtual machine, which depends on which host created it or most recently updated it.

- ▶ Whether or not the virtual machine has been updated to the latest version for the current host.
- ▶ The guest operating system.

The following virtual NIC types are supported:

- ▶ Vlance
- ▶ VMXNET
- ▶ Flexible
- ▶ E 1000
- ▶ Enhanced VMXNET (VMXNET 2)
- ▶ VMXNET 3

If you want to know more about these network adapter types then refer to the following KB article:

`http://kb.vmware.com/kb/1001805`

Getting ready

To step through this recipe, you will need one or more running ESXi Servers, a vCenter Server, and a working installation of vSphere Client. No other prerequisites are required.

How to do it...

To choose a particular virtual network adapter you have two ways, one is while you create a new VM and the other one is while adding a new network adaptor to an existing VM.

To choose a network adaptor while creating a new VM is as follows:

1. Open vSphere Client.
2. Log in to the vCenter Server.
3. Click on the **File** menu, and navigate to **New | Virtual Machine**.

4. Go through the steps and hold on to the step where you need to create network connections. Here you need to choose how many network adaptors you need, which port group you want them to connect to, and an adaptor type.

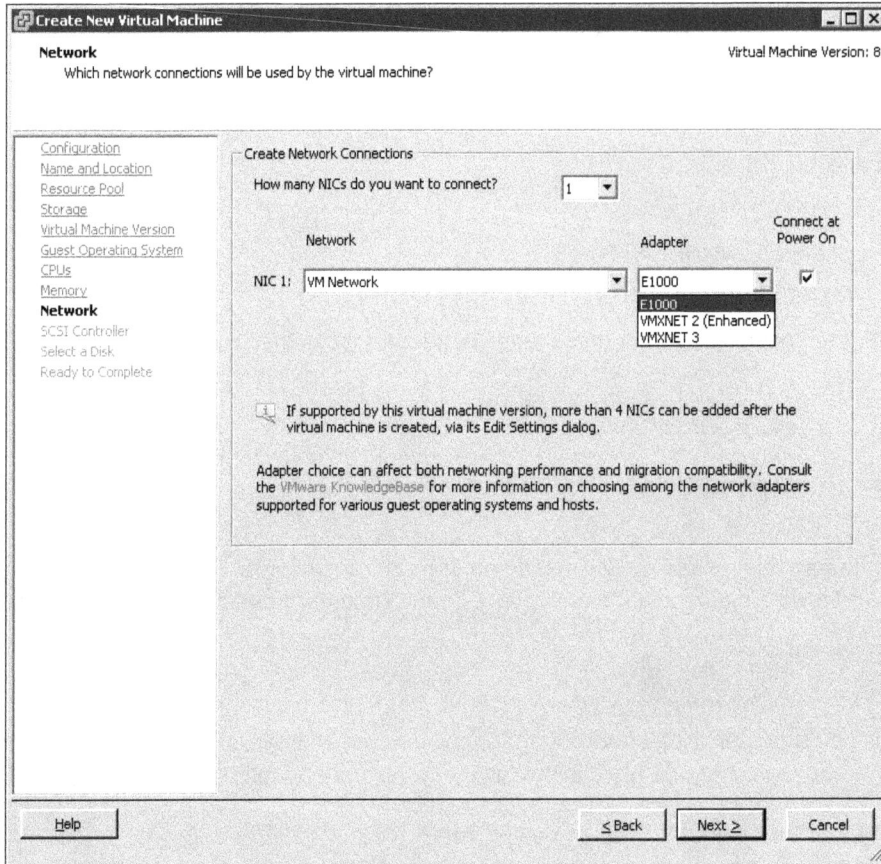

To choose an adaptor type while adding a new network interface in an existing VM you should follow these steps:

1. Open vSphere Client.

2. Log in to the vCenter Server.

3. Navigate to **VMs and Templates** on your home screen.

4. Select an existing VM where you want to add a new network adaptor, right click and select **Edit Settings**.

5. Click on the **Add** button.

6. Select **Ethernet Adaptor**.

7. Select the **Adaptor type** and select the network where you want this adaptor to connect.

8. Click on **Next** and then click on **Finish**

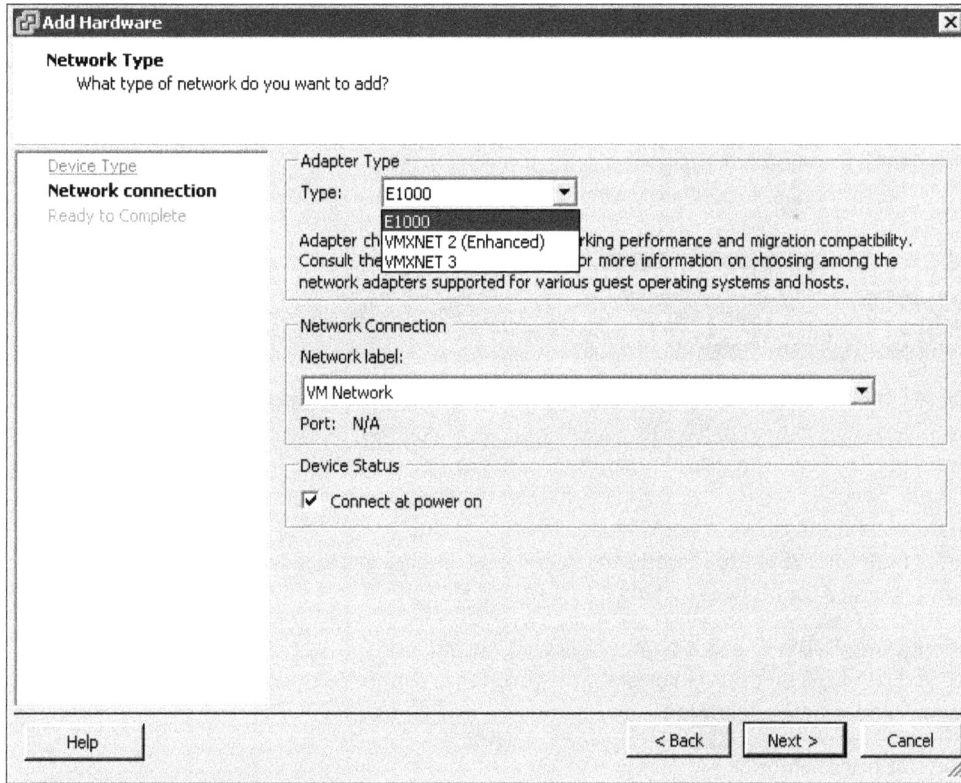

How it works...

Among the entire supported virtual network adaptor types, VMXNET is the paravirtualized device driver for virtual networking. The VMXNET driver implements an idealized network interface that passes through the network traffic from the virtual machine to the physical cards with minimal overhead. The three versions of VMXNET are VMXNET, VMXNET 2 (Enhanced VMXNET), and VMXNET 3.

The VMXNET driver improves the performance through a number of optimizations as follows:

▶ Shares a ring buffer between the virtual machine and the VMkernel, and uses zero copy, which in turn saves CPU cycles. Zero copy improves performance by having the virtual machines and the VMkernel share a buffer, reducing the internal copy operations between buffers to free up CPU cycles.

▶ Takes advantage of transmission packet coalescing to reduce address space switching.

▶ Batches packets and issues a single interrupt, rather than issuing multiple interrupts. This improves efficiency, but in some cases with slow packet-sending rates, it could hurt throughput while waiting to get enough packets to actually send.

▶ Offloads TCP checksum calculation to the network hardware rather than use the CPU resources of the virtual machine monitor. Use vmxnet3 if you can, or the most recent model you can. Use VMware Tools where possible. For certain unusual types of network traffic, sometimes the generally-best model isn't optimal; if you have poor network performance, experiment with other types of vNICs to see which performs best.

Improving performance through VMDirectPath I/O

VMware vSphere DirectPath I/O leverages Intel VT-d and AMD-Vi hardware support to allow guest operating systems to directly access hardware devices. In the case of networking, vSphere DirectPath I/O allows the virtual machine to access a physical NIC directly rather than using an emulated device or a paravirtualized device. An example of an emulated device is the E 1000 virtual NIC, and examples of paravirtualized devices are the VMXNET and VMXNET 3 virtual network adapters. vSphere DirectPath I/O provides limited increases in throughput, but it reduces the CPU cost for networking intensive workloads.

vSphere DirectPath I/O is not compatible with certain core virtualization features. However, when you run ESXi on certain vendor configurations, vSphere DirectPath I/O for networking is compatible with the following:

▶ vSphere vMotion

▶ Hot adding and removing of virtual devices, suspend and resume

▶ VMware vSphere® high availability

▶ VMware vSphere® Distributed Resource Scheduler (DRS)

▶ Snapshots

Typical virtual machines and their workloads do not require the use of vSphere DirectPath I/O. However, for workloads that are networking intensive and do not need the core virtualization features just mentioned, vSphere DirectPath I/O might be useful to reduce CPU usage and/or latency. Another potential use case of this technology is passing through a network card to a guest when the network card is not supported by the hypervisor.

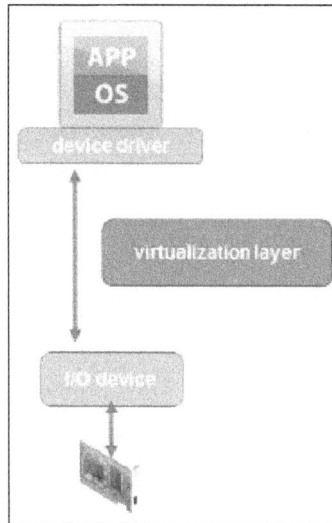

Getting ready

To step through this recipe, you will need one or more running ESXi Servers, the ESXi server hardware should have Intel VT-d or AMD-Vi hardware, a vCenter Server, and a working installation of vSphere Client. No other prerequisites are required.

How to do it...

For configuring VMDirectPath I/O direct PCI device connections for virtual machines you need to follow these steps:

1. Open vSphere Client.

2. Log in to the vCenter Server.

3. On your Home screen, select **Hosts and Clusters**.

4. Select an ESX host from the inventory of VMware vSphere Client.

5. In the **Configuration** tab, click on **Advanced Settings**. The Pass through Configuration page lists all the available pass through devices.

6. Click on **Configure Passthrough**.

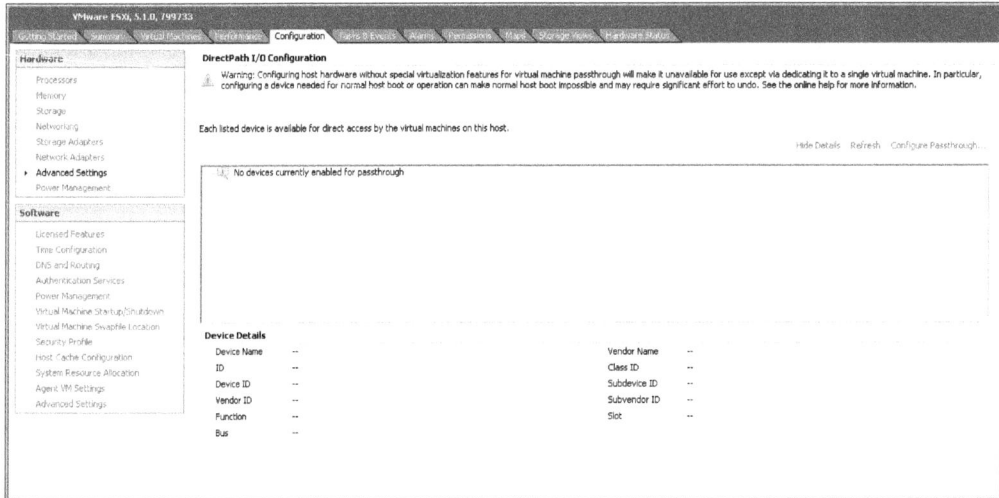

Now you will see a list of devices.

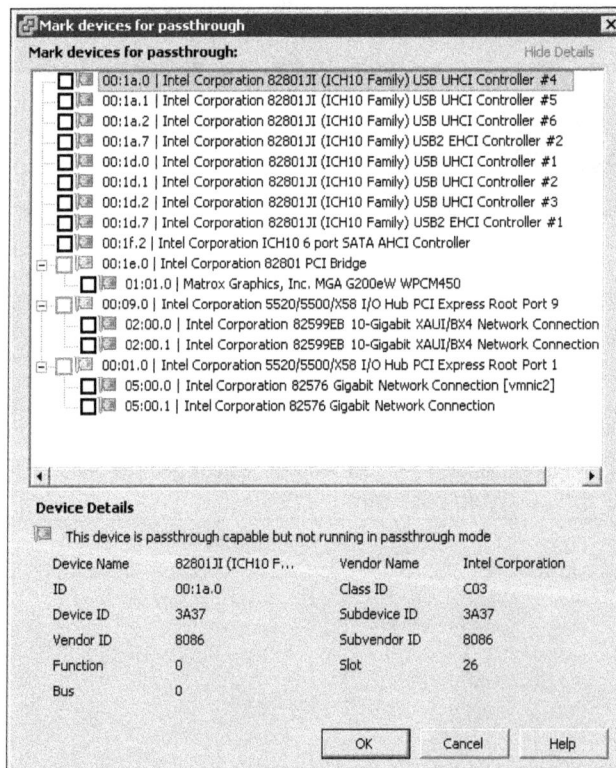

7. Select the devices and click on **OK**.

8. When the devices are selected, they are marked with an orange icon. Reboot the system for the change to take effect. After rebooting, the devices are marked with a green icon and are enabled.

9. To configure a PCI device on a virtual machine:

    1. From the inventory in vSphere Client, right-click on the virtual machine and choose **Edit Settings**. Please note that the VM must be powered off to complete this operation.

    2. Click on the **Hardware** tab.

    3. Click on **Add**.

    4. Choose the PCI device.

10. Click on **Next**.

> When the device is assigned, the virtual machine must have a memory reservation for the full configured memory size.

Improving performance through NetQueue

NetQueue is a performance technology that improves performance in virtualized environments that use 10 GigE adapters which is supported by VMware. NetQueue takes advantage of the multiple queue capability that newer physical network adapters have. Multiple queues allow I/O processing to be spread across multiple CPUs in a multiprocessor system. So while one packet is queued up on one CPU, another packet can be queued up on another CPU at the same time.

Getting ready

To step through this recipe, you will need one or more running ESXi Servers and a working installation of vSphere CLI. No other prerequisites are required.

How to do it...

NetQueue is enabled by default. Disabling or enabling NetQueue on a host is done by using the VMware vSphere **Command-Line Interface** (vCLI).

To enable and disable this feature, you should perform the following activity:

1. Open vSphere CLI.

2. Now run this esxcli system settings kernel with the following command:

   ```
   setting=" netNetqueueEnabled" --value="TRUE"
   ```

3. Use the VMware vSphere CLI to configure the NIC driver to use NetQueue. The following command assumes that you are using the s2io driver:

   ```
   ~ # esxcli system module parameters set -m s2io -p "intr_type=2
   rx_ring_num=8"
   ```

4. Once you set the parameter then use the following command to list the parameters and options:

   ```
   ~ # esxcli system module parameters list -m s2io | more
   ```

```
~ # esxcli system module parameters list -m s2io | more
Name                         Type           Value  Description
----------------------------  -------------  -----  -----------------------------------------------------------
enable_netq                  uint
heap_initial                 int                   Initial heap size allocated for the driver.
heap_max                     int                   Maximum attainable heap size for the driver.
indicate_max_pkts            uint
intr_type                    uint           2
l314hdr_size                 uint
lro                          int
lro_max_bytes                uint
mc_pause_threshold_q0q3      uint
mc_pause_threshold_q4q7      uint
multiq                       uint
napi                         uint
port_type                    uint
rmac_pause_time              uint
rmac_util_period             uint
rst_q_stuck                  uint
rth_mask                     uint
rth_ports                    array of uint
rth_protocol                 uint
rts_frm_len                  array of uint
rx_ring_mode                 uint
rx_ring_num                  uint           8
rx_ring_sz                   array of uint
rx_steering_type             uint
rxsync_frequency             uint
shared_splits                uint
skb_mpool_initial            int                   Driver's minimum private socket buffer memory pool size.
skb_mpool_max                int                   Maximum attainable private socket buffer memory pool size for the driver.
tmac_util_period             uint
tx_fifo_len                  array of uint
tx_fifo_num                  uint
tx_steering_type             uint
ufo                          uint
use_continuous_tx_intrs      uint
vlan_tag_strip               uint
~ #
```

5. Reboot the host.

If you want to disable the NetQueue feature for any reason then you need to follow the proceeding steps:

1. Open vSphere CLI.

2. Now run this esxcli system settings kernel with the following command:

   ```
   set --setting=" netNetqueueEnabled" --value="FALSE"
   ```

3. Now disable the NIC driver to use NetQueue by using the following command:

```
~ # esxcli system module parameters set -m s2io -p "intr_type= rx_
ring_num="
```

4. Now list the parameters as follows to see if it has been taken off or not

```
~ # esxcli system module parameters list -m s2io | more
```

5. Reboot the host

How it works...

NetQueue can use multiple transmit queues to parallelize access that is normally serialized by the device driver. Multiple transmit queues can also be used to get some sort of guarantee. A separate, prioritized queue can be used for different types of network traffic.

NetQueue monitors the load of the virtual machines as they are receiving packets and can assign queues to critical virtual machines. All other virtual machines use the default queue.

Improving network performance using the SplitRx mode for multicast traffic

Multicast is an efficient way of disseminating information and communicating over the network. Instead of sending a separate packet to every receiver, the sender sends one packet which is then distributed to every receiver that has subscribed to this multicast. Multiple receivers can be enabled on a single ESXi host only when you use multicast traffic. Because multiple receivers reside on the same host, packet replication is carried out in the hypervisor instead.

SplitRx mode uses multiple physical CPUs in an ESXi host to process network packets received in a single network queue. As it does not transfer the same copy of the network packet, it provides a scalable and efficient platform for multicast receivers. SplitRx mode improves throughput and CPU efficiency for multicast traffic workloads.

Only the VMXNET 3 network adapter supports SplitRx mode. This feature is disabled by default on vSphere 5.0, however it is enabled in 5.1 by default.

SplitRx mode is individually configured for each virtual NIC.

Getting ready

To step through this recipe, you will need one or more running ESXi Servers, a couple of running virtual machines, a vCenter Server, and a working installation of vSphere Client. No other prerequisites are required.

How to do it...

The behaviur of SplitRx can be enabled or disabled entirely on an ESXi Server using the following steps:

1. Open vSphere Client.
2. Log in to the vCenter Server.
3. Select **Hosts and Clusters** on the home screen.
4. Select the ESXi host you wish to change.
5. Navigate to the **Configuration** tab.
6. Click on **Advanced Settings** in the Software pane.
7. Click on the **Net** section of the left-hand side tree.
8. Find **NetSplitRxMode**.
9. Click on the value to be changed and configure it as you wish.

The possible values of NetSplitRxMode are as follows:

NetSplitRxMode = "0"

This value disables SplitRx mode for the ESXi host.

NetSplitRxMode = "1"

This value (the default) enables SplitRx mode for the ESXi host.

The change will take effect immediately and does not require the ESXi host to be restarted.

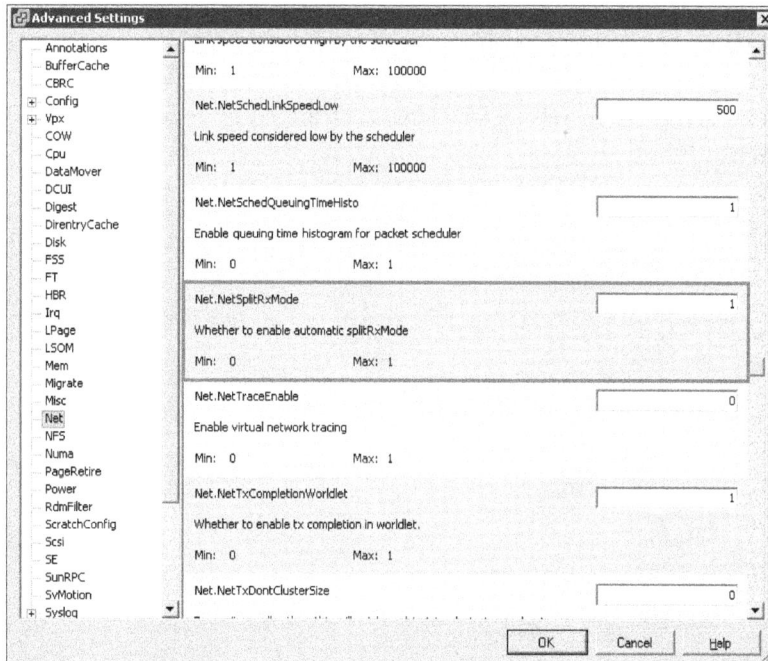

The SplitRx mode feature can also be configured individually for each virtual NIC using the `ethernetX.emuRxMode` variable in each virtual machine's `.vmx` file (where X is replaced with the network adapter's ID).

The possible values for this variable are:

ethernetX.emuRxMode = "0"

This value disables SplitRx mode for ethernetX.

ethernetX.emuRxMode = "1"

This value enables SplitRx mode for ethernetX.

So, if you want to change this value on individual VMs through vSphere Client, you should follow the proceeding steps:

1. Select the virtual machine that you wish to change, and then click on **Edit virtual machine settings.**

2. Go to the **Options** tab.

3. Navigate to **General**, and then click on **Configuration Parameters**.

4. Look for `ethernetX.emuRxMode` (where X is the number of the desired NIC). If the variable isn't present, click on **Add Row** and enter it as a new variable.

5. Click on the value to be changed and configure it as you wish.

> The change will not take effect until the virtual machine has been restarted.

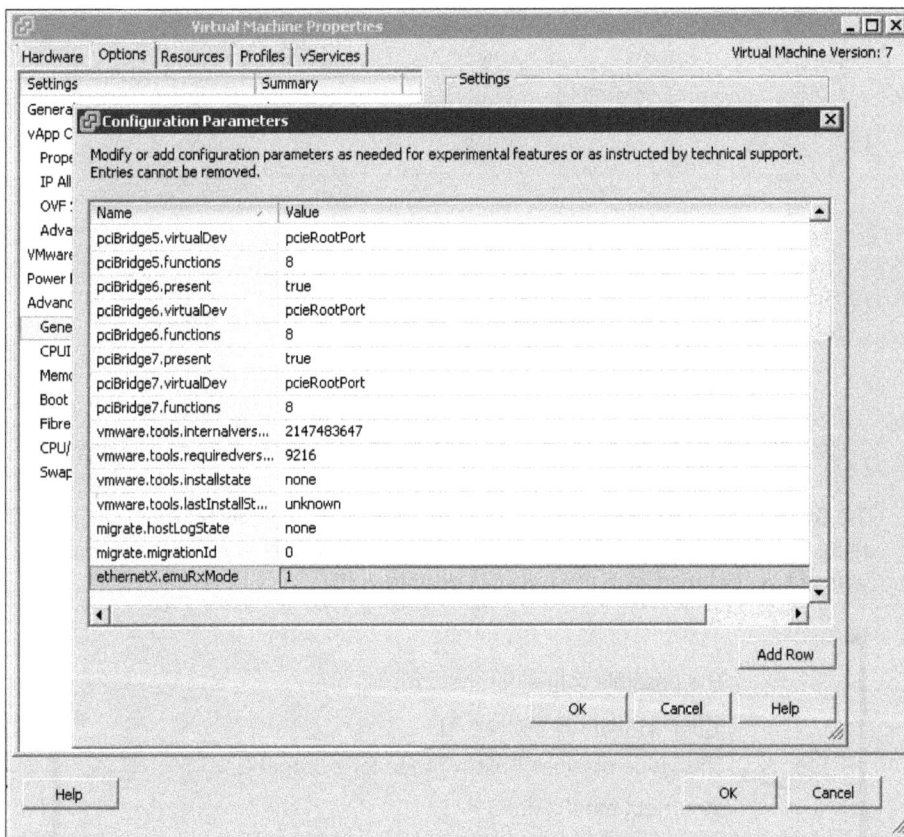

How it works...

SplitRx mode uses multiple physical CPUs to process network packets received in a single network queue. This feature can significantly improve the network performance for certain workloads.

These workloads include:

► Multiple virtual machines on one ESXi host and they are all receiving multicast traffic from the same source.

► Traffic via the DVFilter API between two virtual machines on the same ESXi host.

vSphere 5.1 automatically enables this feature for a VMXNET 3 virtual network adapter (the only adapter type on which it is supported) when it detects that a single network queue on a physical NIC is both heavily utilized and servicing more than eight clients (that is, virtual machines or the vmknic) that have evenly distributed loads.

Designing a multi-NIC vMotion

Before the release of VMware vSphere 5, designing a vMotion network was relatively easy as it was straight-forward. vMotion in VMware vSphere 5.0 is able to leverage multiple NICs.

In vSphere 5.x vMotion balances the operations across all available NICs. It does this for a single vMotion operation and for multiple concurrent vMotion operations. By using multiple NICs it reduces the duration of a vMotion operation.

Getting ready

To step through this recipe, you will need one or more running ESXi Servers, a vCenter Server, and a working installation of vSphere Client. No other prerequisites are required.

How to do it...

So, to create a multi NIC vMotion network, you need to follow the proceeding steps:

1. Open up vSphere Client.
2. Log in to the vCenter Server.
3. Navigate to the **Network** section.
4. Select the distributed switch, right click on it, and then select **New Port Group**.
5. Provide a name, call it `vMotion-01` and confirm it's the correct distributed switch.
6. Enter the VLAN type and specify the VLAN number.
7. Accept all of the other settings as default as of now and then select **Next**
8. Review the settings and click on **Finish**

Once you are done, it will create a vMotion port group, but you need to change the load balancing and failover configuration.

1. Select distributed port group vMotion-01 in the left side of your screen, right-click and select **Edit settings**.

2. Go to **Teaming and Failover** and move the second dvUplink down to mark it as a **Standby uplink**. Verify that load balancing is set to **Route based on originating virtual port**.

3. Click on **OK**.

Repeat the instructions for distributed Port group vMotion-02, but use the VLAN ID used by the IP address of the second VMkernel NIC.

Go to **Teaming and Failover** and configure the uplinks in an alternate order, ensuring that the second vMotion VMkernel NIC is using dvUplink2.

Now once you are done with creating two different distributed port groups, you need to create two vMotion VMK interfaces and tag them to each of these port groups, as follows:

1. Select the first host in the cluster, go to **Configure**, and then click on **Networking**.

2. Click on **vSphere Distributed Switch**.

3. Now click on **Manage Virtual Adaptor**.

4. Click on **Add**.

5. Navigate to **New Virtual Adaptor**.

6. Select the VMkernel and go to **Next**.

7. Now select the port group where you want it to connect to.

8. Select the checkbox **Use this Virtual Adaptor for vMotion** and click on **Next**.

9. Specify the IP address there and click on **Next**.

10. Review the configuration and click on **Finish**.

11. Create the second vMotion enabled VMkernel NIC. Configure it identically, except:

    1. Select the second vMotion port group.

    2. Enter the IP address corresponding to the VLAN ID on distributed port group vMotion-02.

Now you have a ready multi-NIC vMotion Network.

Improving network performance using network I/O control

The 1GigE era is coming to an end and is rapidly being replaced by 10GigE. This means that network traffic with different patterns and needs will merge together on the same network.

This may directly impact performance and predictability due to lack of isolation, scheduling and arbitration. Network I/O control can be used to prioritize different network traffic on the same pipe.

You cannot have a guarantee for a bandwidth as long as you don't limit other traffic so there'll be always enough available bandwidth.

As some traffic (that is, vMotion) might not be used all the time, we'll have temporarily unused bandwidth with the static limits. As long as there is no congestion this doesn't really matter, but if there is, then you're limiting the bandwidth for traffic even when there is bandwidth available which is not really a good way to deal with congestion.

For some VMkernel traffic, VMware recommends dedicated 1GB NICs to guarantee bandwidth for them. So it's very likely that there will be no dedicated NIC any more for VM traffic. Without some **QoS** or guaranteed bandwidth you're wasting the bandwidth with the previous static traffic shaping. So there needs to be a more dynamic solution for it.

So the solution is the **network I/O control** (**NIOC**) for vDS.

	Getting Started	Summary	Networks	Ports	Resource Allocation	Configuration	Virtual Machines	Hosts	Tasks & Events	Alarms	Permissions

Summary

Total number of physical adapters:	4
Total network bandwidth capacity:	40000 Mbps
Network I/O Control:	◇ Disabled

New Network Resource Pool...   Manage Port Groups...   Properties...

Network resource pool	Host limit - Mbps	Physical adapter shares	Shares value	QoS priority tag
System network resource pools				
Fault Tolerance (FT) Traffic	Unlimited	Normal	50	--
iSCSI Traffic	Unlimited	Normal	50	--
Management Traffic	Unlimited	Normal	50	--
NFS Traffic	Unlimited	Normal	50	--
Virtual Machine Traffic	Unlimited	High	100	--
vMotion Traffic	Unlimited	Normal	50	--
vSphere Replication (VR) Traffic	Unlimited	Normal	50	--
User-defined network resource pools				
vSphere Storage Area Network Traff...	Unlimited	Normal	50	--

Network Resource Pool Details   Edit Settings...   Remove

Network resource pool

Origin:	--			
Host limit:	--	Shares value:	--	QoS priority tag:	--

View: Port groups

To control VMware has predefined resource groups, as shown in the previous screenshot.

These traffic groups are based on the vDS ports. So with the connection to a specified port, the traffic on this port belongs to one of these pre-defined groups. This means that if we mount a NFS share inside VM it's treated as a VM traffic instead of NFS traffic. Again, assignment to a group is based on switch port, not on traffic characteristics.

Two values that you can edit for the pre-defined **Network resource pool** are **Physical adapter shares** and **Host limit**.

Shares work like the shares on VMs (CPU and memory). NIOC will sum up all shares and set the shares in relation to the sum. So a value of 50 does not necessarily mean the group is entitled for 50 percent of bandwidth (although it could be possible if the shares of the other groups sum up to 50).

The share does not reflect the # of ports in this group. So it doesn't matter if we have 10 or 100VMs running. The percentage for all will be the same. So inside a resource group there is no sublevel possible.

The defined share values are:

- Normal = 50
- Low = 25
- High = 100
- Custom = any values between 1 and 100

The default share value for VM traffic is 100 and all other traffic is 50, which is normal.

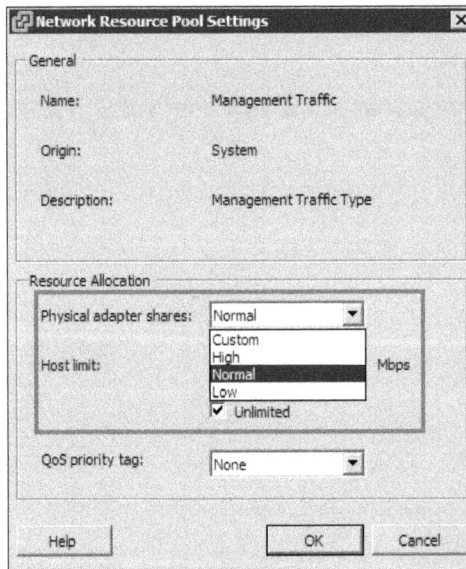

In case some resource groups aren't used at all (that is, no **FT** (**fault tolerance**), no NFS, and no vSphere Replication) the shares still apply but as there will be no traffic claiming bandwidth, the bandwidth will be given to other groups based on the share values.

So if all the traffic together doesn't need the full bandwidth of pNIC there might still be unused bandwidth. But it will be dynamically given to a resource group requesting more bandwidth later. Previously, this bandwidth was not used at all as the limits were configured with peak rates and bursts.

Limits are useful if you don't want to have the other traffic affected too much, that is by vMotion. Let's assume that VM and iSCSI traffic usually uses nearly all available bandwidth. Now, if vMotion starts consuming by default 14 percent of bandwidth, then this will affect the traffic for VMs and iSCSI, so you might want to limit it to 1Gbit/s.

vSphere 5.x comes up with the enhanced network I/O control feature. In addition to the old features in the new NIOC model, you will be able to tag user-defined network resource pools with an 802.1P priority tag (QoS priority flag), which is pTag.

However, it is not performing **Quality of Service**. It is simply tagging these packets with a priority tag to differentiate the different virtual machine traffic. This is very important, as this feature now allows an administrator to determine which VM or group of VMs should have higher priority on the network. Before this release, all the virtual machine traffic was grouped together.

Enhanced network I/O control also includes controls to cap bandwidth for the host-based replication traffic.

> The QoS priority tag is only available with vDS.

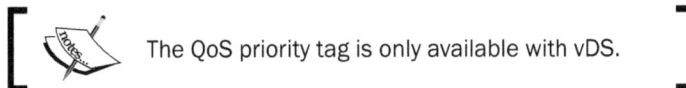

Getting ready

To step through this recipe, you will need one or more running ESXi Servers, a vCenter Server, and a working installation of vSphere Client. Also you need Enterprise and license. No other prerequisites are required.

How to do it...

To check the NIOC resource pool and enable it follow the proceeding steps:

1. Log in to vCenter Server.
2. Select **Networking** on the home screen.
3. Select the appropriate vDS and go to the **Resource Allocation** tab.
4. Navigate to **Properties**.
5. On the Resource Allocation Properties screen, select **Enable Network I/O Control on this vSphere distributed switch**. Click on **OK**.

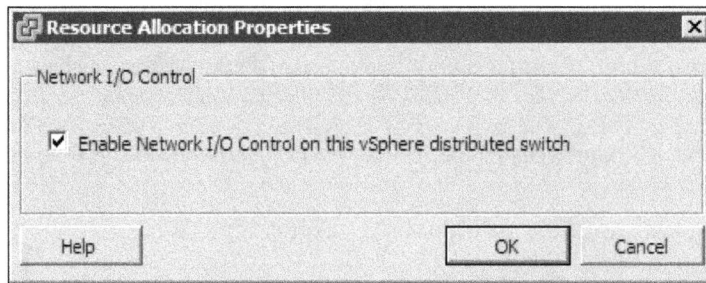

vSphere 5 has the ability to create user-defined network resource pools and to modify the system network resource pools. When editing or creating a new network resource pool, three settings are configurable, as follows:

- ▶ Physical adapter shares: Prioritize the access to the physical NICs when contention arises. One of the four settings can be configured; Low, Normal (default), High, and Custom (a value of 1 to 100 may be specified).

- ▶ Host limit: Host limit places a limit on the amount of network bandwidth (Mbps) that a particular resource pool has access to. The default setting of **Unlimited** puts the onus on the card to control limits.

- ▶ QoS priority tag: Quality of Service tag (802.1p) is associated with all the outgoing packets. This enables compatible upstream switches to recognize and apply the QoS tags. The default setting is **None** and a value between 1 and 7 is configurable.

Perform the following steps to edit an existing network resource pool:

1. Under system network resource pools, right-click the desired resource pool, for example, fault tolerance (FT) traffic, select **Edit Settings**.

2. On the network resource pool settings screen, adjust the settings for **Physical adapter shares**, **Host limit** and **QoS priority tag** as needed.

3. Click on **OK** to apply the changes.

Optionally, an administrator may also create a user-defined network resource pool, as follows:

1. With the **Resource Allocation** tab selected, click on **New Network Resource Pool**.

2. On the Network Resource Pool Settings screen, supply the resource pool name.

3. Adjust the settings for **Physical adapter shares**, **Host limit**, and **QoS priority tag** as needed.

4. Click on **OK** to apply the changes.

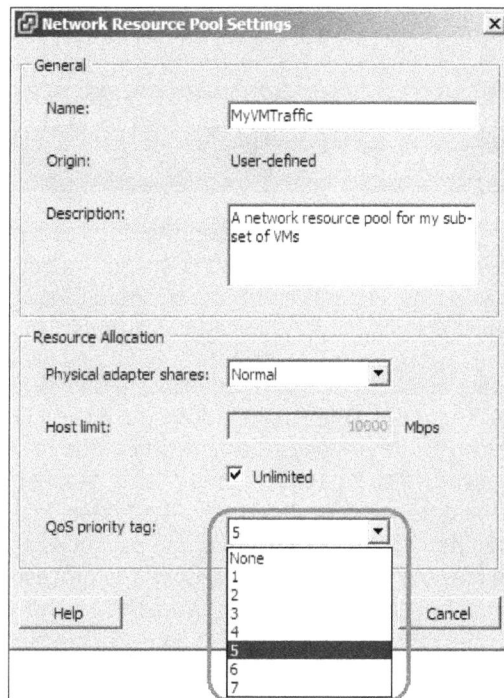

Once a user-defined resource pool has been selected, perform the following steps to associate a port group with it:

1. From the **Networking** view, select the appropriate vDS.

2. Right-click the appropriate port group, navigate to **Edit Settings**.

3. On the port group's **Settings** screen, navigate to **Resource Allocation**.

4. Click on the drop-down menu associated with network resource pool and select the appropriate resource pool. Click on **OK**.

5. If multiple user-defined network resource pools have been created, click on **Assign multiple** to associate port groups with multiple resource pools.

User-defined network resource pools			
MyVMTraffic	Unlimited Normal	50	5

Network Resource Pool Details			Edit Settings... Remove

MyVMTraffic

Origin:	User-defined network resource pool		
Host limit:	Unlimited	Shares value: 50	QoS priority tag: 5

View: Port groups

Name, Port binding, VLAN ID, Number of VMs, Number of ports or Alarm actions contains: ▾ [   ] Clear

Name	Port binding	VLAN ID	Number of VMs	Number of ports	Alarm actions
VM Traffic	Static binding	VLAN access : 0	4	128	Enabled

Monitoring network capacity and performance matrix

Network performance is dependent on the application workload and network configuration. Dropped network packets indicate a bottleneck in the network. To determine whether packets are being dropped, use resxtop/esxtop or the VMware vSphere Client advanced performance charts to examine the droppedTx and droppedRx network counter values.

If packets are being dropped, adjust the virtual machine CPU shares. This is just intensifying the problem for other VMs. The root solution is to reduce the overall CPU load on the host. If you just adjust CPU shares up for this VM, you'd expect other VMs to start dropping packets or having higher CPU latency (**%RDY**). If packets are not being dropped, check the size of the network packets and the data received and transmitted rates. In general, the larger the network packets, the faster the network speed. When the packet size is large, fewer packets are transferred, which reduces the amount of CPU required to process the data. When network packets are small, more packets are transferred, but the network speed is slower because more CPU is required to process the data. In some instances, large packets can result in high latency. To rule out this issue, check the network latency.

If packets are being dropped and the data received rate is also slow, the host may lack the CPU resources required to handle the load. Check the number of virtual machines assigned to each physical NIC. If necessary, perform load balancing by moving the virtual machines to different virtual switches or by adding more NICs to the host. You can also move virtual machines to another host or increase the CPU resources of the host or virtual machines.

Check the following key metrics. These are the significant network statistics in a vSphere environment:

- ▶ Network usage
- ▶ Host droppedRx (received packets dropped)
- ▶ Host droppedTx (transmitted packets dropped)
- ▶ Net packets received
- ▶ Net packets transmitted

You can use the vSphere Client performance charts to track the network statistics per host, per virtual machine, or per NIC (virtual or physical). However, a single chart can display either physical objects (host and vmnic#) or virtual objects (virtual machine and virtual NIC). Track these counters to determine network performance as follows:

- ▶ Network packets transmitted: Number of packets transmitted in the sampling interval
- ▶ Network packets received: Number of packets received in the sampling interval
- ▶ Network data transmit rate: Amount of data transmitted in Kbps
- ▶ Network data receive rate: Amount of data received in Kbps
- ▶ droppedTx: Number of outbound packets dropped in the sampling interval
- ▶ droppedRx: Number of inbound packets dropped in the sampling interval

Getting ready

To step through this recipe, you will need one or more running ESXi Servers, a vCenter Server, and a working installation of vSphere Client. No other prerequisites are required.

How to do it...

Now to check the network statistics of the ESXi Server or VM you should follow the proceeding steps:

1. Open up vSphere Client.
2. Log in to the vCenter Server.
3. Navigate to **Hosts and Clusters** on the home screen.
4. Choose the ESXi Server where you want to monitor the utilization and performance of network.
5. Go to the **Performance** tab on the right-hand side.
6. Select **Network** from the drop-down menu.
7. Click on the **Advanced** tab, and navigate to **Chart Options**.

8. Now select the metrics, and click on **OK** to continue.

9. Counters which you need to select are:

   ❑ **Usage**

   ❑ **Data receive rate**

   ❑ **Data transmit rate**

   ❑ **Packets transmitted**

   ❑ **Packets received**

   ❑ **Transmit packets dropped**

   ❑ **Receive packets dropped**

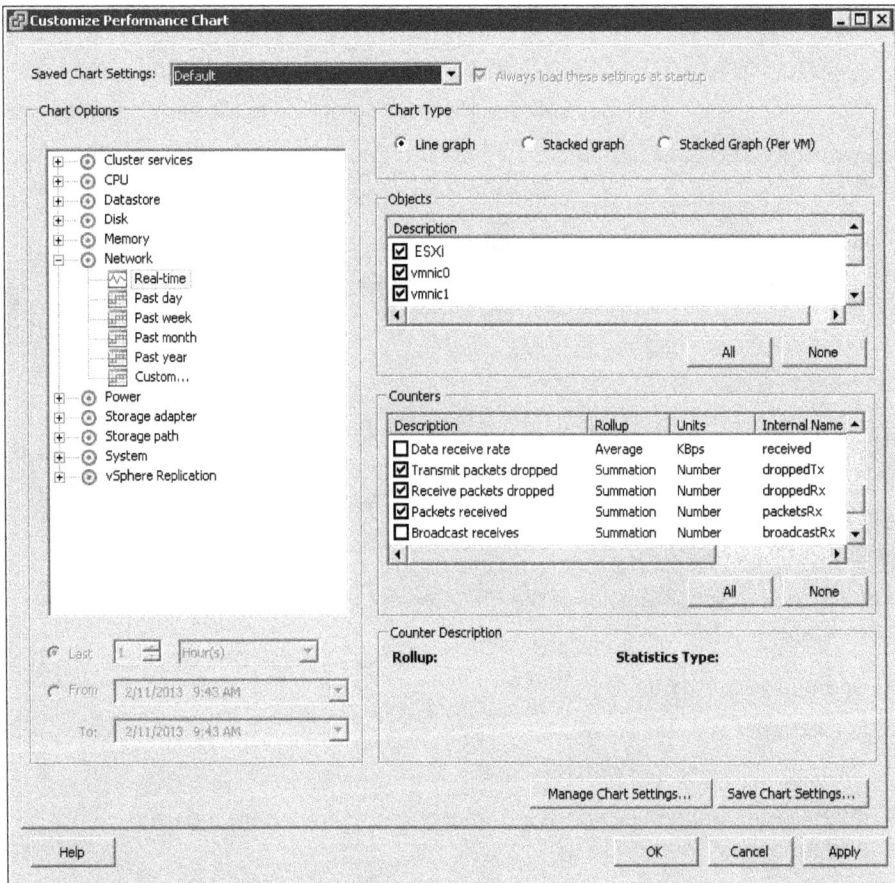

Following is an example screen shot where you can see the utilization of the ESXi network:

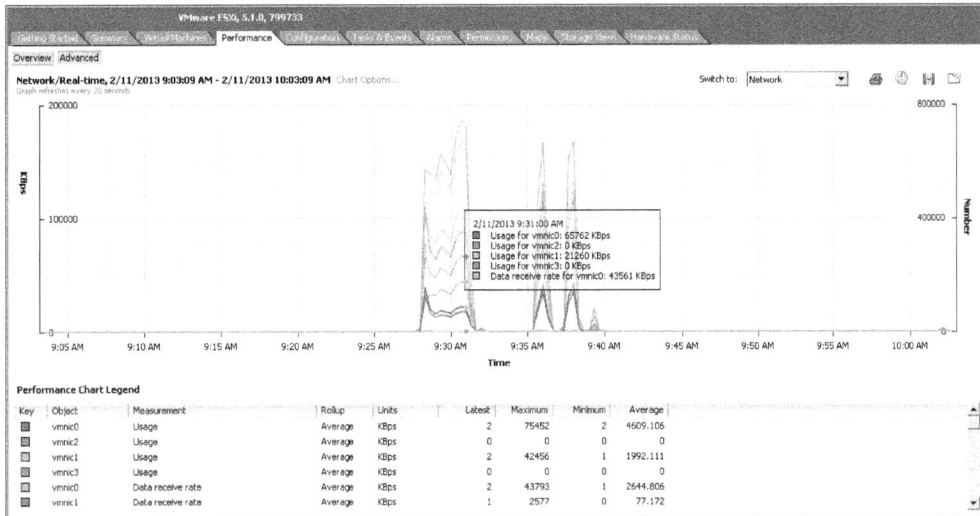

It's worth noting that in practice, dropped packets should be exactly zero. Also, in practice, network usage for typical VMs is a trivial load on the host compared to storage I/O, CPU, and memory demand. Network is the least likely physical bottleneck, as long as it's configured reasonably.

4

DRS, SDRS, and Resource Control Design

In this chapter, we will cover the tasks related with DRS, SDRS and Resource Control Design. You will learn the following aspects of DRS and SDRS Design:

- ▸ Using DRS algorithm guidelines
- ▸ Using resource pool guidelines
- ▸ Avoid using resource pool as folder structure
- ▸ Choosing the best SIOC latency threshold
- ▸ Using storage capability and profile driven storage
- ▸ Anti-affinity rules in the SDRS cluster
- ▸ Avoiding the use of SDRS I/O Metric and array-based automatic tiering together
- ▸ Using VMware SIOC and array-based automatic tiering together

Introduction

ESXi provides several mechanisms to configure and adjust the allocation of CPU, memory, and network and storage resources for virtual machines running within it. Resource management configurations can have a significant impact on virtual machine performance.

In this lesson we will discuss the guidelines for resource allocation settings such as shares, reservation, and limits.

We will also discuss guidelines for the DRS algorithm, and resource pools. Some of the advanced storage concepts will also be unveiled.

Using DRS algorithm guidelines

The **Distributed Resources Scheduler** (**DRS**) aligns resource usage with business priority by automatically load balancing across hosts. It continuously monitors utilization across vSphere ESXi servers and intelligently allocates available resources among virtual machines according to business needs.

It aggregates vSphere ESXi host resources into clusters and automatically distributes these resources to virtual machines by monitoring utilization and continuously optimizing virtual machine distribution across vSphere ESXi hosts. DRS operates on a continuous 60 minute cycle in a default configuration.

It also continuously balances computing capacity in resource pools to deliver a level of performance, scalability, and availability which is not possible with a physical infrastructure.

So, when you choose the DRS Migration threshold, remember these two things:

- ▶ Moderate threshold, which is also the default setting, works well for most of the cases, for an example, the majority of business applications that exhibit stable workload characteristics.

- ▶ However, you may wish to change the migration threshold for the following type of workloads in order to provide a more balanced workload distribution:

  - ❑ Clusters which are homogenous
  - ❑ Where resource demand for VMs is relatively constant
  - ❑ Have few affinity and anti-affinity rules

Use affinity and anti-affinity rules only when absolutely necessary. The more rules that are used, the less flexibility DRS has when determining on which hosts to place virtual machines.

Also, always make sure that DRS is in automatic mode, cluster-wide. If you need more control over your critical virtual machines, override the cluster-wide setting by setting manual or partially automated mode on selected virtual machines.

Now with that automatic mode cluster wide setting, DRS can make migration recommendations "only" for the virtual machines that can be migrated with vMotion.

The following are some things to consider before allowing DRS to use vMotion:

▸ Ensure that the hosts in the DRS cluster have compatible CPUs. Within the same hardware platform (Intel or AMD), there might be differences in CPU family, which means different CPU feature sets. As a result, virtual machines will not be able to migrate across hosts. However, **Enhanced vMotion Compatibility** (**EVC**) automatically configures server CPUs with Intel FlexMigration or AMD-V Extended Migration technologies to be compatible with older servers. EVC works by masking newer CPU features. Enabling EVC may require VM downtime if those newer features are in use. This prevents migrations with vMotion from failing due to incompatible CPUs.

▸ Leave some unused CPU capacity in your cluster for vMotion operations. When a vMotion operation is in progress, ESXi opportunistically reserves CPU resources on both the source and destination hosts. CPU resources are reserved to ensure the ability of vMotion operations to fully utilize the network bandwidth. The amount of CPU reservation thus depends on the number of vMotion NICs and their speeds: 10 percent of a processor core for each Gigabit Ethernet network interface is reserved. 100 percent of a processor core for each 10 Gigabit Ethernet network interface is reserved.

▸ The network configuration should be consistent across all hosts in your DRS cluster. In addition, the virtual machine network and the datastores on which the virtual machines reside should be available on all the hosts in your cluster.

▸ Disconnect virtual machine devices that map to local host devices, such as the local CD-ROM drive, the local floppy drive, local serial ports, and local USB ports.

Getting ready

To step through this recipe, you will need couple of ESXi Servers, an instance of vCenter Server, and a working installation of vSphere Client. No other prerequisites are required.

How to do it...

To create a DRS Cluster, you need to carry out the following steps:

1. Open up the vSphere client and log in to the **vCenter Server**.
2. Select **Hosts and Clusters** on the home screen.
3. Select the datacenter object where you want to create the cluster.
4. Right-click on the object and select **New Cluster**.

5. Give a name to this cluster and select **Turn On VMware DRS** checkbox.

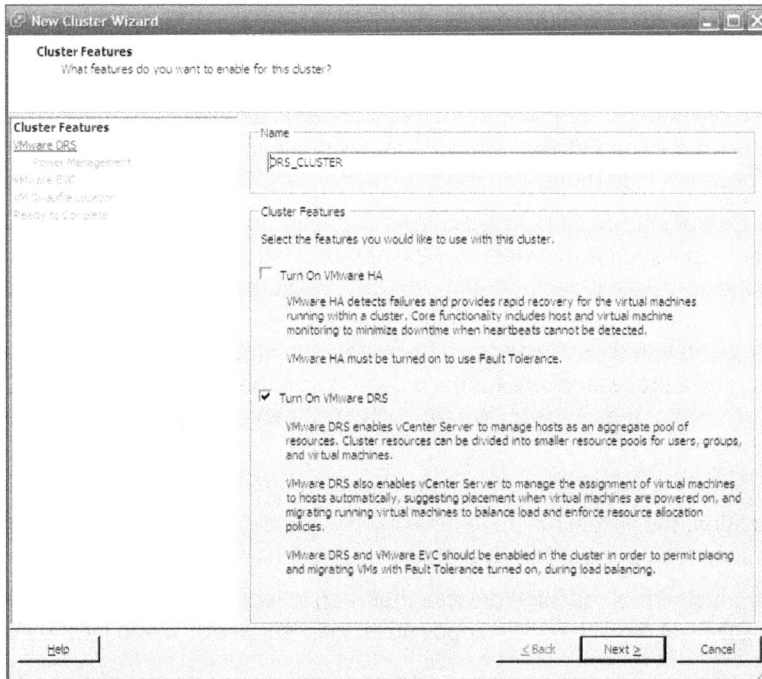

6. Click on **Next** and select the **Automation level** and **Migration Threshold**.

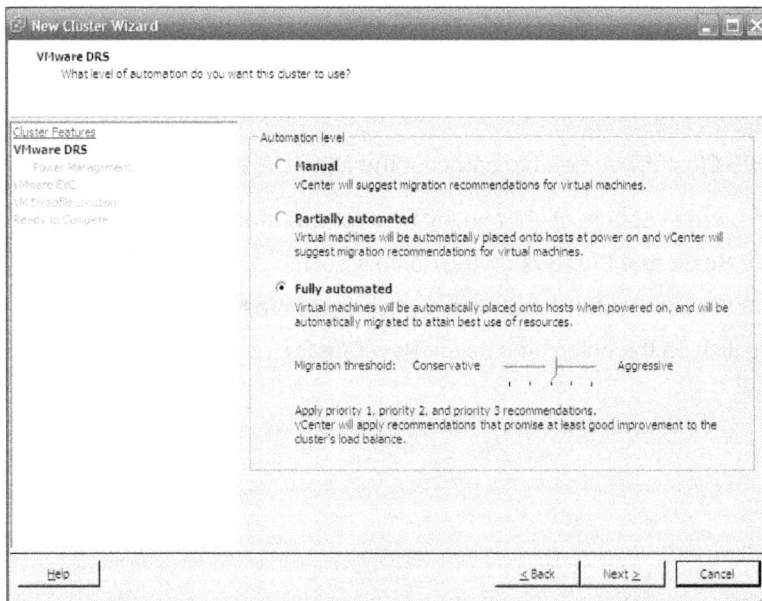

7. Click on **Next**, and then select the **Power Management** options.

8. At this point you need to select the **EVC** settings. If you are using homogenous hosts then select **Disable EVC**; otherwise, select the appropriate EVC mode for your processor.

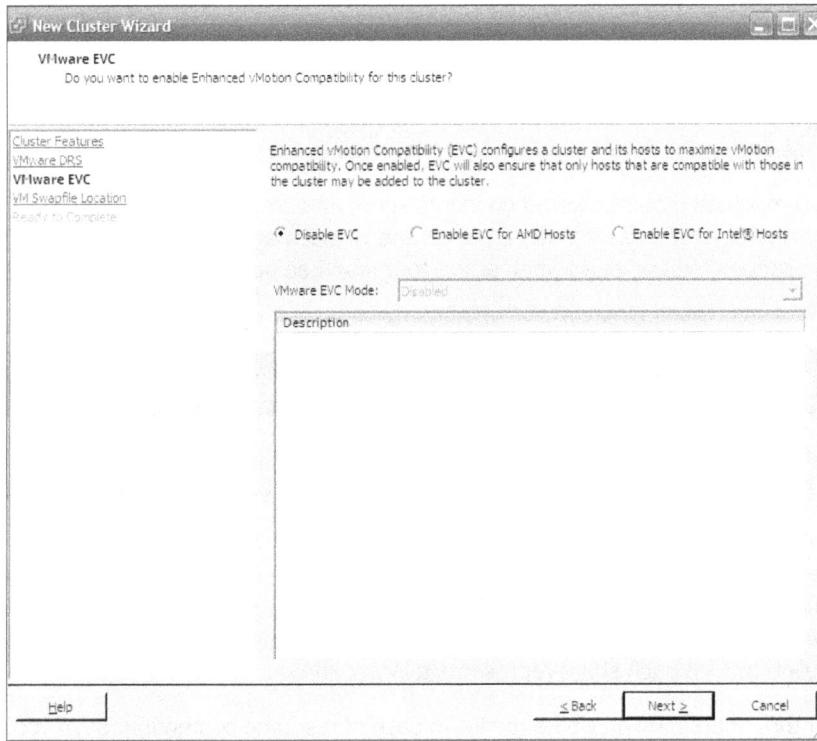

9. Select the **VM Swapfile Location**, and then click on **Next**.

10. Finally review the configuration, and then click on **Finish**

How it works...

For a better DRS placement algorithm you need to always remember these points:

Always choose homogenous hosts, which include the same CPU and Memory Architecture. However, differences can exist in the memory cache architecture of hosts in your DRS cluster. For example, some of your hosts in the DRS cluster might have NUMA architecture and others might not. This difference can result in differences in performance numbers across your hosts. DRS does not consider memory cache architecture because accounting for these differences results in minimal benefits at the DRS granularity of scheduling.

If you have more hosts in your cluster, then DRS will get more opportunities to place your virtual machines. The maximum number of hosts in a cluster is 32.

If your DRS cluster consists of hosts that vary in terms of the number of CPUs and memory sizes, then DRS tries to place your virtual machines on the largest host first. The idea here is that DRS wants the virtual machine to run on a host with excess capacity to accommodate any changes in resource demands of the virtual machine.

Virtual machines with smaller memory sizes and/or fewer vCPUs provide more opportunities for DRS to migrate them in order to improve balance across the cluster. Virtual machines with larger memory sizes and/or more vCPUs add more constraints in migrating the virtual machines.

Every virtual machine that is powered on incurs some amount of memory overhead. This overhead is not factored in as in order a part of the virtual machine's memory usage. You can very easily overlook the overhead when sizing your resource pools and when estimating how many virtual machines to place on each host.

Using resource pool guidelines

ESXi provides several mechanisms to configure and adjust the allocation of CPU and memory resources for virtual machines. Thus, resource management configurations have a significant impact on virtual machine performance.

If you expect flexibility in the total available resources, then use shares but not reservations. It will allocate resources fairly across virtual machines. Even if you upgrade the hardware, each virtual machine stays at the same relative priority using shares. The relative priority remains the same even though each share represents a larger amount of memory or CPU.

Remember that shares will only be effective in case of resource contention. So, if you think you can get immediate effect on resources for a VM by increasing the number of shares, you are mistaken. Share values are used in order to determine the dynamic entitlement of a VM. The dynamic entitlement is used in order to determine fairness, but also to opportunistically distribute unused resources. Therefore, while shares are enforced during contention, their configured priority is also leveraged in non-contentious situations as well.

You may want to use reservations to specify the minimum amount of guaranteed CPU or memory. After all resource reservations have been met, the VMkernel allocates the remaining resources based on the number of shares and the limits configured for the virtual machine.

If you choose to have a reservation for your VM, then just remember that you may limit the ability of the DRS cluster for placement of other VMs.

So carefully specify the memory limit and memory reservation. If these two parameters are misconfigured, users might observe ballooning or swapping, even when the host has plenty of free memory. For example, a virtual machine's memory might be reclaimed when the specified limit is too small or when other virtual machines reserve too much host memory. If a performance-critical virtual machine needs a guaranteed memory allocation, the reservation must be specified carefully because it might affect other virtual machines.

Getting ready

To step through this recipe, you will need a couple of ESXi Servers, an instance of installed vCenter Server, and a working installation of vSphere Client. No other prerequisites are required.

How to do it...

Now let's get started with the implementation of the guidelines.

1. Log in to the **vCenter server** using **vSphere Client**.
2. Select **Hosts and Clusters** on the home screen.
3. Select the **Cluster** where you want to create the **Resource Pool**.
4. Right-click on the resource pool, and select **New Resource Pool**.

In order to create a resource pool, you need to have the following information in hand:
Name: Name of the resource pool

Shares: Number of shares to be allocated to every VM

Reservation: Minimum resources guaranteed to VM's

Expandable Reservation: There are two options check/uncheck, if you check, reservation of existing resource pools are not available and they can be used from the parent resource pool. If you uncheck, then the host won't be able to power on the VM.

Limit: Maximum resources any VM under this resource pool will get.

Similar options are available for memory configuration. Once this step is completed you might see a yellow warning triangle, which suggests that something is incorrect.

How it works...

Resource pools hierarchically partition the available CPU and memory resources. When you configure separate resource pools, you have more options when you need to choose between resource availability and load balancing.

You may want to use resource pools to isolate performance. Isolation can prevent one virtual machine's performance from affecting the performance of other virtual machines. This way your defined limits provide more predictable service levels and less resource contention. If you define limits on your resource pool then it also protects the resource pool from a virtual machine going into a runaway condition. You also may want to set a firm limit on a resource pool, which reduces the negative effect that the virtual machine might have on the resource pool.

VMware recommends that resource pools and virtual machines should not be made siblings in a hierarchy. Instead, each hierarchy level should contain only resource pools or only virtual machines. By default, resource pools are assigned share values that might not compare appropriately with those assigned to virtual machines, potentially resulting in unexpected performance.

Avoiding using resource pool as folder structure

Many of you use resource pools to create a folder structure in the host and cluster view of vCenter and categorize your virtual machines. You Administrators may place these Virtual machines into these resource pools for sorting. But this is not the true sense of using resource pools. Resource pools should be used to prioritize virtual machine workloads, guarantee and/or limit the amount of resources available to a group of virtual machines. The issue is that even though a particular resource pool may have a higher level of shares, but by the time the pool is subdivided and finally the VM ends up with fewer shares than a VM that resides in a resource pool with a lower number of shares.

If you create a resource pool with the default settings, then by default this resource pool will be assigned 4000 shares. Also, a VM has a default of 1,000 shares. In this way, if you place three VMs on a resource pool, even with default settings, the resources will be divided by three. This means that each VM will get one-third of the resources assigned by default to that RP.

Now if you take one VM out of that RP, it will get a performance impact.

How to do it...

Now let's get started with the configuration of the Folders rather than Resource Pool.

1. Open up **vSphere Client** and log in to the **vCenter Server**.
2. Select **VMs and Templates** on the home screen.
3. Select the **Datacenter** where you want to categorize the VMs.
4. Right-click on the **Datacenter** and select **New Folder**.
5. Give a name to this folder.
6. Now move the existing VMs into this folder based on the categorization.

How it works...

Let's say you create a resource pool with all the default settings. Now you add eight virtual machines to this RP called Prod. Now if you have another resource pool and some other virtual machines at the root resource pool (Cluster) then your RP will get by default 4,000 shares, and those VMs which are in the root RP will get 1,000 shares.

In this case, the percent of shares for the RP will be same for all RPs. But if you keep on placing VMs inside the RP then it will be divided amongst all of them. Following is an example of what could happen in this situation.

For an example if you have a "Prod" Resource Pool with 1,000 shares of CPU and four VMs within that, and a "Dev" Resource Pool with 4,000 shares of CPU and 50 VMs.

"Prod": 1000 shares, 4 VMs greater than equal to 250 units per VM (small pie, a few big slices):

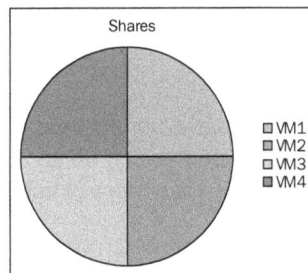

"Dev": 4000 shares, 50 VMs greater than equal to 80 units per VM (bigger pie, many small slices):

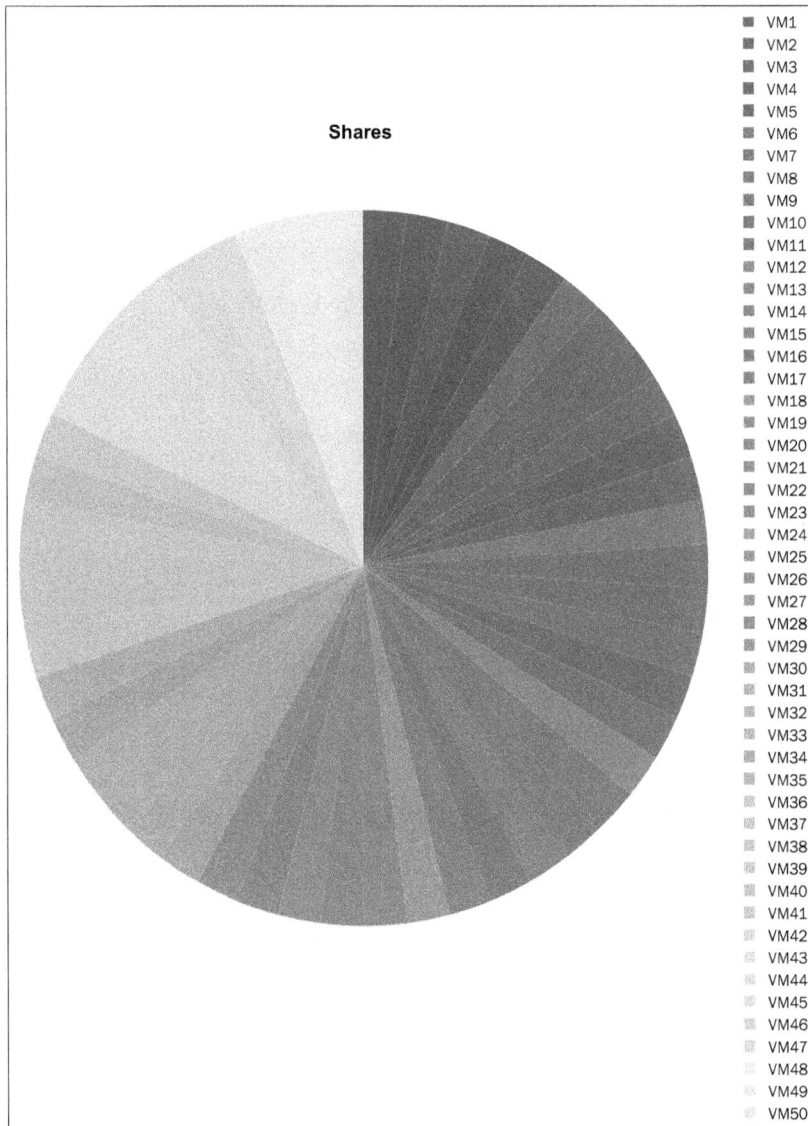

Also note that Shares will only come into play when there is contention. However, if the shares for the VMs aren't allocated properly, this can be an issue. It may happen that your non-production VMs may get higher priority than more critical VMs.

Folders provide a simple structure and nothing else. You can have as many folders as you want.

Choosing the best SIOC latency threshold

Storage I/O Control extends the constructs of shares and limits to handle storage I/O resources. Storage I/O Control is a proportional share IOPS scheduler that, under contention, throttles IOPS. You can control the amount of storage I/O that is allocated to virtual machines during periods of I/O congestion. Controlling storage I/O ensures that more important virtual machines get preference over less important virtual machines for I/O resource allocation.

There are two thresholds: one for standalone Storage I/O Control and one for Storage DRS. For Storage DRS, latency statistics are gathered by Storage I/O Control for an ESXi host and sent to vCenter Server and stored in the vCenter Server database. With these statistics, Storage DRS can make the decision on whether a virtual machine should be migrated to another datastore.

The default latency threshold for Storage I/O Control is 30 milliseconds. The default setting might be acceptable for some storage devices, but other devices might reach their latency threshold well before or after the default setting is reached. For example, **Solid State Disks** (**SSD**) typically reach their contention point sooner than the default setting protects against. Not all devices are created equally.

Getting ready

To step through this recipe, you will need one or more running ESXi servers, a couple of datastores are attached to the ESXi, a fully functioning vCenter Server and a working installation of vSphere Client.

How to do it...

To enable Storage I/O Control on a datastore:

1. In the **Datastores and Datastore Clusters** inventory view, select a datastore and click on the **Configuration** tab.
2. Click on the **Properties** link.
3. Under **Storage I/O Control**, select the **Enabled** checkbox.
4. Click on the **Close** button.

To set the storage **I/O shares and limits**, carry out the following steps:

1. Right-click on the virtual machine in the inventory, and select **Edit Settings**.
2. In the **Virtual Machine Properties** dialog box, click on the **Resources** tab.

By default, all virtual machine shares are set to Normal (1000), with unlimited IOPS.

How it works...

Storage I/O Control provides quality of service capabilities for storage I/O in the form of I/O shares and limits that are enforced across all virtual machines accessing a datastore, regardless of which host they are running on. Using Storage I/O Control, vSphere administrators can ensure that the most important virtual machines get adequate I/O resources, even in times of congestion.

In vSphere 5.1, Storage I/O Control can automatically determine the optimal latency threshold by using injector-based models to determine the latency setting. In vSphere 5.1 this injector determines and sets the latency threshold when 90 percent of the throughput is reached. This is not the case in vSphere 4.1 or 5.0.

When SDRS is enabled, Storage I/O Control is set to stats only mode by default. Stats only mode collects and stores statistics, but does not perform throttling on the storage device. Storage DRS can use the stored statistics immediately after the initial configuration, or when new datastores are added.

When you enable Storage I/O Control on a datastore, ESXi begins to monitor the device latency that hosts observe when communicating with that datastore. When device latency exceeds a threshold, the datastore is considered to be congested, and each virtual machine that accesses that datastore is allocated I/O resources in proportion to their shares.

When you allocate storage I/O resources, you can limit the IOPS that are allowed for a virtual machine. By default, the number of IOPS allowed for a virtual machine is unlimited. If the limit that you want to set for a virtual machine is in terms of megabytes per second instead of IOPS, you can convert megabytes per second into IOPS based on the typical I/O size for that virtual machine. For example, a backup application has a typical I/O size of 64KB. To restrict a backup application to 10MB per second, set a limit of 160 IOPS (10MB per second per 64KB I/O size, which is equal to 160 I/OS per second). However, this setting needs an eye on it as an application with a 4KB IO size would be very slow if limited to 160 IOPs. An IOPs limit is applied to the sum of the limits for all of the virtual disks attached to a VM.

Using storage capability and profile driven storage

It is always a cumbersome task to manage datastores and match the SLA requirements of virtual machines with the appropriate datastore. vSphere 5.0 introduced Profile Driven Storage, which allows for rapid and intelligent placement of virtual machines based on SLA, availability, performance or other requirements and provided storage capabilities.

You can request various storage characteristics, typically defined as a tier, in a virtual machine storage profile using Profile Driven Storage. These profiles are used during provisioning, cloning, and Storage vMotion to ensure that only those datastores or datastore clusters that are compliant with the virtual machine storage profile are made available.

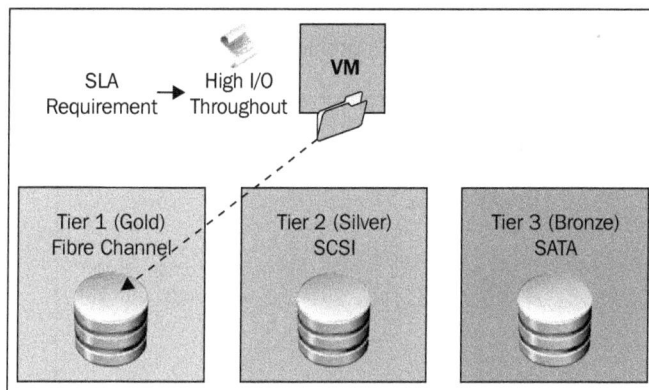

Profile-driven storage is achieved by using two key components: storage capabilities and virtual machine storage profiles.

Storage capability outlines the quality of service that a storage system can deliver. It is a guarantee that the storage system can provide a specific set of characteristics. The two types of storage capabilities are system-defined and user-defined.

A system-defined storage capability is one that comes from a storage system that uses a **VASA (vStorage API for Storage Awareness)** vendor provider. The vendor provider informs vCenter Server that it can guarantee a specific set of storage features by presenting them as a storage capability. The vCenter Server recognizes this capability and adds it to the list of storage capabilities for that storage vendor. The vCenter Server assigns the system-defined storage capability to each datastore that you create from that storage system.

A user-defined storage capability is one that you can define and associate with datastores. Examples of user-defined capabilities are as follows:

- Storage array type
- Replication status
- Storage tiers, such as gold, silver, and bronze datastores

A user-defined capability can be associated with multiple datastores. It is possible to associate a user-defined capability with a datastore that already has a system-defined capability.

Storage capabilities are used to define a virtual machine storage profile. A virtual machine storage profile lists the storage capabilities that virtual machine home files and virtual disks require to run the applications on the virtual machine. A virtual machine storage profile is created by an administrator, who can create different storage profiles to define different levels of storage requirements. The virtual machine home files (`.vmx`, `.vmsd`, `.nvram`, `.log`, and so on) and the virtual disks (`.vmdk`) can have separate virtual machine storage profiles.

With a virtual machine storage profile, a virtual machine can be checked for storage compliance. If the virtual machine is placed on storage that has the same capabilities as those defined in the virtual machine storage profile, the virtual machine is storage-compliant.

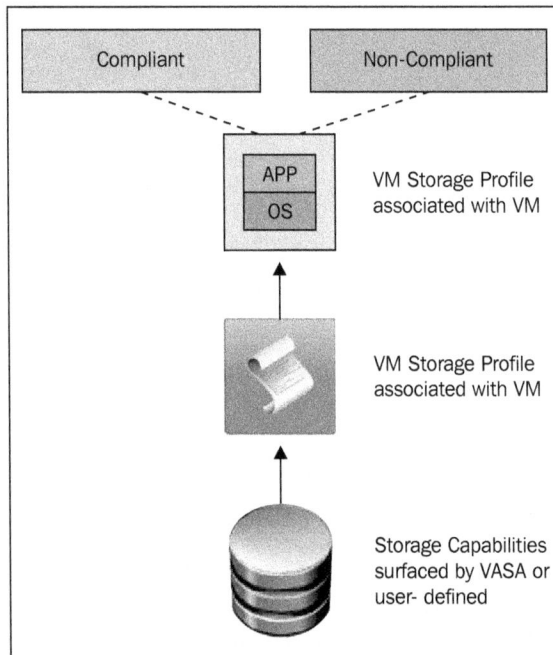

Getting ready

To step through this recipe, you will need one or more running ESXi Servers, a couple of datastores attached to these ESXi servers, a vCenter Server, and a working installation of vSphere Client. No other prerequisites are required.

How to do it...

Let's get started:

1. Create the user-defined storage capabilities. From the vSphere UI, click on the **VM Storage Profiles icon**. This will take you to the **VM Storage Profiles** view.

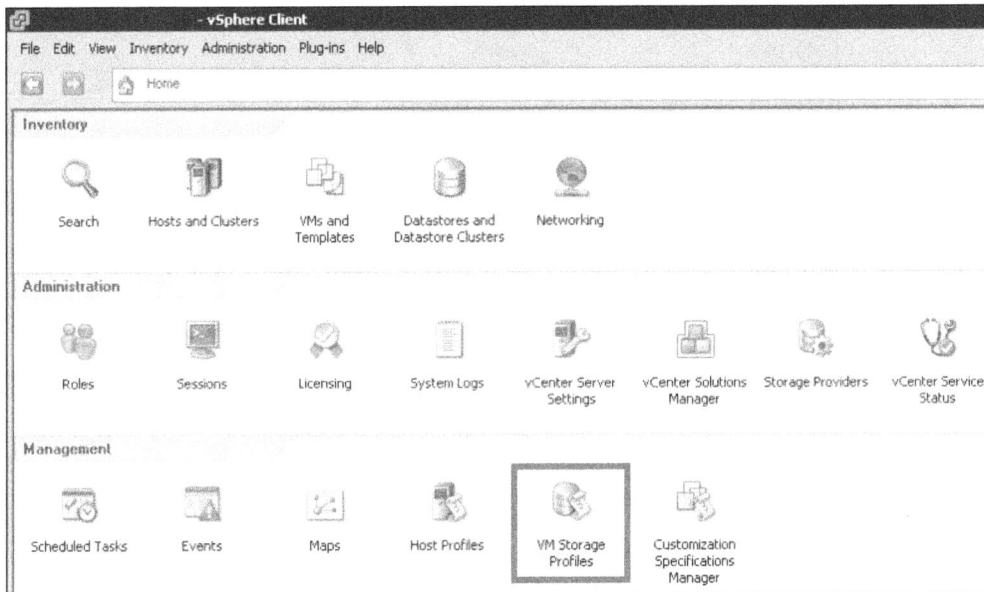

2. The next step is to start adding the user-defined storage capabilities (or business tags).To do this, select **Manage Storage Capabilities**, and add them in. If we stick with the gold/silver/bronze example, here is how you would create a `Bronze` user-defined storage capability.

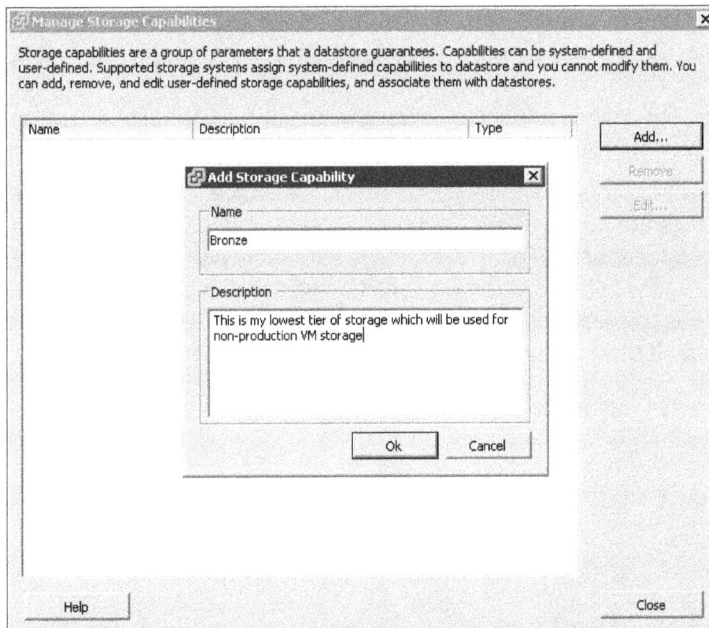

If you create additional storage capabilities, you can use them to classify different types of storage.

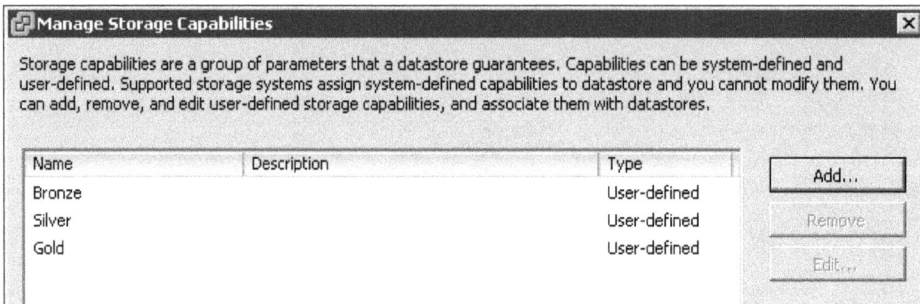

Manage Storage Capabilities ☒

Storage capabilities are a group of parameters that a datastore guarantees. Capabilities can be system-defined and user-defined. Supported storage systems assign system-defined capabilities to datastore and you cannot modify them. You can add, remove, and edit user-defined storage capabilities, and associate them with datastores.

Name	Description	Type	
Bronze		User-defined	**Add...**
Silver		User-defined	Remove
Gold		User-defined	Edit...

3. Create a VM Storage Profile. To create a profile, select the option **Create VM Storage Profile** in the **VM Storage Profiles** view seen earlier. First give it a name and a description, and then select the storage capabilities for that profile.

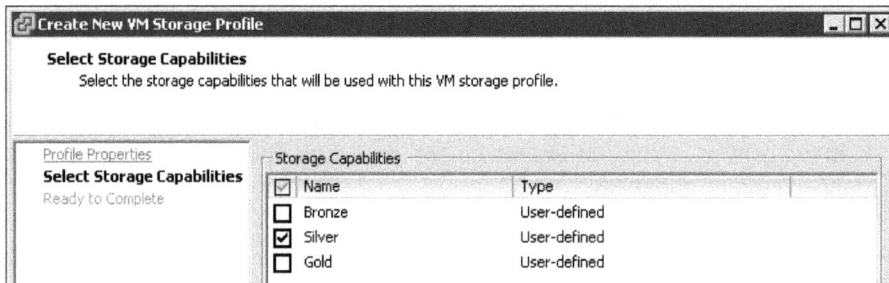

Create New VM Storage Profile _ ☐ ☒

Select Storage Capabilities
Select the storage capabilities that will be used with this VM storage profile.

Profile Properties
Select Storage Capabilities
Ready to Complete

Storage Capabilities

☑ Name	Type	
☐ Bronze	User-defined	
☑ Silver	User-defined	
☐ Gold	User-defined	

4. Add the user-defined capability to the datastore. Simply right-click on the desired datastore, and select the option **Assign User-Defined Storage Capability**.

5. Using the VM Storage Profile. At this point, the profile is created and the user-defined capabilities are added to the datastore. Now we can use the profile to select the correct storage for the VM. The profile is automatically attached to the VM during the deployment phase. Later, we can check if the datastore on which the VM is placed has the same capabilities as the profile. If it does, then the VM is said to be compliant. If they do not, then the VM is said to be non-compliant.

    VM Storage Profiles can be used during deployment or during migrations, or can be attached on-the-fly.

How it works...

Profile-driven storage enables the creation of datastores that provide varying levels of service. With profile-driven storage, you can use storage capabilities and virtual machine storage profiles to ensure that virtual machines use storage that provides a certain level of capacity, performance, availability, redundancy, and so on.

Profile-driven storage minimizes the amount of storage planning that the administrator must do for each virtual machine. For example, the administrator can use profile-driven storage to create basic storage tiers. Datastores with similar capabilities are tagged to form gold, silver, and bronze tiers. Redundant, high-performance storage might be tagged as the gold tier, and non-redundant, medium performance storage might be tagged as the bronze tier.

It can be used during the provisioning of a virtual machine to ensure that a virtual machine's disks are placed on the storage that is best for its situation. For example, profile-driven storage can help you ensure that the virtual machine running a critical I/O-intensive database is placed in the gold tier. Ideally, the administrator wants to create the best match of predefined virtual machine storage requirements with available physical storage properties.

Anti-affinity rules in the SDRS cluster

Storage DRS makes sure that a virtual machine's data is assigned to the optimal storage location initially and then uses ongoing load balancing between datastores to avoid bottlenecks. Storage DRS provides smart virtual machine placement and load balancing mechanisms based on I/O and space utilization.

Similar to the vSphere DRS, SDRS aggregates the resources of several datastores into a single datastore cluster to simplify storage management at scale with vSphere SDRS. During virtual machine provisioning Storage DRS provides intelligent virtual machine placement based on the IO load and the available storage capacity of the datastores. Storage DRS performs ongoing load balancing between datastores to ensure space and/or I/O bottlenecks are avoided as per pre-defined rules that reflect business needs and changing priorities.

Similar to the vSphere DRS, SDRS also has a mechanism for placing the Virtual Machines. data. It is similarly called Affinity and Anti Affinity rule. But affinity and anti-affinity rule works on VMDK and datastores.

By default, all of a virtual machine's disks can be on the same datastore. However an end user might want the virtual disks on different datastores. For example, a user can place a system disk on one datastore and place the data disks on another. In this case, the user can set up a virtual machine disk (VMDK) anti-affinity rule, which keeps a virtual machine's virtual disks on separate datastores.

If you change the default setting of keeping VMDKs together, then Storage DRS will have far more options for moving virtual disks around, as it can make decisions per disk instead of per VM. By changing the default, Storage DRS will find the optimal placement per disk.

Virtual machine anti-affinity rules keep virtual machines on separate datastores. This rule is useful when redundant virtual machines are available.

The following is a full table of how it behaves in different options:

Intra-VM VMDK Affinity	Intra-VM VMDK Anti-Affinity	VM Anti-Affinity
Keep a Virtual Machine's VMDKs together on the same datastore	Keep a VM's VMDKs on different datastores	Keep VMs on different datastores
Maximize virtual machine availability when all disks are needed in order to run	Rule can be applied to all, or a subset of, a VM's disks	Rule is similar to the DRS anti-affinity rule
Rule is on by default for all VMs		Maximize availability of a set of redundant VMs

Intra-VM VMDK Affinity   Intra-VM VMDK Anti-Affinity   VM Anti-Affinity

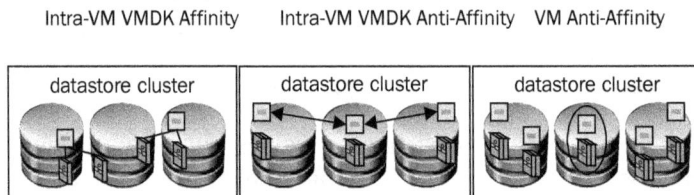

Getting ready

To step through this recipe, you will need one or more running ESXi Servers, more than one Datastore attached to the ESXi, a couple of VMs on those datastores, a vCenter Server, and a working installation of vSphere Client. No other prerequisites are required.

How to do it...

To change the default setting of the SDRS affinity rule you need to carry out the following steps:

Log in to the **vCenter Server** using **vSphere Client**.

1. Select **Datastores and Datastore Cluster** on the home screen.
2. Select the **Datastore Cluster** where you want to change the setting.

3. Right-click on the datastore cluster, and select **Edit Settings**.

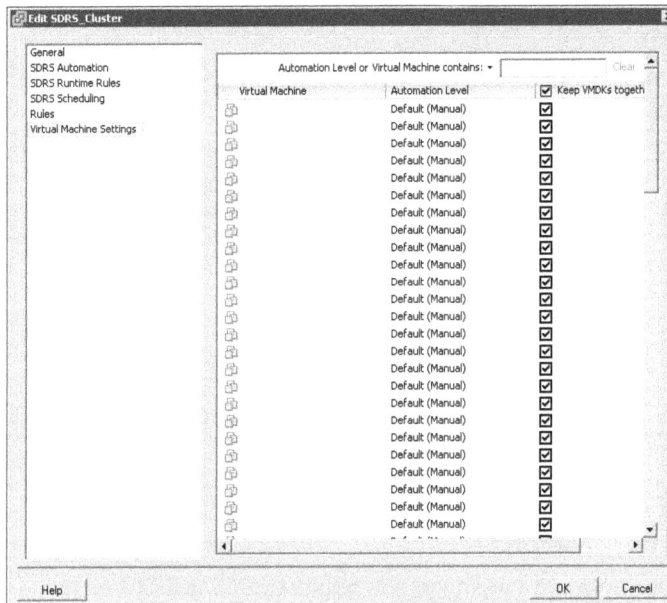

4. Select **Virtual Machine Settings** and change the default setting for the VMDK affinity rule.

5. Select the **Rule**, and specify your desired rules for other VMs.

Avoiding the use of SDRS I/O Metric and array-based automatic tiering together

While we can employ array-based automatic LUN tiering and VMware Storage DRS, we need to disable the I/O Metric-based calculation in SDRS. So, in this way we would not employ both of them doing the same job. Now let us see what it does in the back end.

SDRS triggers action on either capacity and/or latency. Capacity stats are constantly gathered by vCenter, where the default threshold is 80 percent. I/O load trend is evaluated (by default) every eight hours, based on the past day's history; the default threshold is 15ms. This means that the Storage DRS algorithm will be invoked when these thresholds are exceeded. Now in the case of "utilized space", this happens when vCenter collects the datastore statistics and notices that the threshold has been exceeded, in the case of I/O load balancing.

Every eight hours, Storage DRS will evaluate the I/O imbalance and will make recommendations if and when the thresholds are exceeded. Note that these recommendations will only be made when the difference between the source and destination is at least five percent and the cost/ risk/benefit analysis has a positive result.

I/O Latency is the datastore's response time, measured in milliseconds. The default value is 15ms, which means that the datastore will not consider relocations until the datastore restore time exceeds 15ms, and the imbalance rules are also satisfied.

In some cases, it might be best to avoid the latency assessment because of variability in the application workload or storage configuration. For example, auto-tiered storage can provide varied I/O response times, depending on the class of storage used by the tiered device. Additionally, tiered storage is designed to migrate blocks at a sub-LUN level. Since both SDRS and FAST address the same problem, although at a slightly different level, use only one of them to perform the migrations to avoid duplicate relocation operations, do not allow both SDRS and FAST to perform automated relocations.

When using EMC FAST VP, use SDRS, but disable I/O metric. This combination gives you the simplicity benefits of SDRS for automated placement and capacity balancing.

So, the thumb rule is DO NOT enable I/O metric for SDRS recommendations. Let that be done by Array-based Automatic LUN tiering at the storage layer.

Getting ready

To step through this recipe, you will need one or more running ESXi servers, a couple of Datastores attached to the ESXi, a fully functioning vCenter Server, and a working installation of vSphere Client. No other prerequisites are required. However we presume that FAST is enabled on the Storage side. Showing how to enable FAST on Storage side is not in scope of this recipe.

How to do it...

To do this you need to carry out the following steps:

1. Open up **vSphere Client** and log in to the **vCenter Server**.
2. Select **Datastores and Datastore Cluster** on the home screen.
3. Right-click on your datacenter object, and select **New datastore Cluster**.
4. Give a name to this **Datastore Cluster** and click on **Next**.
5. Select your **Automation level** and click on **Next**.

> Manual mode indicates that Storage DRS will only make recommendations and the user will need to apply these. Fully Automated means that Storage DRS will make recommendations and apply these directly, by migrating virtual machines or virtual disks to the proposed destination datastore.

6. Click on **Show Advanced Options**.

7. Here do not select the **I/O Metric Inclusion**.

8. Accept all of the default settings, and click on **Next**.

9. Select the cluster to which you want to add this **Datastore Cluster**.

10. Select the datastores that should be part of this **Datastore Cluster**.

11. Review your selections, ensure that all hosts are connected to the datastores in the datastore cluster and click on **Finish**.

12. The datastore cluster will now be created and a new object should appear on the **Datastores and Datastore Clusters** view. This object should contain the selected datastores.

Using VMware SIOC and array-based automatic tiering together

Storage IO Control and array-based automatic tiering always complement each other and we should use it wherever possible.

Fully-automated storage tiering for Virtual Pools, or FAST VP, intelligently manages data placement at the sub-LUN level, thus increasing overall performance. When implemented on a storage system, FAST VP measures, analyzes, and implements a storage-tiering policy much faster and more efficiently than any user could.

Depending on the performance characteristics, FAST VP puts drives of varying performance levels and cost into storage pools. LUNs use the capacity from these pools as needed. FAST VP collects statistics based on I/O activity, in 1 GB slices. This is only specific to newer EMC Arrays, such as VNX or VMAX and so on. These statistics are then used to determine which slices will be promoted to a higher tier of storage.

At the user's discretion, relocation of the data can be initiated—either manually or by an automated scheduler.

FAST VP is a licensed feature available on the VNX series, supporting a unified approach to automatic tiering for both file and block data.

All data goes through a lifecycle and experiences varying levels of activity over that lifetime.

For example, when data is first created it is typically used heavily and as it ages data is accessed less often. FAST dynamically matches these data characteristics to the tier of disk drives best suited to the data access patterns. Disk drives are segregated into tiers based on the frequency of the data access.

Disk drives also offer varying degrees of performance, and are placed in tiers accordingly. Flash or SSD drives perform the fastest, followed by SAS and NL-SAS respectively.

Data that requires a high response time and has a high rate of IOPs should be optimized by allowing FAST VP to migrate this data to these drives.

Storage I/O Control

| APP OS | CPU shares: High
 Memory shares: High
 I/O shares: High | APP OS | CPU shares: Low
 Memory shares: Low
 I/O shares: Low |

16GHz
8GB

Datastore A

Fast optimization

Storage Pool

Storage System

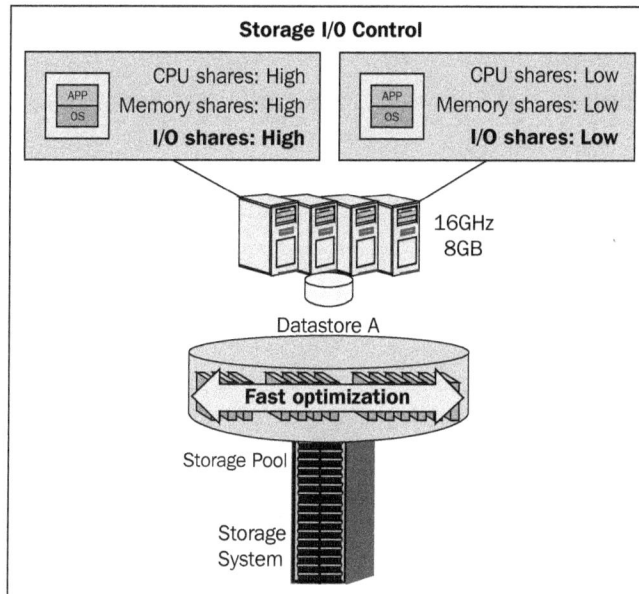

Getting ready

To step through this recipe, you will need one or more running ESXi servers, a couple of datastores are attached to the ESXi, a fully functioning vCenter Server, and a working installation of vSphere Client. No other prerequisites are required. However we presume that FAST is enabled on the Storage side. Configuring FAST VP on EMC storage is not in the scope of this recipe.

How to do it...

Let's get started

1. Open up **vSphere Client** and log in to the **vCenter Server**.
2. In the **Inventory** section, select **Datastores**.

3. Choose the **Datastores** from the list of datastores in the left panel where you want to prioritize the I/O.

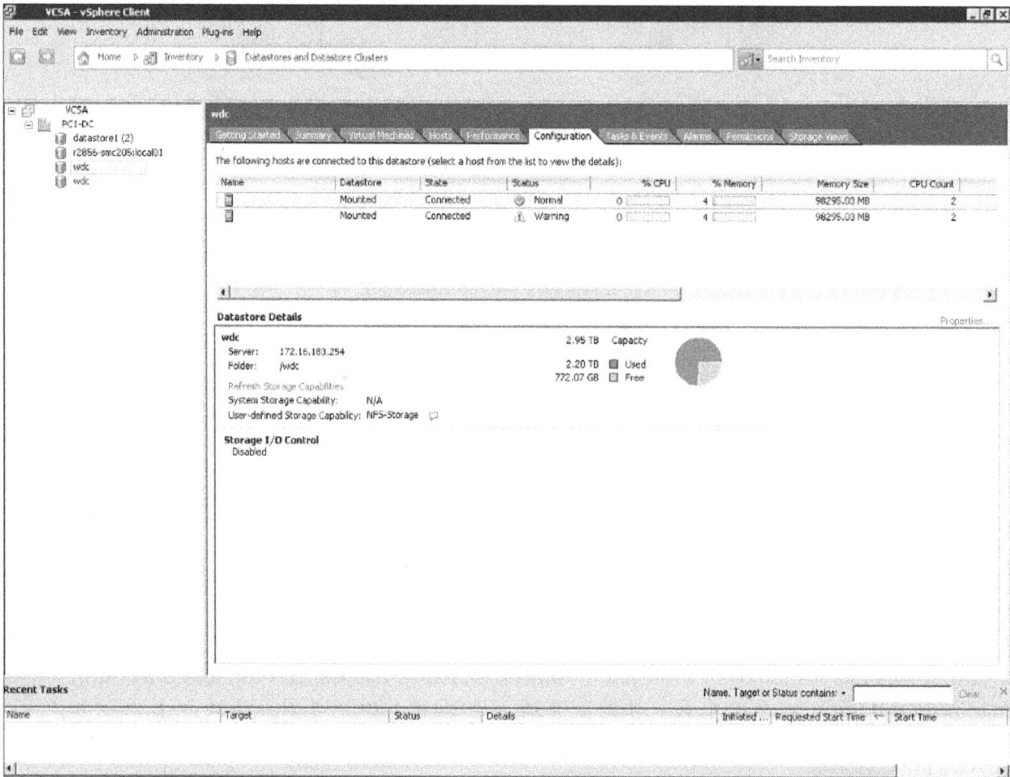

4. Select a **Datastore**, click on its corresponding **Configuration** tab, and then click on the **Properties** link to bring forward the **Properties** window, as shown in the following screenshot.

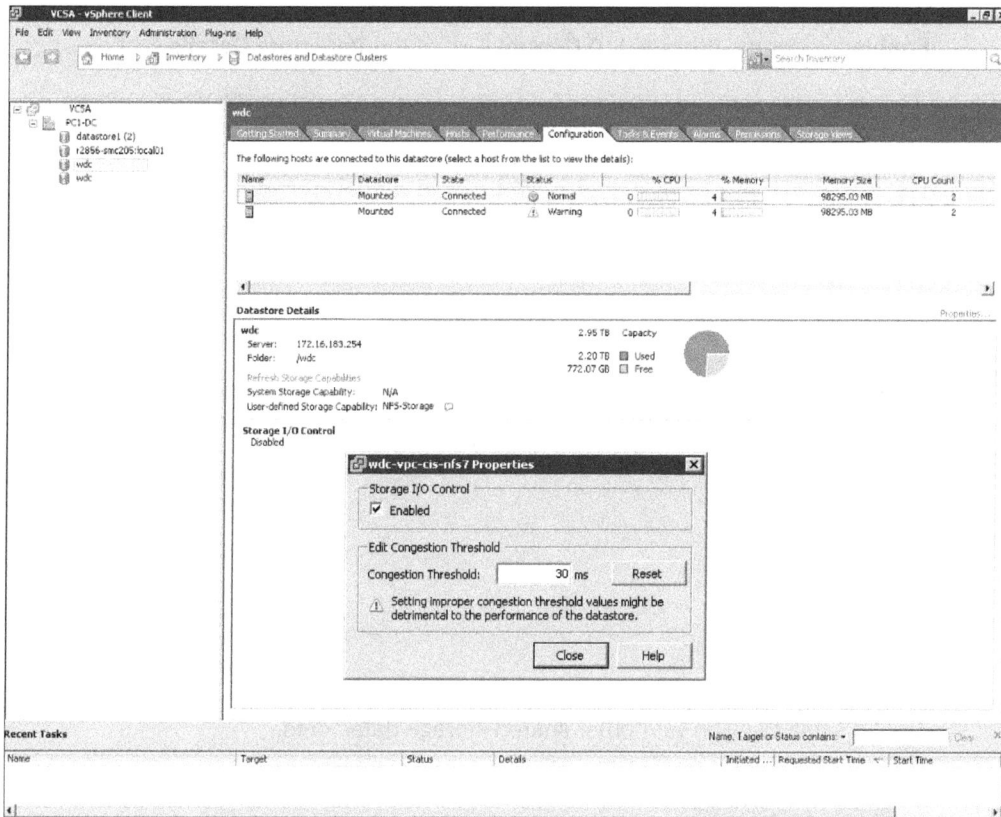

5. At this stage you can enable the **Storage I/O Control** by simply selecting the checkbox labeled **Enabled**. Click on the **Close** button when you're done.

6. You'll know you were successful if, in the **vSphere client** window, you now see **Enabled** under the **Storage I/O Control** item of the **Datastore Details** section.

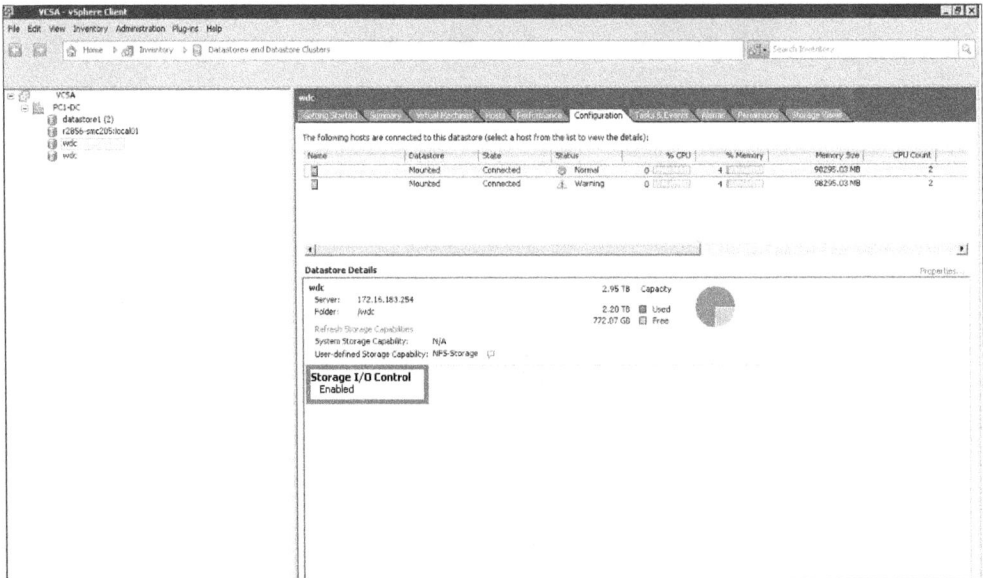

7. Do the same thing on your other shared storage datastores.

How it works...

FAST supports **Storage I/O Control** (**SIOC**). SIOC is a technology on the VMware-side that allows users to configure I/O shares at a datastore level, so that the critical VM receives the I/O throughput and response time when needed, without worrying that another VM on that same datastore would hinder the performance of a critical VM. One works at the VM level and the other works at the drive level—both complement each other.

For example, let's say you have two VMs, each running SQL, however one VM is critical and the other is not.

FAST will service the I/O from both SQL databases equally. However, you can design these VMs as HIGH and LOW in SOIC and ensure the correct performance is given to your VMs.

This is probably a situation where we either need to assign a response time value based upon the weakest link (NL-SAS). So if we expect the performance/response time for

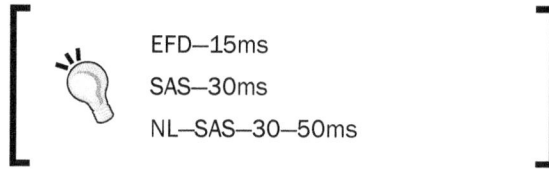

$$\left[\begin{array}{l} \text{EFD—15ms} \\ \text{SAS—30ms} \\ \text{NL—SAS—30—50ms} \end{array} \right]$$

In this case, FAST VP Pool with NL-SAS would need to be set to 50.

Of course it does not help if all of the data resides on EFD and the LUN experiences contention.

5
vSphere Cluster Design

In this chapter, we will cover the tasks related to vSphere Cluster Design for best performance. You will learn the following aspects of vSphere Cluster Design:

- ▸ Trade-off factors while designing scale up and scale out clusters
- ▸ Using VM Monitoring
- ▸ vSphere Fault Tolerance design and its impact
- ▸ DPM and its impact
- ▸ Choosing the reserved cluster failover capacity
- ▸ Rightly choosing a vSphere HA cluster size

Introduction

Downtime always brings significant costs to any environment. Thus, implementing a high availability solution is always necessary. However, traditionally it brings complexity, in terms of manageability and cost.

VMware vSphere High Availability (vSphere HA) makes it simpler, easier, and cheaper to provide high availability for your important applications. You can configure it with a couple of simple steps through VMware vCenter Server. You can create a vSphere HA Cluster with multiple ESXi Servers, which will enable you to protect virtual machines and the services running inside them. In the event of a failure of one of the hosts in the cluster, impacted virtual machines are automatically restarted on other ESXi hosts within that same VMware vSphere Cluster.

However, it is not that easy to determine size of a vSphere HA Cluster, keeping an amount of resource in a safe vault, and considering some other features such as vSphere Fault Tolerance (also known as FT) and Distributed Power Management (also known as DPM). In this chapter you will learn what you need to know about these to make sure you are running a balanced environment, and thus achieving a good performance in your vSphere Cluster.

Trade-off factors while designing scale up and scale out clusters

You should take an initial design decision when you design your vSphere HA cluster. Now the decision is whether you should design a small cluster with larger hosts, or a large cluster with smaller hosts.

We call the first cluster as scale up cluster, and the second one as scale out cluster. There are many factors that work as a catalyst when you choose a scale up or a scale out cluster. Some of them are as follows:

- Depending on the cost, which hardware is ideal for lowering cost, a few larger hosts or a large number of smaller hosts? Though this answer varies in different situations.

- What is the operational cost and complexity over the period of time in maintaining any of these two models?

- What about the other infrastructure components, such as power, cooling, and floor space?

- What is the purpose of this cluster? Is it a Desktop Virtualization Cluster or a Server Virtualization Cluster?

The design decision that you choose depends on the answer. If you choose to virtualize servers then this typically requires large number of hosts with fair capacity. This cluster typically hosts fewer virtual machines per host. However, the picture is totally different when you virtualize desktops, where you choose fewer hosts with large capacity to host more virtual machines per host. You should also consider the maximum capacity of a host in HA cluster.

Getting ready

To step through this recipe, you need to have two different set of ESXi servers: some of them should be rich and thick (four socket servers with more memory) in terms of capacity, and other should be thin (two socket servers with less memory) in terms of capacity. A vCenter Server and a working installation of vSphere Client, no other prerequisites are required.

How to do it...

Perform the following steps to create a scale up cluster and a scale out cluster:

1. Using vSphere Client, log in to the vCenter Server.
2. Select the **Hosts and Clusters** view on the **Home** screen.
3. Right-click on the **Datacenter** in the Inventory tree and click on **New Cluster**.
4. Name this cluster as scale up in the Cluster Creation Wizard.

5. By default **Turn on vSphere HA** and **Turn on vSphere DRS** will be selected; click on **Next**.

6. From this stage, leave the default settings, and click on **Next**.

7. Select all of the default settings and move to the **Finish** screen.

8. Review the cluster configuration and click on **Finish**.

9. Once your cluster is created, right-click on it and select **Add Host**.

10. Specify the Hostname/IP Address of the ESXi hosts that you select for the scale up cluster (thick hosts) and click on **Next**.

11. Choose the default configuration for the rest of the steps and click on **Finish**.

12. Repeat this step for rest of the scale up hosts' addition.

Now you are ready with a cluster that has fewer hosts with rich configurations/capacity for your server workload.

To create a Scale Out cluster, repeat the previous steps:

1. Change the name of the cluster in Step 4.

2. Choose the scale out (thin hosts) hosts in step 10 and add subsequent hosts there.

How it works...

A scale up and a scale out cluster has its advantages and disadvantages.

Primary advantage for a scale up cluster is that it takes less effort to manage and monitor, and thus it is less expensive (in terms of operational cost) as well. When it comes to the other infrastructure components, such as power, cooling, and space, this cluster is also beneficial as it might consume less than a scale out cluster. If you choose to virtualize user desktops, then a scale up cluster is preferable.

However, a scale up cluster has disadvantages as well. Try to consider the failure domain of a scale up cluster. A single host failure in a scale up cluster can affect many virtual machines at the same time. vSphere HA can take time to restart those failed virtual machines. Also, the reservation of failover capacity is also huge, as reserving a single host also impacts the cluster resource reservation.

DRS migration choice is very limited in a scale up cluster. In this case, balancing your virtual machines on those hosts will be inefficient.

You may need to consider the HA maximum virtual machine limit as well. Sometimes (More than 4,000 VMs in the cluster) in a scale up cluster, you will end up reaching that limit very fast, and then HA will not be able to restart those VMs after a failure.

Similarly, a scale out cluster also has several advantages and disadvantages. As opposed to the scale up cluster, only fewer virtual machines are affected in a scale out cluster by a single host failure, and failover takes quickly as well. Also, fewer resources will be reserved for the failover.

> Note that in any cluster with many VMs, the probability that more than one host will fail simultaneously goes up.

With DRS enabled, a scale out cluster has the option to give more choice to virtual machines, in terms of migration and load balancing. Also, it is hard to reach the per-host virtual machines limits in a scale out cluster.

However, it can consume more power, cooling, and floor space. For example, four socket servers takes 4U space in the rack, and two socket server takes 2U space in the rack. Additional cost could be network port cost. Operational complexity and costs are also high for a scale out cluster.

Using VM Monitoring

When you enable VM Monitoring, the VM Monitoring service, which is serviced by VMware Tools, evaluates whether each virtual machine in the cluster is running or not. Regular heartbeats and I/O activity from the VMware Tools process will be checked by the VM Monitoring service to determine the running guest.

Sometimes, VM heartbeats or I/O activity are not received by the VM Monitoring Service because the guest operating system has failed or VMware Tools is not being allocated time to complete its tasks. If the VM Monitoring Service does not get to listen to those heartbeats, then it declares that the virtual machine has failed and the virtual machine is rebooted to restore service.

The VM Monitoring service also monitors a virtual machine's I/O activity just to avoid unnecessary resets. If there are no heartbeats received within the failure interval, the I/O stats interval (a cluster level attribute) is checked. The I/O stats interval (by default 120 seconds) determines if any disk or network activity has occurred for the virtual machine during the previous two minutes. If not, then the virtual machine is reset.

> This default value (120 seconds) can be changed using the advanced attribute **das.iostatsinterval**.

You should enable VM Monitoring to restart a failed virtual machine. To be effective, the application or service running on the virtual machine must be capable of restarting successfully after a reboot.

The default monitoring and restart settings are acceptable. Virtual machine monitoring does not adversely affect virtual machines that are protected by FT and MSCS. FT and Microsoft Clustering Services (also known as MSCS) monitors for virtual machine failure, but they detect and react to a virtual machine failure well before vSphere HA virtual machine monitoring.

You can also configure the level of monitoring. If you select high as the sensitivity then a fast conclusion will be reached regarding the failure occurrence. However, it may result in negative impact as the monitoring service might not get a heartbeat because of resource constraints and may trigger a false alarm. Low sensitivity monitoring results in longer interruptions in service between actual failures and virtual machines being reset. You should select an option that is an effective compromise for your needs.

VM Monitoring Settings are as follows:

Setting	Failure Interval (seconds)	Reset Period
High	30	1 hour
Medium	60	24 hours
Low	120	7 days

Getting ready

You should have an existing vSphere Infrastructure, and an existing vCenter Server. No other prerequisites are required.

How to do it...

To configure VM Monitoring while creating a vSphere HA Cluster, you should carry out the following steps:

1. Using vSphere Client, log in to the vCenter Server.
2. Select the **Hosts and Clusters** view on the **Home** Screen.
3. Right-click on the **Datacenter** in the Inventory tree, and click on **New Cluster**.
4. Give a name to this cluster.
5. By default **Turn on vSphere HA** and **Turn on vSphere DRS** will be selected; click on **Next**.
6. Leave the default settings for **DRS Automation** level and click on **Next**.
7. Click on **Next** on the **Power Management** page.
8. Review the overall **HA Configuration** page and select **Next**.
9. Select the default HA cluster setting and click on **Next**.

10. On the **VM Monitoring** page, select **VM Monitoring** as **Enabled** (by default it will be disabled) from the drop-down menu.

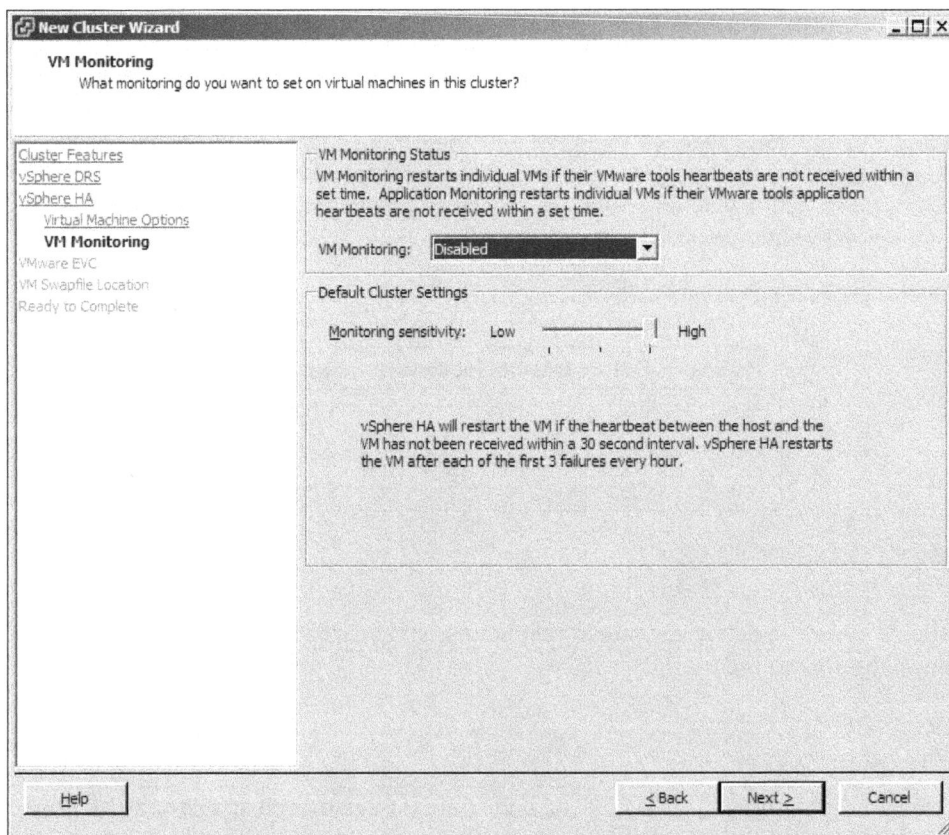

11. Choose the default **Monitoring sensitivity** as **Low**, **Medium**, or **High** and click on **Next**.

12. On the **EVC** page select the default and click on **Next**.

13. On the **Swapfile** page again select the default and click on **Next**.

14. Review the cluster configuration and click on **Finish**.

vSphere Fault Tolerance design and its impact

It all depends on the workloads whether you want to configure Fault Tolerance (FT) protected Virtual Machines. One of the major reasons to choose FT is, if you require zero or near zero downtime for a critical workload. If you perform a current state analysis of an existing infrastructure and found some critical workloads already protected in physical infrastructure, it is most likely that these workloads require protection in a VMware virtual infrastructure as well. FT is simple to configure and can offer a wide range of workloads to be protected. However, FT works for uniprocessor VMs, which is a deal killer for most VMs that would otherwise get FT.

However, there are number of limitations associated with the configuration of FT. Many fundamental virtualization benefits are lost, including the use of virtual machine snapshots and VMware vSphere Storage vMotion.

There are number of prerequisites and configurations on the infrastructure side which should be in place before you configure FT and they are as follows:

- ▶ FT can only be configured in a vSphere HA Cluster. You should have at least three hosts in the cluster because if one host fails there will be two hosts servicing two FT virtual machines (one vCPU limitation per VM).

- ▶ For avoiding performance problems, every host that you have in the HA cluster should have a similar CPU configuration. If you have some slower CPUs on some hosts and faster CPUs on some other hosts, the then when the secondary virtual machine runs on slower CPU host, primary machine have to stop continuously to allow the secondary server to catch up.

- ▶ ESXi hosts must have access to the same datastore and networks.

There is varied number of infrastructure impacts on the FT. One of them, which is crucial is, contention on the FT logging network. VMware requires at least one physical 1GB Ethernet network for the logging network. You should have another 1GB Ethernet for vMotion. Also, vMotion and FT should be on separate subnet.

VMware also recommends that you configure no more than four FT protected virtual machines per host, with a 1GB logging network. The number of virtual machines that are protected by FT that you can safely run on each host is based on the sizes and workloads of the ESXi host and the virtual machines.

To reduce the contention over the FT network, you should configure a 10Gbps logging network, which increases the available bandwidth. Also, you should distribute the primary hosts across multiple physical hosts because logging traffic is asymmetric. Distributing primaries across different hosts allows the logging network to benefit from Ethernet's bidirectional capability.

Getting ready

You should have an existing vSphere Infrastructure, an existing vCenter Server, a couple of ESXi servers connected to vCenter Server and the HA Cluster. Shared storage is required; a dedicated gig Ethernet required; the same version of ESXi required for all three hosts; VM to protect needs to be one per CPU. No other prerequisites are required.

How to do it...

Before you start configuring FT in your vSphere Infrastructure, you should have the prerequisites configured.

Infrastructure prerequisites:

1. Your ESXi host should support vLockstep technology to support FT.
2. CPU clock speeds between the two hosts must be within 400MHz of each other to ensure that the hosts can stay in sync.
3. All of your ESXi hosts should be running on the same build and should have a license to run FT virtual machines.
4. Shared storage in between ESXi hosts.
5. Should have HA cluster enabled for FT to work
6. Dedicated NIC for the FT logging network and a separate vMotion network.
7. Host certificate checking must be enabled in vCenter Server.

Virtual Machine Prerequisites:

1. VMs must be single processor. FT does not support vSMP.
2. The VM's disk must be in Eager zeroed thick format. Thin disk is not supported by FT.
3. There are no non-replayable devices on the VM.
4. Snapshots must be removed before FT can be enabled on the VM.
5. vMotion is supported on FT enabled VMs, but you cannot vMotion both the primary and secondary VMs at the same time. SvMotion is not supported on FT enabled VMs.

Once the requirements have been met then you can work on the actual FT configuration.

1. Using vSphere Client, log in to the vCenter Server.
2. Select **Hosts and Clusters** on the Home Screen.
3. Select an ESXi host and select **Configuration** from the right tree.
4. Select **Networking** within the **Configuration** tab.

5. Choose an existing vSwitch and click on **Properties**.

6. In the vSwitch properties window click on **Add**.

7. Select the **VMkernel** option and click on **Next**.

8. Give **VMkernel port** a label "FT" and specify a VLAN number (optional).

9. Select the check box **Use this port group for Fault Tolerance logging** and click on **Next**.

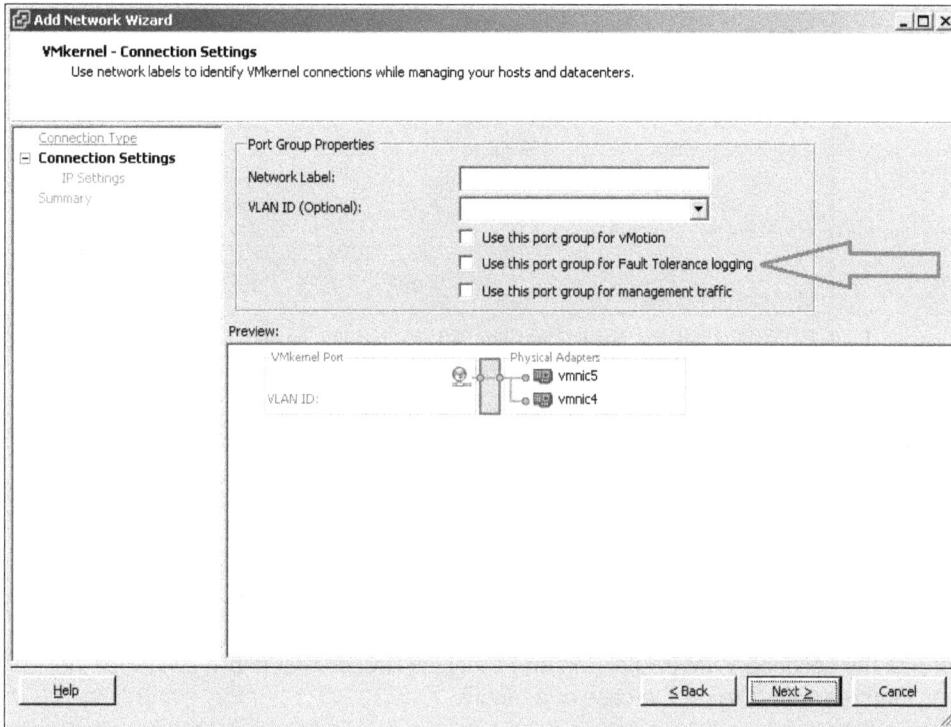

10. Specify the IP Address, and Subnet Mask on the **IP Settings** page and click on **Next**.

11. Review the configuration and click on **Finish**.

Now as you have configured VMkernel for FT logging, you should be able to enable your VM for FT protection, as follows:

1. Choose the VM, right-click on it and navigate to **Fault Tolerance | Turn on Fault Tolerance**.

2. Once the set-up is complete, you will be able to see the **vLockstep Interval** and **Log Bandwidth** information for the VM in the lower-right corner.

Fault Tolerance

Fault Tolerance Status: **Protected**

Secondary Location: esx3

Total Secondary CPU: 0 MHz
Total Secondary Memory: 563.00 MB

vLockstep Interval: 0.029 seconds
Log Bandwidth: 279 KBps

VM Storage Profiles

Refresh

VM Storage Profiles: lun
Profiles Compliance: Compliant (4/8/2013 10:12:48 AM)

---

3. To test the FT feature you should right-click on the VM, select **Fault Tolerance** and click on **Test Failover**.

How it works...

FT creates a secondary VM on another ESX host that shares the same virtual disk file as the primary VM, and then transfers the CPU and virtual device inputs from the primary VM (record) to the secondary VM (replay) via an FT logging NIC, so that it is in sync with the primary and ready to take over in case of a failure.

Data from the primary VM is copied to the secondary VM using a special FT logging network that is configured on each ESXi server.

VMware has a formula that you can use to determine the FT logging bandwidth requirements:

VMware FT logging bandwidth = (Avg disk reads (MB/s) × 8 + Avg network input (Mbps)) × 1.2 [20% headroom]

DPM and its impact

VMware vSphere Distributed Power Management (also known as vSphere DPM) continuously monitors resource requirements and power consumption across a VMware vSphere DRS cluster. When your vSphere HA cluster needs fewer resources, it consolidates workloads and powers off unused ESXi hosts so that it can reduce power consumption. However, virtual machines are not affected because DRS moves the running VMs around without downtime as needed, while hosts power off and on. ESXi hosts are kept powered off during periods of low resource use. But when there is a need of more resources then DPM powers on those ESXi hosts for the virtual machines to use. vSphere DPM uses three techniques to bring the host out of standby mode and those techniques are as follows:

- ▶ Intelligent Platform Management Interface (IPMI)
- ▶ Hewlett-Packard Integrated Lights-Out (iLO)
- ▶ Wake on LAN (WOL)

If a host supports all of them then the order of the technique chosen for use by DPM is as ordered above. However, for each of these protocols you need to perform specific configuration on each host before you can enable vSphere DPM for the cluster.

You need to make a note that vCenter Server marks those hosts as Standby which has been powered off by DPM, but standby mode indicates that the host is available for power on in case it is required.

Getting ready

To step through this recipe, you will need couple of ESXi server which supports either of IPMI, iLO, or WOL, a vCenter Server, and a working installation of vSphere Client. No other prerequisites are required.

How to do it...

To enable DPM on a vSphere Cluster, you need to perform the following steps:

1. Using vSphere Client, log in to the **vCenter Server**.
2. Select **Hosts and Clusters** on the **Home** Screen.
3. Right-click on the vSphere Cluster, and select **Edit Settings**.
4. Select **vSphere DRS** and select **Power Management**.
5. Select **Manual** or **Automatic** as the **DPM** option.

6. If you want to override a cluster's power management settings for individual hosts then choose the host from **Host Overrides** section and select the appropriate **Power Management** setting for.

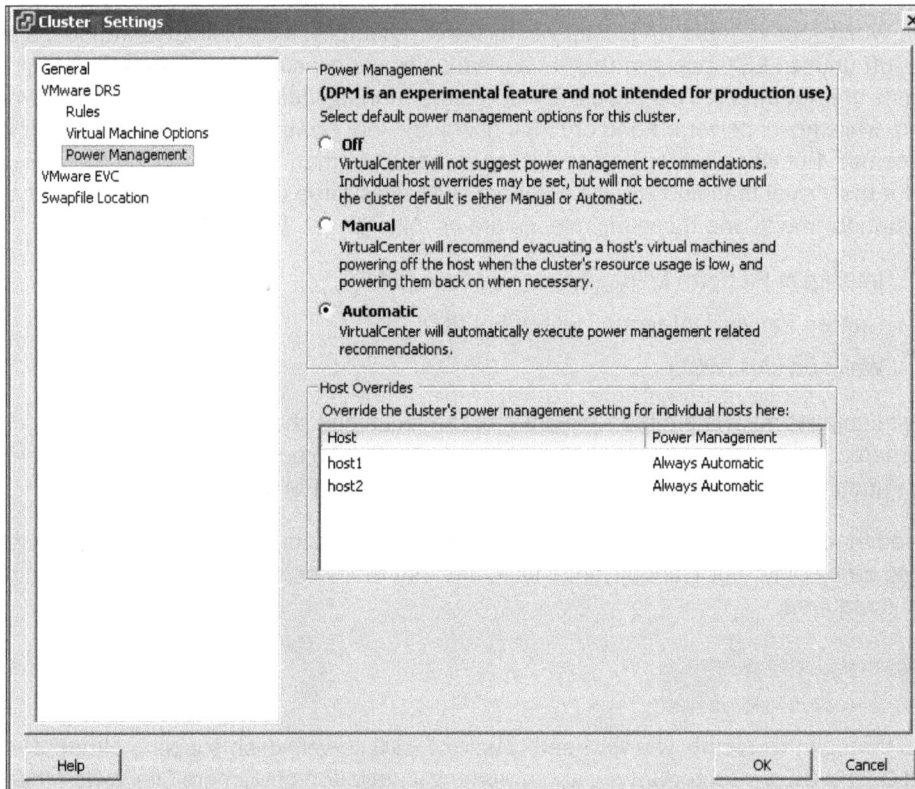

7. Once you are done, click on **OK**.

   Note that once you are done with Cluster configuration, you need to configure IPMI/iLO for each host as well.

8. On the **Home** screen of vCenter Server, select **Hosts and Clusters**.

9. Select the Host for which you want to enable IPMI/iLO (you should configure IPMI/iLO on all hosts in your cluster).

10. Click on the **Configuration** tab and select **Software**, and then go to **Power Management**.

11. Click on **Properties**.

12. Enter the **Username, Password, BMC IP Address**, and **BMC MAC Address** (use colons) fields. Click on **OK**. You will get immediate feedback if this was unsuccessful.

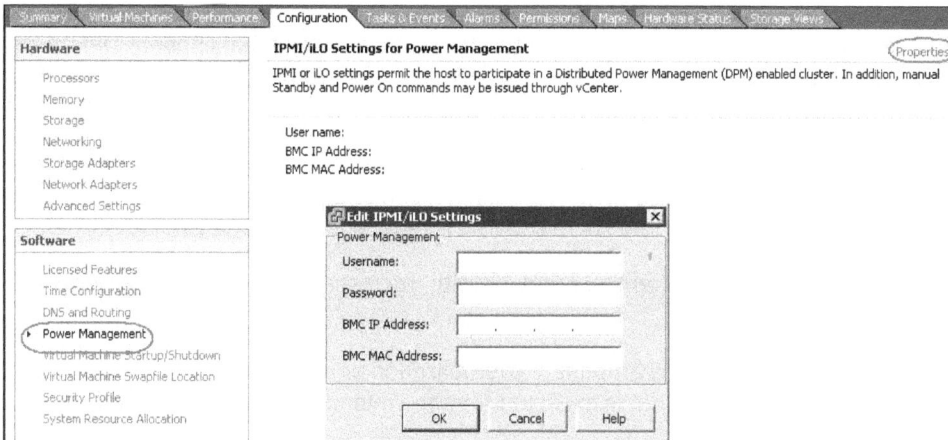

If you want to test DPM configuration then you need to carry out the following steps:

1. Right-click on a host within the cluster, and select **Enter Standby mode**.

2. Once complete, the host will have a moon icon next to the name.

3. Right-click on the host, and select **Power On**.

4. Right-click on the cluster containing the DPM-enabled cluster, and select **Edit Settings**.

5. Select **vSphere DRS**, go to **Power Management**, and select **Host Options**.

6. Verify that the host's **Last Time Exited Standby** is updated with the most recent attempt, and that it was successful.

How it works...

vSphere DPM awakes an ESXi host from a powered off state through Wake On LAN (WOL) packets. WOL packets are broadcast traffic and require that the vCenter and ESXi hosts be in the same layer 2 network. The vMotion VMkernel interface is used to send these WOL packets to other hosts, so vSphere DPM keeps at least one host powered on at all times. VMware recommends that you need to test the "exit standby" procedure for the host where DPM is going to be enabled. You need to make sure it can be successfully powered on through Wake on LAN.

The vSphere DPM algorithm does not frequently power servers on and off in response to transient load variations. Rather, it powers off a server only when it is very likely that it will stay powered off for some time. The history of the cluster workload is used to account this.

To minimize the power cycling frequency across all of the hosts in the cluster, vSphere DPM cycles through all comparable hosts enabled for vSphere DPM hosts when trying to find a power-off candidate.

In conjunction with vSphere HA, if HA Admission Control is disabled, then failover constraint are not passed on to DPM and thus those constraints are not enforced. vSphere DPM does not care about failover requirements, and put hosts into standby mode.

With cluster configuration settings, users can define the reserve capacity to always be available. Users can also define the time for which load history can be monitored before the power-off decision is made. Power-on is also triggered when not enough resources are available to power on a virtual machine, or when more spare capacity is required for vSphere HA.

You should enable DPM only after you are done with the testing of standby mode and wake on protocol configuration.

Priority ratings are based on the amount of overutilization or underutilization found in the DRS cluster, and the improvement that is expected from the intended host power state change.

When you disable vSphere DPM, hosts are taken out of standby mode. Taking hosts out of standby mode ensures that when vSphere DPM is disabled, all the hosts are powered on and are ready to accommodate load increases. You can use the Schedule Task: Change Cluster Power Settings wizard to create scheduled tasks to enable and disable vSphere DPM for a cluster.

Also when you enable vSphere DPM, hosts in the DRS cluster inherit the power management automation level of the cluster by default.

VMware strongly recommends that you disable any host with a Last Time Exited Standby status of Never, until you ensure that WOL is configured properly. You do not want vSphere DPM to power off a host for which wake has not been successfully tested.

Choosing the reserved cluster failover capacity

By now, we all know that VMware has introduced a Percentage-based cluster resource reservation model. Using this setting, you need to specify how much resource you want to reserve for accommodating host failure. It also allows us to select different percentages for CPU and Memory.

You might wonder how would you calculate how much resource you want to reserve for your HA cluster. While it was a straight-forward approach when we used to select number of hosts reserve for servicing a host failure, we have seen disadvantages as well. If you use the number of ESXi hosts failure in your HA cluster, you will reserve those completely, thus it will not be efficient to tune in your HA cluster or put it into best use. Also it avoids the commonly experienced slot size issue, where values are skewed due to a large reservation.

Percentage-based reservation is also much more effective as it considers actual reservation per virtual machine to calculate available failover resources, which means that clusters dynamically adjusts when resources are added.

What you get is an option to specify a percentage of failover resources for both CPU and memory. Prior to vSphere 5, this was not the case.

```
┌─ Admission Control Policy ──────────────────────────────────────────┐
│                                                                      │
│   Specify the type of policy that admission control should enforce.  │
│                                                                      │
│   ○  Host failures the cluster tolerates:        ┌────────┐          │
│                                                  │   1  ⬍ │          │
│                                                  └────────┘          │
│                                                                      │
│   ◉  Percentage of cluster resources             ┌────────┐          │
│      reserved as failover spare capacity:        │  25  ⬍ │  %  CPU  │
│                                                  └────────┘          │
│                                                  ┌────────┐          │
│                                                  │  25  ⬍ │  %  Memory│
│                                                  └────────┘          │
│                                                                      │
│   ○  Specify failover hosts:          0 hosts specified. Click to edit. │
│                                                                      │
└──────────────────────────────────────────────────────────────────────┘
```

The 25 percent is by default, which means that 25 percent of your total CPU and total memory resources across the entire cluster is reserved for your cluster. This means if you have an 8 node cluster, 25 percent of your resources are reserved for an HA event. If there is a 32 node cluster and if that is balanced, resources that equate to 8 nodes will be reserved, as 8 is 25 percent of 32. So keep that in mind before deciding what number to put there.

> You can use the following formula to calculate the percentage of resource you should keep there.
>
> ((Total amount of available resources – total reserved virtual machine resources) / total amount of available resources) < = (percentage HA should reserve as spare capacity)
>
> For those virtual machines that do not have a reservation, a default of 32 MHz will be used for CPU and a default of 0 MB plus memory overhead will be used for Memory. The total reserved virtual machine resources includes the default reservation of 32 MHz plus the memory overhead of the virtual machine.

Getting ready

You should have an existing vSphere Infrastructure, an existing vCenter Server, a couple of ESXi servers connected to vCenter Server and in a HA Cluster. No other prerequisites are required.

How to do it...

To set a percentage-based Admission Control you need to follow these steps:

1. Log in to the vCenter Server.
2. Click on **Hosts and Clusters** on the **Home** Screen.

3. Right-click on the **Datacenter** and select **New Cluster**.

4. Name this cluster in the Cluster Creation Wizard.

5. By default **Turn on vSphere HA** and **Turn on vSphere DRS** will be selected. Accept these defaults, and then click on **Next**.

6. Choose the default settings on the **DRS** page and click on **Next**.

7. Choose the default on the **Power Management** page and click on **Next**.

8. On the vSphere HA page, select **Admission Control Policy** as **Percentage of cluster resources reserved as failover spare capacity**.

9. Specify the percentage of resource for CPU and memory which you want to reserve for failover and click on **Next**.

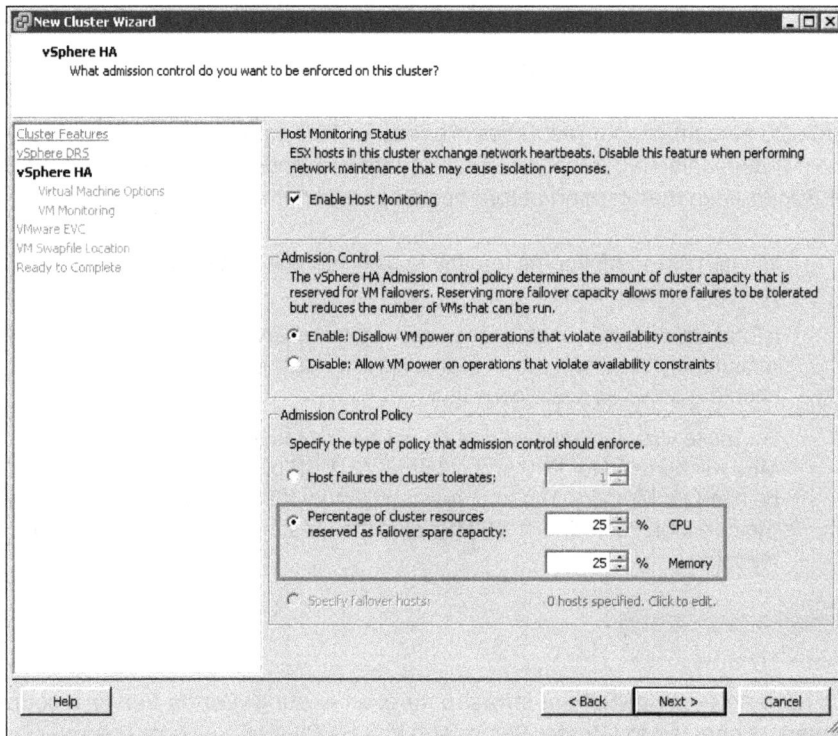

10. Select the rest of the configuration as per your requirement and click on **Finish** at the end.

How it works...

Let me show you how it works by way of an example scenario and a diagram.

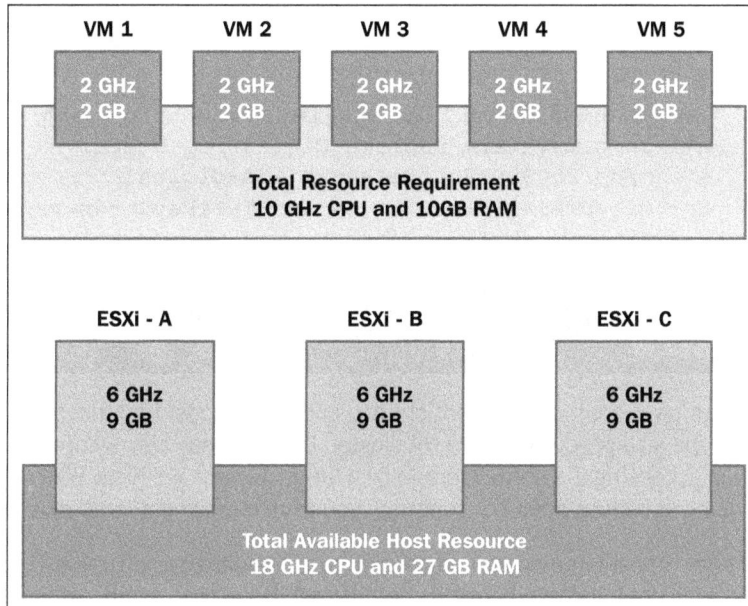

In this example, we have three ESXi hosts in a vSphere HA cluster. All of the hosts are identical, and has 6 GHz of CPU and 9 GB of memory.

There are five powered-on virtual machines which are also identical (in reality, getting identical VM requirements are rare, this is for academic purpose only). Each VM requires 2 GHz of CPU and 2 GB of memory, and a reservation is also set for the entire allocated CPU and Memory.

So you have now gathered how much resource you have and how much you need.

Based on this, the current CPU failover capacity is ((18 GHz-10 GHz)/18GHz = 44%, and the current memory failover capacity is ((27 GB-10 GB)/27 GB) = 62%.

Now, because your cluster was configured with 25 percent failover capacity, 19 percent CPU resource is still available to power on additional virtual machines. Also, you still have 37 percent memory resources for additional virtual machines.

See also

▶ For more information on the percent of resources to keep, see the following:

  ❑ The Setting Correct Percentage of Cluster Resources Reserved at `http://frankdenneman.nl/2011/01/20/setting-correct-percentage-of-cluster-resources-reserved/`

  ❑ The VMware vSphere 5.1 Clustering Deepdive at `http://www.amazon.com/VMware-vSphere-Clustering-Deepdive-ebook/dp/B0092PX72C/ref=sr_1_1?s=digital-text&ie=UTF8&qid=1367261445&sr=1-1&keywords=vsphere+5.1`

Rightly choosing the vSphere HA cluster size

With vSphere 5, we have seen a significant change in the HA model and that does relax the constraint on the size of your vSphere HA cluster. But, you may ask, what about storage bottlenecks while accessing the same storage by a large cluster? We have VAAI to handle that now, and that being in picture does not constrain you from choosing a large cluster.

Also a crucial factor is that large cluster creates more scheduling opportunities for DRS and a bigger cluster does not impose a heavy lift on the cost. Does that mean, we suggest "ONLY" bigger cluster and not many smaller clusters? Well, not really. It all boils down to what you are going to use on that cluster, and what is your requirement. If you are implementing View Manager and are going to use Linked Clone then you are limiting yourself with eight hosts, as with Linked Clone only eight hosts can access one single file. This restriction is not there in vSphere 5.1.

There are a few other factors that you need to look for before you decide your HA cluster size and one of them is Operational Complexity. Maintaining a large cluster in a production environment is not an easy task. You need to have all hosts in a cluster updated and in the same change window. This may conflict with your change management process. Also, the time required to update a cluster depends on the cluster size, the amount of time required to evacuate a host, the number of resources available to perform concurrent host updates, and so on.

Getting ready

To step through this recipe, you will need to have ESXi servers, a vCenter Server, and a working installation of vSphere Client. No other prerequisites are required.

How to do it...

Perform the following steps to create your desired cluster with a determined size:

1. Using vSphere Client, log in to the vCenter Server.
2. Select the **Hosts and Clusters** view on **Home** Screen.
3. Right-click on the **Datacenter** in the Inventory tree, and click on **New Cluster**.
4. Name this cluster in the Cluster Creation Wizard.
5. By default **Turn on vSphere HA** and **Turn on vSphere DRS** will be selected, click on **Next**.
6. Accept the **default settings**, and click on **Next**.
7. Select all of the default settings, and move to the **Finish** screen.
8. Review the cluster configuration and click on **Finish**.
9. Once your cluster is created, right-click on it and select **Add Host**.
10. Specify the **Hostname and IP Address** of the ESXi hosts that you selected for your cluster and click on **Next**.
11. Choose the default configuration for the rest of the steps and click on **Finish**.
12. Repeat steps 9 to 11 for rest of the host's addition.

So, in a nutshell, if you limit the number of hosts in a vSphere HA Cluster then this reduces the number of load balancing opportunities. However, if you exceed the number of ESXi hosts beyond what you actually need, then this will cause CPU strain on your vCenter Server because DRS performs load balancing calculations every five minutes for each cluster. So this needs to be balanced according to your requirements.

6
Storage Performance Design

In this chapter, we will cover the tasks related to storage performance design. You will learn the following aspects of storage performance design:

- ► Designing the host for a highly available and high performing storage
- ► Designing a highly available and high performance iSCSI SAN
- ► Designing a highly available and high performing FC storage
- ► Performance impact of queuing on storage array and host
- ► Factors that affect storage performance
- ► Using VAAI to boost storage performance
- ► Selecting the right VM disk type
- ► Monitoring command queuing
- ► Identifying a severely overloaded storage

Introduction

Storage can limit the performance of enterprise workloads. Storage is one of the most common bottlenecks in performance. You should know how to design a storage system, monitor a host's storage throughput, and troubleshoot problems that result in overloaded storage and slow storage performance.

There are many catalysts that affect storage performance. These are:

- ► Improper configuration of a storage device
- ► Storage protocols

▸ Queuing and LUN queue depth

▸ Load balancing across available storage

▸ VMFS configuration:

    ❑ Characteristics of VMFS and RDMs

    ❑ SCSI reservations

▸ Virtual disk types

▸ Placing more I/O demand than the storage is architected to deliver

Designing the host for a highly available and high-performing storage

VMware ESXi enables multiple hosts to share the same physical storage through its optimized storage stack and VMware VMFS distributed filesystem. Centralized storage of virtual machines can be accomplished by using VMFS and/or NFS. Centralized storage enables virtualization capabilities such as VMware vMotion, VMware Distributed Resource Scheduler (DRS), and VMware High Availability.

Several factors have an effect on storage performance:

▸ Storage protocols

▸ Proper configuration of your host device and storage devices

▸ Load balancing across available storage processors

▸ Storage queues

Getting ready

To step through this recipe, you will need one or more running ESXi Servers, HBA Card, an NIC Card, and a FC or iSCSI Storage. No other prerequisites are required.

How to do it...

High availability requires at least two HBA connections to provide redundant paths to the SAN or storage system.

Follow the proceeding steps to design a high performing storage:

1. Having redundant HBAs mitigate the single point of failure and also increases performance. If you use more than one single-port HBA then it helps to isolate port and path failure, and may provide performance benefits. However multiport HBA provides a component cost savings and efficient port management, which results in operational simplicity. If you have only a few available I/O bus slots in your host then multiport HBAs are useful, but you also have to consider a single point of failure. A single port HBA failure would affect only one port.

2. You should put HBAs on separate host buses for performance and availability. This may not be possible on hosts that have a single bus or a limited number of bus slots. However, the likelihood of a bus failure is arguably so small as to be negligible.

3. You should always use an HBA that equals or exceeds the bandwidth of the storage network. That means you should not use 2 GB/s or slower HBAs for connections to 4 GB/s SANs. This is mainly because FC SANs reduce the speed of the network path to the HBA's speed, or to the storage system's frontend port if directly connected. It may create a performance bottleneck when you focus to optimize bandwidth.

4. Always use most current HBA firmware and driver from the manufacturer.

5. You can use NICs and/or iSCSI HBA for iSCSI environments. The differences include cost, host CPU utilization, and features such as security.

6. Ethernet networks will auto negotiate down to the lowest common device speed thus a slower NIC may bottleneck the storage network's bandwidth. If you use TOE then it offloads TCP packet segmentation, checksum calculations, and optionally IPSec from the host CPU to themselves. So if you use TOE then your CPU cycles will be used exclusively for application processing.

7. For avoiding a single point of failure, you should use Redundant NICs, iSCSI HBAs, and TOEs wherever possible. You can use either single or multiport NICs. Typically, each NIC or NIC port is configured to be on a separate subnet and this applies to IP storage and not ESXi networking in general. If you have more than one NIC then you should place them on separate host buses. Note this may not be possible on smaller hosts having a single bus or a limited number of bus slots, or when the on board host NIC is used.

Designing a highly available and high-performance iSCSI SAN

Main advantage why people use iSCSI SANs is that they handle longer transmission distances and are less expensive over Fiber Channel SANs.

iSCSI SAN's performance mainly gets affected by network congestion. Most of the time network congestion is usually the result of an inappropriate network configuration or improper network settings.

For example, a common problem what we see is a switch in the data path into the storage system that is fragmenting frames. It happens most of the time for jumbo frames, and network oversubscription also plays a crucial role there. A slow switch somewhere in the path can reduce the overall speed of the network connection because of this slowest link.

Getting ready

To step through this recipe, you will need one or more running ESXi Servers, an iSCSI SAN, and couple of VLANs provisioned on the network switch side. No other prerequisites are required.

How to do it...

For better performance and security you should use separate Ethernet networks to ensure redundant communications between hosts and storage systems. In addition, paths should be handled by separate switching, if direct connections are not used.

You should use a dedicated storage network, otherwise put the iSCSI traffic in either separated network LAN segments, or a **virtual LAN** (**VLAN**). VLAN allows more than one logical L2 network to share the same physical network while maintaining separation of the data and reducing the broadcast domain and collisions.

Ethernet connections to the storage system should use separate subnets depending on, if they are workload or storage system management related. You should consider separating the **storage processor** (**SP**) management ports into separate subnets from the iSCSI front end network ports.

Do this by placing each port from SP-A on a different subnet. Place the corresponding ports from SP-B on the same set of subnets. The 10.x.x.x or 172.16.x.x through 172.31.255.255 private network addresses are completely available.

For example, a typical configuration for the iSCSI ports on a storage system with two iSCSI ports per SP would be:

   ▸   A0: 172.18.48.10 (Subnet mask 255.255.255.0; Gateway 172.18.48.1)

   ▸   A1: 172.18.49.10 (Subnet mask 255.255.255.0; Gateway 172.18.49.1)

   ▸   B0: 172.18.48.11 (Subnet mask 255.255.255.0; Gateway 172.18.48.1)

   ▸   B1: 172.18.49.11 (Subnet mask 255.255.255.0; Gateway 172.18.49.1)

The above configuration could survive two errors: loss of routing on one network and loss of a single SP.

There is also a restriction on 192.168.0.0/16 subnets. The only restricted addresses are 192.168.1.1 and 192.168.1.2 and the rest of the 192.168.x.x address space is usable with no problems.

Following is how a simple network topology should be achieved:

▸ Network conditions and latency affects bandwidth and throughput rates.

▸ iSCSI performance is commonly affected by the network contentions, routing, and so on. Look at your MTU configuration and if possible use jumbo frames.

▸ Routed iSCSI traffic increases latency. In an ideal configuration you should put the host and the iSCSI frontend port on the same subnet, and there should not be any gateways defined on the iSCSI ports. If they are not on the same subnet, users should define static routes.

▸ iSCSI based storage system performance gets affected largely by latency in the storage network.

For a balanced bandwidth configuration, you should follow the proceeding points:

▸ A balanced bandwidth iSCSI configuration is when the host iSCSI initiator's bandwidth is greater than or equal to the bandwidth of its connected storage system's ports. One storage system port should be configured as active/active wherever supported.

▸ Network settings also affect performance. Follow these points to mitigate it.

❑ Use jumbo frames

❑ Disable pause frames

❑ Disable TCP delayed Ack

How it works...

Let us discuss how jumbo frames, pause frames, and TCP delayed Ack can improve iSCSI network bandwidth

Jumbo frames

Standard Ethernet network uses a frame size of 1500 bytes. Jumbo frames allow packet configurable up to 9000 bytes in length.

To use jumbo frames, all switches and routers in the network path of the iSCSI storage system must be configured for jumbo frames. However, you may hit into a worse performance problem if every hop in the path cannot pass the jumbo frames without breaking them down (fragmenting them).

Pause frames

Pause frames should be disabled on the iSCSI network used for storage, considering the characteristic flow of the iSCSI traffic. They may cause delay of traffic unrelated to a specific host port to the storage system links. That means if Host A could send a pause frame, it would cause the array to stop sending data to Host B and other hosts too, even though Host B has no trouble handling the desired data rate.

TCP delayed Ack

TCP delayed Ack delays an acknowledgement for a received packet for the ESXi host.

So certainly TCP delayed Ack should be disabled on the iSCSI network used for storage.

If you have this feature enabled then an acknowledgment for a packet is delayed up to 0.5 seconds or until two packets are received. Sending an acknowledgment after 0.5 seconds is a sign that the network is congested. Because there was no communication between the host computer and the storage system during those 0.5 seconds, the host computer issues inquiry commands to the storage system for all LUNs based on the delayed Ack. When there is congestion in the network and recovery of dropped packets, delayed Ack can slow down the recovery considerably, resulting in further performance degradation.

To implement this workaround in ESXi 5.x, use the vSphere Client to disable delayed ACK as follows:

1. Log in to vSphere Client and select the host.
2. Navigate to the **Configuration** tab.
3. Select **Storage Adapters**.
4. Select the iSCSI vmhba to be modified.
5. Click on **Properties**.
6. Modify the delayed Ack setting, using the option that best matches your site's needs as follows:

    ❑ Modify the delayed Ack setting on a discovery address (recommended) as follows:

    1. On a discovery address, click on the **Dynamic Discovery** tab.
    2. Navigate to the **Server Address** tab.
    3. Click on **Settings**.
    4. Click on **Advanced**.

    ❑ Modify the delayed Ack setting on a specific target as follows:

    1. Navigate to the **Static Discovery** tab.
    2. Select the target.

3. Click on **Settings**.
4. Click on **Advanced**.

   ❏ Modify the delayed Ack setting globally as follows:

   1. Navigate to the **General** tab.
   2. Click on **Advanced**.

7. In the **Advanced Settings** dialog box, scroll down to the delayed Ack setting.
8. Uncheck **Inherit from parent**.
9. Uncheck **DelayedAck**.
10. Reboot the host.

Designing a highly available and high-performing FC storage

Availability refers to the storage system's ability to provide user access to data in the case of a hardware or software fault. Midrange systems are classified as highly available, because they provide access to data without any single point of failure. However, the following configuration settings can improve performance under degraded mode scenarios.

Single **Disk Array Enclosure** (**DAE**) provisioning, which is a disk storage system that contains multiple disk drives, is the practice of restricting the placement of a RAID group within a single enclosure. This is sometimes called horizontal provisioning. Single DAE provisioning is the default method of provisioning RAID groups and because of its convenience and high availability attributes, is the most commonly used method. However you may need to check vendor configuration for this.

In Multiple DAE provisioning, two or more enclosures are used. An example of multiple DAE provisioning requirements is where drives are selected from one or more additional DAEs because there are not enough drives remaining in one enclosure to fully configure a desired RAID group. Another example is SAS backend port balancing. The resulting configuration may or may not span backend ports depending on the storage system model and the drive to enclosure placement.

Following is a typical multiple DAE connected to SP:

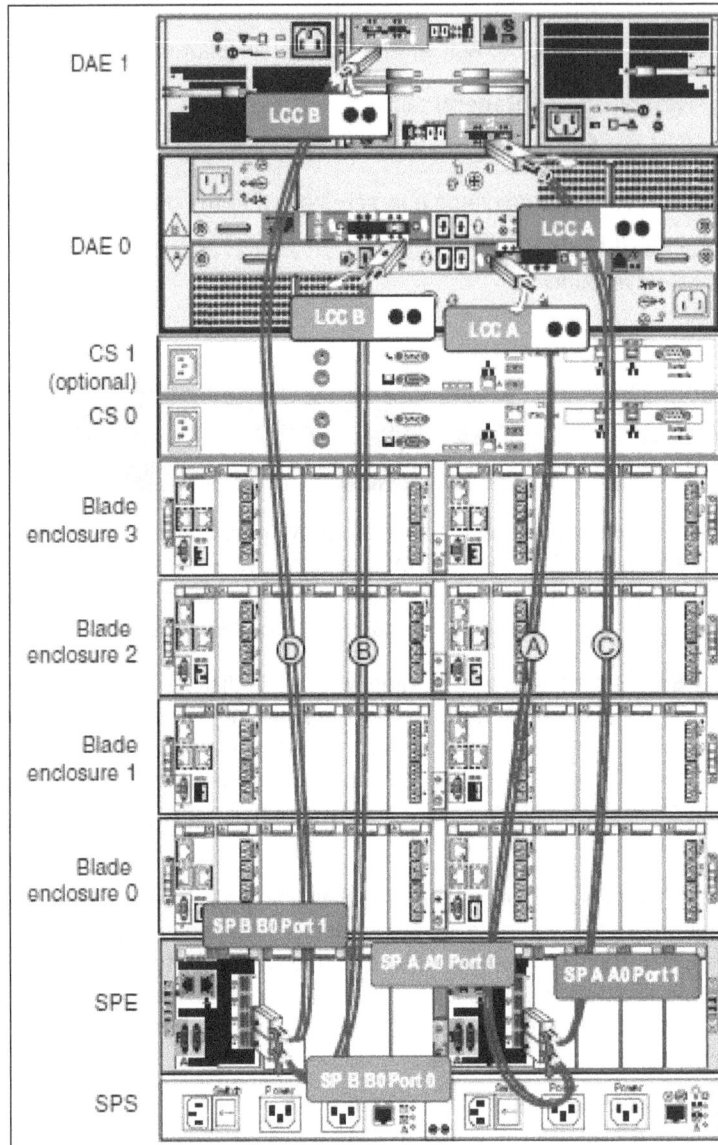

- ▸ Connection from SP A A0 Port 0 goes to DAE 0 LCC A, which is defined as (A)
- ▸ Connection from SP B B0 Port 0 goes to DAE 1 LCC B, which is defined as (B)
- ▸ Connection from SP A A0 Port 1 goes to DAE 0 LCC A, which is defined as (C)
- ▸ Connection from SP B B0 Port 1 goes to DAE 1 LCC B, which is defined as (D)

A **Link Control Card** (**LCC**) controls data flow to and from the DAE, and connects the drives in a DAE to one SP's SAS backend port; the peer LCC connects the DAE's drives to the peer SP. In a single DAE LCC failure, the peer storage processor still has access to all the drives in the DAE, and RAID group rebuilds are avoided. The storage system automatically uses its lower director capability to reroute around the failed LCC and through the peer SP. The peer SP experiences an increase in its bus loading while this redirection is in use. The storage system is in a degraded state until the failed LCC is replaced. When direct connectivity is restored between the owning SP and its LUNs, data integrity is maintained by a **background verify** (**BV**) operation.

Request forwarding's advantages of data protection and availability result in a recommendation to horizontally provision. In addition, note that horizontal provisioning requires less planning and labor.

If vertical provisioning was used for compelling performance reasons, provision drives within RAID groups to take advantage of request forwarding. This is done as follows:

- RAID 5: At least two (2) drives per SAS backend port in the same DAE
- RAID 6: At least three (3) drives per backend port in the same DAE
- RAID 1/0: Both drives of a mirrored pair on separate backend ports

Getting ready

To step through this recipe, you will need a couple of ESXi Servers, an HBA Card, and a Fiber Channel storage system. No other prerequisites are required.

How to do it...

1. Maintain at least two paths between the host and the storage system for high availability. Ideally, the cabling for these paths should be physically separated.

2. Make sure that these paths should be handled by separate switching, if not directly connecting hosts and storage systems. This includes redundant, separate HBAs, and attachment to both of the storage system's storage processors. Make sure path management software, such as PowerPath and dynamic multi-pathing software on hosts (to enable failover to alternate paths and load balancing), are available.

3. Run `# esxcli storage core path list` to get detailed information regarding the paths.

4. Run `# esxcli storage core path list -d <naaID>` to list the detailed information for the corresponding Paths for a specific device.

5. Run `# esxcli storage nmp device list` to lists of LUN multipathing information.

How it works...

RAIDlevel data protection

If you use EMC Storage then all of the LUNs bound within a virtual provisioning pool will have data loss from a complete failure of a pool RAID group.

The larger the number of private RAID groups within the pool, the bigger the failure domain would be.

The tradeoff factors in choosing a RAID Level are:

- ▸ Availability
- ▸ Performance
- ▸ Capacity utilization

If the priority is absolutely on availability then RAID 6 is the recommendation at the cost of performance.

If it is capacity utilization or performance, and we have solid design for data protection in place (backups, replication, hot spares, and so on), then having a RAID level 5 is likewise a sound decision.

RAID 10, for example, is fast and crash proof; however, it eats disk space. If you need more protection for your storage, or faster storage performance, RAID 10 is a simple, relatively cheap fix.

There are three levels of data protection available for pools, which is nothing but using RAID levels and those are:
RAID 5 has good data protection capability and has excellent read performance. However it does not have much write performance and that is due to parity calculations. As it uses parity, if one drive of a private RAID group fails, no data is lost. RAID 5 is appropriate for small to moderate sized pools.

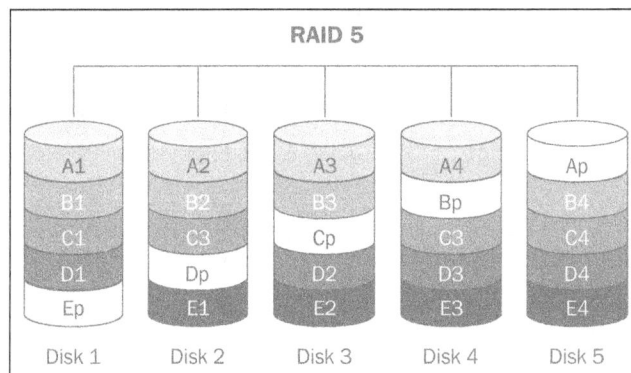

- RAID 6 provides the highest data availability. RAID 6 is similar to RAID 5; however, it uses striping with parity and uses two parity drives. With the second parity drive, up to two drives may fail in a private RAID group and result in no data loss. RAID 6 is appropriate for any size pool, including the largest possible.

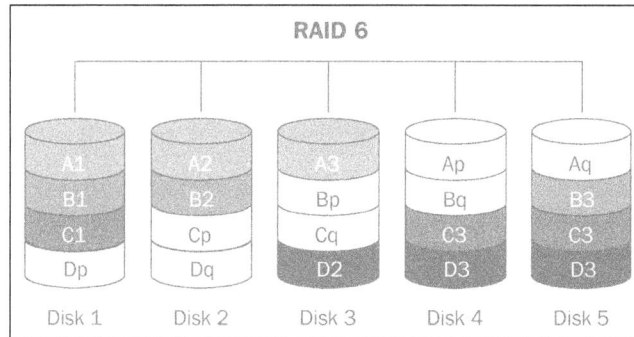

- RAID 1/0 or RAID 10 has high data availability. In this RAID two drives are mirrored together and then those are striped. Because of this design, you can achieve high I/O rates (especially small random write I/Os). A single disk failure in a private RAID group results in no data loss. However, a primary and its mirror cannot fail together and if they fail then data will be lost.

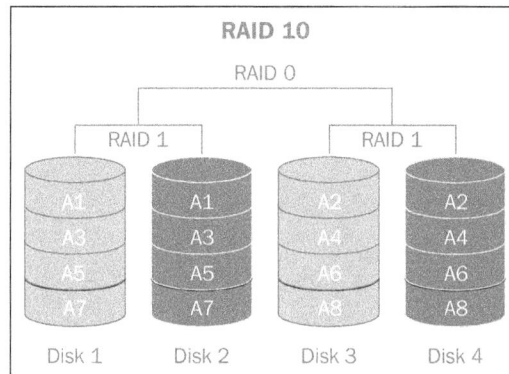

Performance impact of queuing on the storage array and host

There are several storage queues:

- ▸ Device driver queue
- ▸ Kernel queue
- ▸ Storage array queue

The device driver queue is used for low-level interaction with the storage device. This queue controls the number of active commands that can be on a LUN at the same time. This number is effectively the concurrency of the storage stack. If you set the device queue to 1 then each storage command becomes sequential.

The kernel queue is an overflow queue for the device driver queues. This queue enables features that optimize storage (it doesn't include them; they are built using the queue). These features include multi-pathing for failover and load balancing, prioritization of storage activities, which is based on virtual machine and cluster shares, and optimizations to improve efficiency for long sequential operations.

For example, batching several incoming read requests and doing hashes 1, 4-7, and 14 together because they're all on nearby parts of the disk, then doing hash 2:

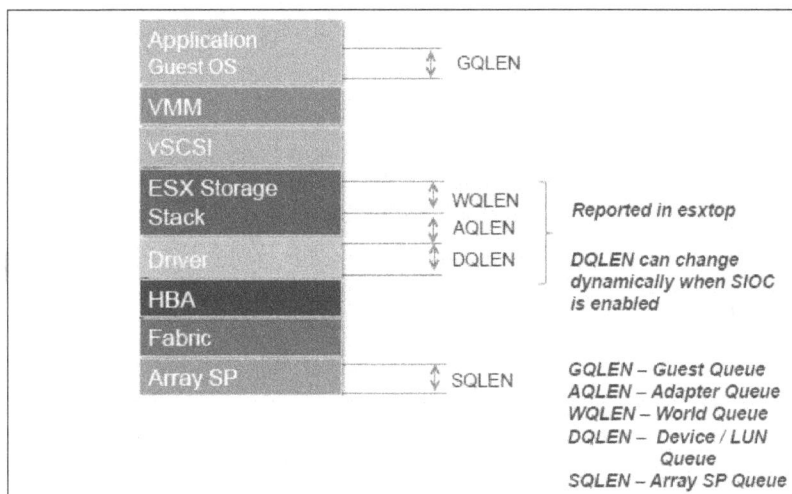

SCSI device drivers have a configurable parameter called the LUN queue depth that determines how many commands can be active at one time to a given LUN. The default value is 32. If the total number of outstanding commands from all virtual machines exceeds the LUN queue depth, the excess commands are queued in the ESXi kernel, which increases latency.

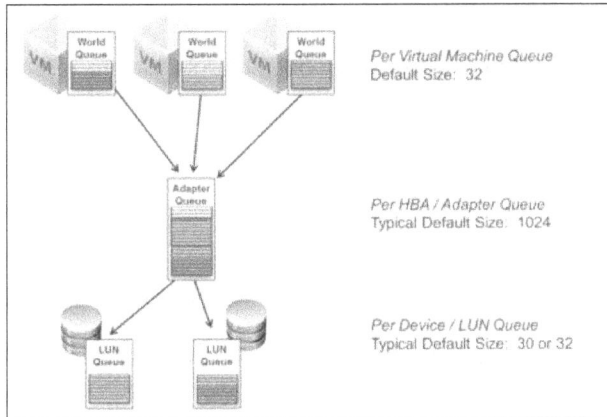

Getting ready

To step through this recipe, you will need one or more running ESXi Servers, a vCenter Server, and a working installation of vSphere Client. No other prerequisites are required.

How to do it...

If the performance of your hardware bus adapters (HBAs) is unsatisfactory, or your SAN storage processors are overutilized, you can adjust your ESXi/ESX hosts' maximum queue depth value. The maximum value refers to the queue depths reported for various paths to the LUN. When you lower this value, it throttles the ESXi/ESX host's throughput and alleviates SAN contention concerns if multiple hosts are overutilizing the storage and are filling its command queue.

In a way this solves the problem, but in a way it just pushes the problem closer to the demand. Now instead of the SP failing to deliver all the I/O power that is wanted, it's the hosts that are failing to deliver I/O as fast as the VMs want. Tweaking queue depths is mostly just an easy thing to do that doesn't actually deliver better performance overall.

You should consider re-architecting the storage infrastructure to meet the higher demand (for example, using faster drives, more spindles, or higher-performance RAID), or investigate if you can lower the demand by tuning the applications or moving VMs to other storage arrays.

To adjust the queue depth for an HBA, perform the following steps:

1. Verify which HBA module is currently loaded by entering one of these commands:

    For QLogic:

    ```
    # esxcli system module list | grepqla
    ```

    For Emulex:

    ```
    # esxcli system module list | greplpfc
    ```

2. Run one of these commands:

    Note: The examples show the QLogic qla2xxx and Emulex lpfc820 modules. Use the appropriate module based on the outcome of the previous step.

    For QLogic:

    ```
    # esxcli system module parameters set -p ql2xmaxqdepth=64 -m
    qla2xxx
    ```

    For Emulex:

    ```
    # esxcli system module parameters set -p lpfc0_lun_queue_depth=64
    -m lpfc820
    ```

3. In this case, the HBAs represented by ql2x and lpfc0 have their LUN queue depths set to 64.

    If all Emulex cards on the host need to be updated, apply the global parameter, `lpfc_lun_queue_depth` instead.

4. Reboot your host.

5. Run this command to confirm that your changes have been applied:

    ```
    # esxcli system module parameters list -m driver
    ```

    where driver is your QLogic or Emulex adapter driver module, such as `lpfc820` or `qla2xxx`.

    The output appears similar to:

    ```
    Name                            Type Value Description
    --------------------------- ---- ----- ----------------------------
    ---------------------
    ..... ql2xmaxqdepth                   int   64    Maximum queue
    depth to report for target devices.

    .....
    ```

When one virtual machine is active on a LUN, you only need to set the maximum queue depth. When multiple virtual machines are active on a LUN, the `Disk.SchedNumReqOutstanding` value is also relevant. The queue depth value, in this case, is equal to whichever value is the lowest of the two settings: adapter queue depth or `Disk.SchedNumReqOutstanding`.

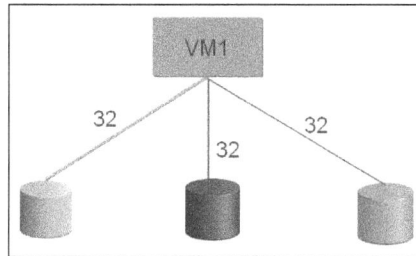

In this example, you have 32 Active commands simultaneously to each LUN. But you still have only 32 Active commands simultaneously to the LUN. It is the Sum Total of all Commands. And this is where you need `Disk.ShedNumReqOutstanding`.

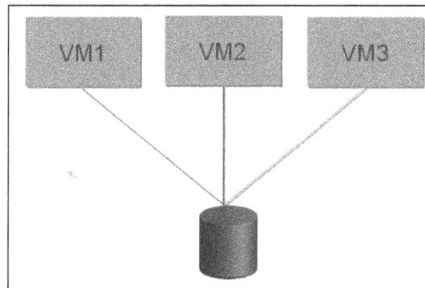

But you will still have only 32 Active commands simultaneously to the LUN if you do not change the LUN queue depth as well.

> For more information on `Disk.SchedNumReqOutstanding`, read the following blog:
>
> `http://www.yellow-bricks.com/2011/06/23/disk-schednumreqoutstanding-the-story/`

The following procedures only apply to the ESXi/ESX host that the parameters are changed on. You must make the same changes to all other ESXi/ESX hosts that have the datastore/LUN presented to them.

To set the VMkernel limit for vSphere 5:

1. In the vSphere Client, select the host in the inventory panel.

2. Click on the **Configuration** tab, and then click on **Advanced Settings** under **Software**.

3. Click on **Disk** in the left panel and scroll down to **Disk.SchedNumReqOutstanding**.

4. Change the parameter value to the number of your choice and click on OK.

For more information on an example value/scenario, read the following blog:

`http://www.boche.net/blog/index.php/2011/06/16/disk-schednumreqoutstanding-and-queue-depth/`

How it works...

To understand the effect of queuing on the storage array, take the situation in which the virtual machines on an ESXi host is generating a constant number of SCSI commands equal to the LUN queue depth, which means that the LUN queue buffer is constantly full (# commands in the LUN queue buffer = LUN queue depth). This is an example of device driver queue. If multiple ESXi hosts share the same LUN, SCSI commands to that LUN from all hosts are processed by the storage processor on the storage array, which means multiple commands begin queuing up, resulting in high latencies.

When you use a shared LUN to place all of your virtual machines then the total number of outstanding commands permitted from all virtual machines on a host to that LUN is governed by the `Disk.SchedNumReqOutstanding` configuration parameter, which can be set in VMware vCenter Server.

If you want to reduce latency then make sure that the sum of the active commands from all virtual machines does not consistently exceed the LUN queue depth. If you are using vSphere SIOC (Storage I/O Control) then that takes care of any manual queue depth configuration. However this is only available with Enterprise and license. SIOC has been covered in *Chapter 4, DRS, SDRS and Resource Control Design*, already.

However, if you want to know the calculation of queue depth then it is the result of the combination of number of host paths, execution throttle value, and number of presented LUNs through the host port must be less than the target port queue depth. Which means it is T = P * q * L.

T = Target port queue depth

P = Paths connected to the target port

Q = Queue depth

L = number of LUN presented to the host through this port

But in a vSphere infrastructure, multiple ESXi hosts communicate with the storage port, therefore the queue depth should be calculated by the following formula:

T = ESX Host 1 (P * Q * L) + ESX Host 2 (P * Q * L) ..... + ESX Host n (P * Q * L)

Factors that affect storage performance

Storage performance is affected by many factors; however, some of them are really important. These are:

- VMFS partition alignment
- Spanned VMFS volumes
- SCSI reservation

Getting ready

To step through this recipe, you will need one or more running ESXi Servers, a vCenter Server, and a working installation of vSphere Client. No other prerequisites are required.

How to do it...

The first thing you have to counter is the VMFS partition alignment as follows:

1. The alignment of your VMFS partitions can affect performance and it happens only if you create the datastore using CLI since the vSphere Client is not impacted by misalignment. Like other disk-based file systems, VMFS suffers a penalty when the partition is unaligned. Using the VMware vSphere Client to create VMFS datastores avoids this problem because it automatically aligns the datastores along the 1 MB boundary.

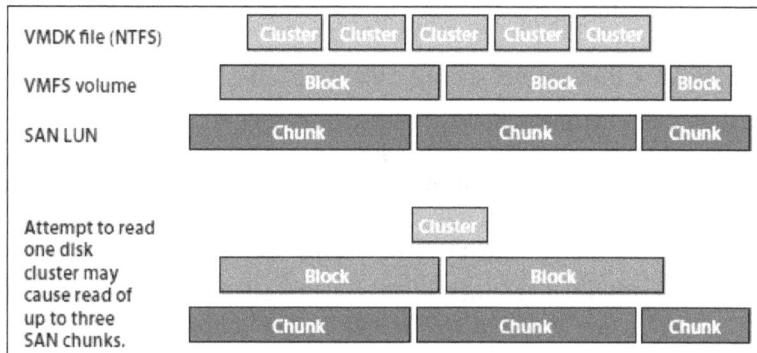

If you are using Windows 2008 in Guest OS then it automatically aligns partitions using a default starting offset of 1 MB, however prior to Windows 2008 manual alignment is required using `Diskpart.exe` (or `diskpar.exe`).

To manually align your VMFS partitions, check your storage vendor's recommendations for the partition starting block. If your storage vendor makes no specific recommendation, use a starting block that is a multiple of 8 KB.

> To align your VMFS filesystem use this paper:
>
> http://www.vmware.com/pdf/esx3_partition_align.pdf

Once you have aligned your VMFS volume and Guest OS disk, your alignment will look like this:

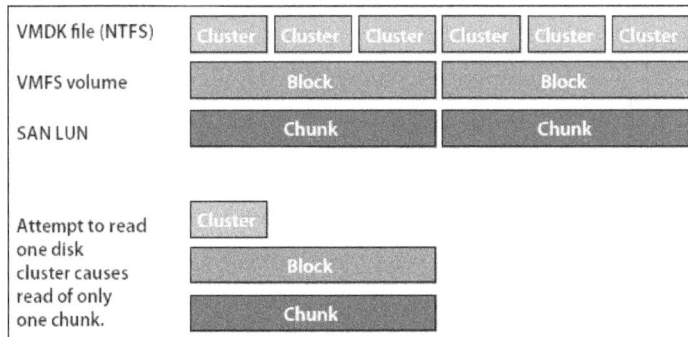

2. Before performing an alignment, carefully evaluate the performance effect of the unaligned VMFS partition on your particular workload. The degree of improvement from alignment is highly dependent on workloads and array types. You might want to refer to the alignment recommendations from your array vendor for further information.

   If a VMFS3 partition was created using an earlier version of ESXi that aligned along the 64 KB boundary, and that filesystem is then upgraded to VMFS5, it will retain its 64 KB alignment. 1 MB alignment can be obtained by deleting the partition and recreating it using vSphere Client and an ESXi host.

3. Now you need to take care of spanned VMFS volumes.

   A spanned VMFS volume includes multiple extents (part or an entire LUN). Spanning is a good feature to use if you need to add more storage to a VMFS volume while it is in use. Predicting performance with spanned volumes is not straightforward, because the user does not have control over how the data from the various virtual machines is laid out on the different LUNs that form the spanned VMFS volume.

   For example, consider a spanned VMFS volume with two 100 GB LUNs. Two virtual machines are on this spanned VMFS, and the sum total of their sizes is 150 GB. The user cannot determine the contents of each LUN in the spanned volume directly. Hence, determining the performance properties of this configuration is not straightforward.

   Mixing storage devices of different performance characteristics on the same spanned volume could cause an imbalance in virtual machine performance. This imbalance might occur if a virtual machine's blocks were allocated across device boundaries, and each device might have a different queue depth.

4. The last but not the least part is SCSI reservation.

    VMFS is a clustered filesystem and uses SCSI reservations as part of its distributed locking algorithms. Administrative operations, such as creating or deleting a virtual disk, extending a VMFS volume, or creating or deleting snapshots, result in metadata updates to the filesystem using locks and thus result in SCSI reservations. A reservation causes the LUN to be available exclusively to a single ESXi host for a brief period of time. Although an acceptable practice is to perform a limited number of administrative tasks during peak hours, postponing major maintenance to off-peak hours in order to minimize the effect on the virtual machine performance is better.

    The impact of SCSI reservations depends on the number and nature of storage or VMFS administrative tasks being performed, as follows:

    ❏   The longer an administrative task runs (for example, creating a virtual machine with a larger disk or cloning from a template that resides on a slow NFS share), the longer the virtual machines are affected. Also, the time to reserve and release a LUN is highly hardware-dependent and vendor-dependent.

    ❏   Running administrative tasks from a particular ESXi host does not have much effect on the I/O intensive virtual machines running on the same ESXi host.

    SCSI reservation conflicts used to be a big problem in a lot of real cases in ESX 2.x days, but it is not a problem in the recent releases of VMware vSphere ESXi, especially with VMFS5 (atomic test and set, opportunistic locking/pre-allocating sectors in metadata). Also VAAI plays a major role there. We have countered VAAI in a different recipe in this chapter.

Using VAAI to boost storage performance

Various storage functions, such as cloning and snapshots, are performed more efficiently by the storage array (target) than by a host (initiator). In a virtualized environment, since virtual disks are files on VMFS and disk arrays cannot interpret the VMFS on-disk data layout; you cannot leverage hardware functions on a per-VM or per-virtual disk (file) basis.

The **vStorage APIs for Array Integration** (**VAAI**) are a set of new protocol interfaces between ESXi and storage arrays, and new application programming interfaces in the VMkernel. Using a small set of primitives (fundamental operations) that can be issued to the array using these interfaces, ESXi is able to improve its offering of storage services.

The fundamental operations are:

▶   **Atomic test & set** (**ATS**) – new locking mechanism

▶   Clone blocks/full copy/XCOPY

▶   Zero blocks/write same

The goal of VAAI is to help storage vendors provide hardware assistance to speed up VMware I/O operations that are more efficiently accomplished in the storage hardware. VAAI plugins can improve the performance of data transfer, and are transparent to the end user.

Atomic test & set (ATS)

ATS is a mechanism to modify a disk sector to improve the performance of the ESXi host when doing metadata updates.

Clone blocks/full copy/XCOPY

This does full copy of blocks and the ESXi host is guaranteed to have full space access to the blocks. Default offloaded clone size is 4 MB.

Zero blocks/write same

This basically writes zeroes. This will address the issue of time falling behind in a virtual machine when the guest operating system writes to the previously unwritten regions of its virtual disk. This primitive will improve your MSCS in virtualization environment solutions where we need to zero out the virtual disk. Default zeroing size is 1 MB.

Getting ready

To step through this recipe, you will need one or more running ESXi servers, a vCenter server, and a working installation of vSphere Client. You also need a VAAI supported storage array connected to these ESXi Servers and a SSH Client. No other prerequisites are required.

How to do it...

VAAI is a storage compatible feature. So first check with your vendor whether your storage is VAAI supported or look at VMware HCL for that.

However, you also need to check the vSphere side to see if it is enabled there as well. By default, it is enabled in the ESXi host.

1. Open the VMware vSphere Client.
2. In the **Inventory** pane, navigate to the ESXi host.
3. Click on the **Configuration** tab.

4. Under **Software**, click on **Advanced Settings**.

5. Click DataMover.

6. Check the value of the **DataMover.HardwareAcceleratedMove** setting and that should be 1.

7. Check the value of the **DataMover.HardwareAcceleratedInit** setting and that should be 1.

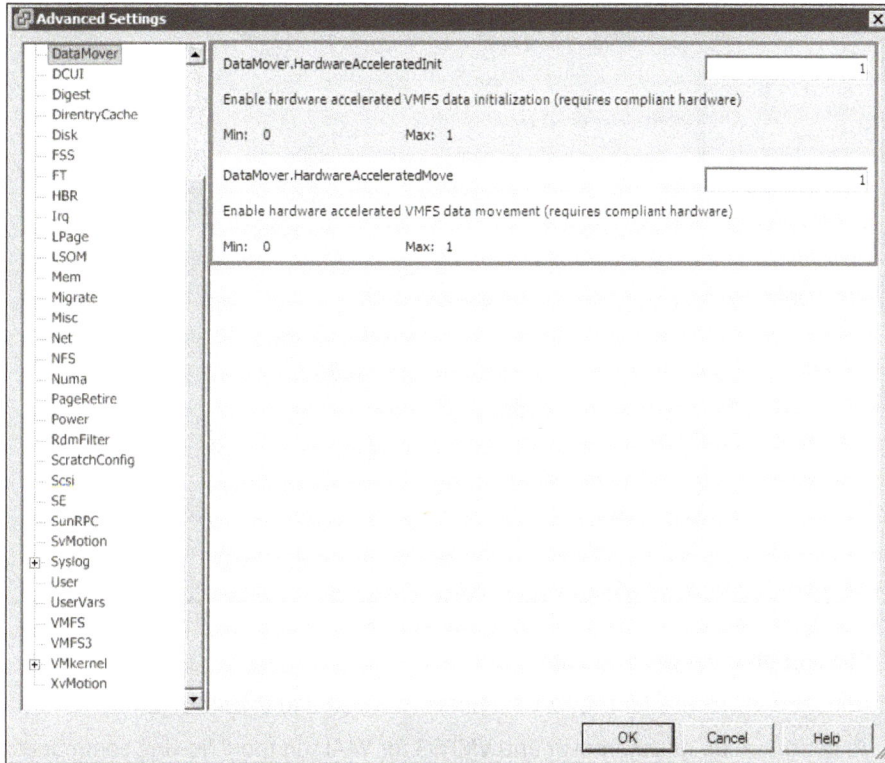

8. Click on **VMFS3**.

9. Check the value of the **VMFS3.HardwareAcceleratedLocking** setting and that should be 1.

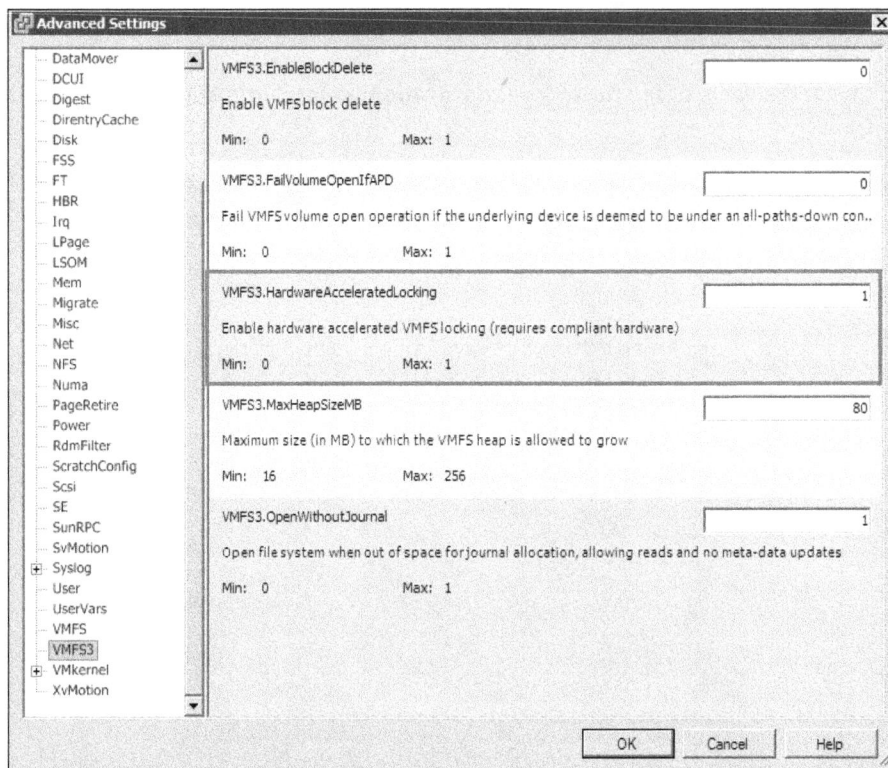

10. Click on **OK** once you are done.

11. Repeat this process for the all ESXi hosts connected to the storage.

12. To get the value of Datamover and VMFS3 for VAAI run the following commands:

```
# vicfg-advcfg -g /DataMover/HardwareAcceleratedMove
# vicfg-advcfg -g /DataMover/ HardwareAcceleratedInit
# vicfg-advcfg -g /VMFS3/HardwareAcceleratedLocking
```

13. If you are using VAAI capable/supported storage then you should be able to see this status in vSphere Client by following the proceeding steps:

   1. Login to the vCenter Server.

   2. Select **Hosts and Clusters** on the home screen.

   3. Navigate to an ESXI host.

   4. Click on the **Configuration** tab.

5. Navigate to **Storage** in the **Hardware** section.

6. Check the **Hardware Acceleration Status**. It should be **Supported**

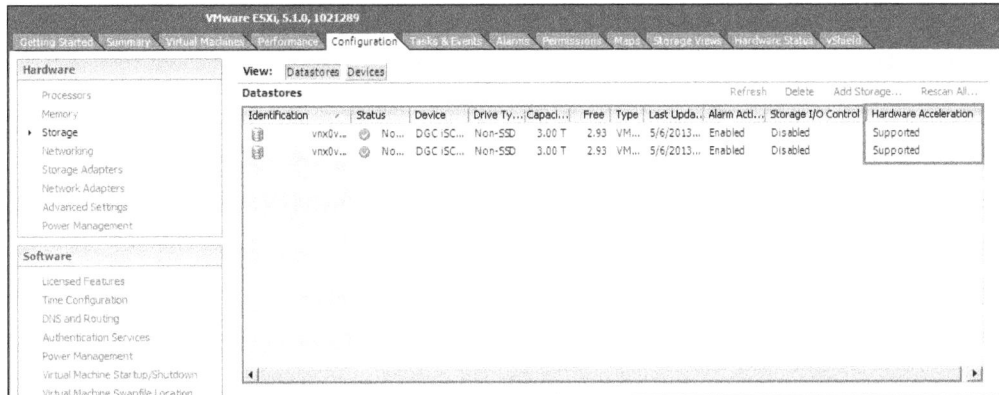

How it works...

The VMkernel core data mover has traditionally done software data movement. Now, with the hardware primitives in place, the data mover can use these primitives to offload certain operations to the array. When a data movement operation is invoked and the corresponding hardware offload operation is enabled, the data mover will first attempt to use the hardware offload. If the hardware offload operation fails, the data mover falls back to the traditional software method of data movement.

If using the hardware offload does succeed, the hardware data movement should perform significantly better than the software data movement. It should consume less CPU cycles and less bandwidth on the fabric. Improvements in performance can be observed by timing operations that use these primitives and `esxtop` to track values such as CMDS/s, READS/s, WRITES/s, MBREAD/s, and MBWRTN/s of storage adapters during the operation.

VMFS uses the data mover to handle certain data operations. One application that invokes these operations is `disklib`. It is in turn used by utilities such as `vmkfstools` and `hostd` to manipulate the virtual machine disks.

Now you may ask what those operations are where it will be leveraged. The following functionality leverages VMFS data movement services:

► Creating a full clone of a VM

► Importing a VMDK using `vmkfstools -i`

► Importing a VM or provisioning a VM off of a VM template in vSphere Client

► Creating `eagerzeroedthick` disks via `vmkfstools` or by provisioning a Fault Tolerant virtual machine

> ► Storage VMotion of a Virtual Machine

> ► Committing redo logs or when snapshots and linked clones are deleted

Selecting the right VM disk type

When you create a virtual disk, you can specify disk properties, such as size, format, clustering features, and more. However the most important is the format.

The type of virtual disk used by your virtual machine can have an effect on the I/O performance, thus it plays a vital role in maintaining the disk performance. Type of disks which are available today are:

> ► Eagerzeroed thick

> ► Lazyzeroed thick

> ► Thin

You need to carefully evaluate the workload and the performance factors for each disk before you choose one.

Getting ready

To step through this recipe, you will need one or more running ESXi Servers, a vCenter Server, and a working installation of vSphere Client. No other prerequisites are required.

How to do it...

When you create a disk inside a VM, you have the option to select the type of disk as follows:

1. Open up vSphere Client and log in to the vCenter Server.
2. Select **Hosts and Clusters** on the home screen.
3. Navigate to the ESXi host where you want to create a new VM.
4. Click on **File | New | Virtual Machine**.
5. Specify the name of the VM, **Resource Pool**, where you want to place it, select the Datastore where you want to put it in, select the VM hardware version, **Guest OS**, **CPU**, **Memory**, **Network**, and **SCSI controller**.
6. Navigate to **create a new virtual disk**.
7. Select the size of the VM hard disk.

8. At this point, you have to select one of the mentioned types of disk. By default **Thick Provision Lazy Zeroed** is selected. However, you have the option to select any one of the three types.

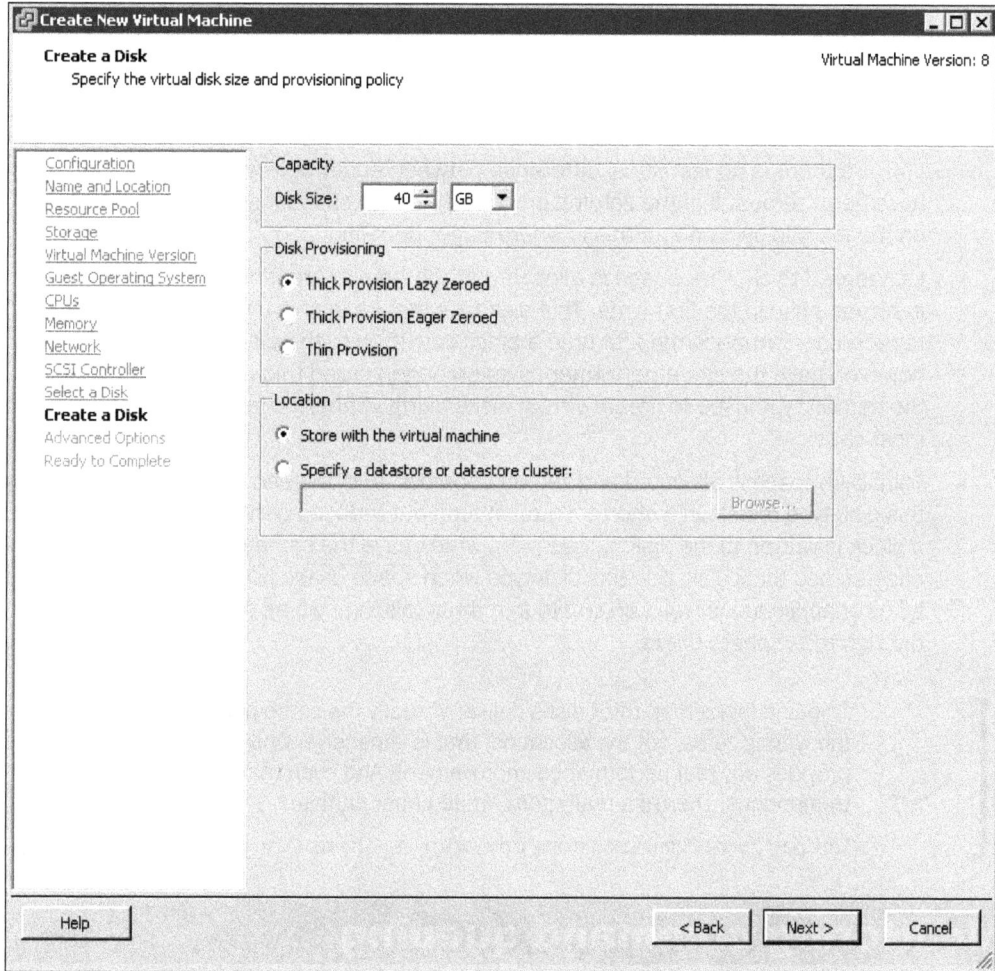

9. Select the virtual device node and mode, and click on **Finish** to complete the operation.

How it works...

Let us look at the different types of disks:

- ▶ Eagerzeroed thick: Disk space is allocated and zeroed out at the time of creation. Although this extends the time it takes to create the disk, using this disk type results in more consistent performance, even the first time we write to each block. The primary use of this disk type is for quorum drives in an MSCS cluster. You can create eagerzeroed thick disks at the command prompt with vmkfstools. As per VMware there is no statistical difference between eager or lazy once all blocks have been zeroed. It is the zeroing process that creates inconsistent performance on the lazy file system and this is where eager benefits.

- ▶ Lazyzeroed thick: Disk space is allocated at the time of creation, but each block is zeroed only on the first write. This disk type results in shorter creation time but reduced performance the first time a block is written to the disk. Subsequent writes, however, have the same performance as an eagerzeroed thick disk. This disk type is the default type used to create virtual disks using vSphere Client and is good for most cases.

- ▶ Thin: Disk space is allocated and zeroed upon demand, instead of upon creation. Using this disk type results in a shorter creation time but reduced performance the first time a block is written to the disk. Subsequent writes have the same performance as an eagerzeroed thick disk. Use this disk type when space usage is the main concern for all types of applications. You can create thin disks (also known as thin-provisioned disks) through the vSphere Client.

> Thin and lazyzeroed thick disks deliver virtually the same performance. It's the writing zeros, not the allocation, that is expensive. Only eagerzeroed provides any real performance improvement. And even that is usually not tremendous. There's a really good white paper on this:
>
> `http://www.vmware.com/pdf/vsp_4_thinprov_perf.pdf`

Monitoring command queuing

There are metrics for monitoring the number of active disk commands and the number of disk commands that are queued. These metrics provide information about your disk performance. They are often used to further interpret the latency values that you might be observing.

Number of active commands: This metric represents the number of I/O operations that are currently active. This includes operations for which the host is processing. This metric can serve as a quick view of storage activity. If the value of this metric is close to or at zero, the storage subsystem is not being used. If the value is a nonzero number, sustained over time, then constant interaction with the storage subsystem is occurring.

Number of commands queued: This metric represents the number of I/O operations that require processing but have not yet been addressed. Commands are queued and awaiting management by the kernel when the driver's active command buffer is full. Occasionally, a queue will form and result in a small, nonzero value for **QUED**. However, any significant average of queued commands means that the storage hardware is unable to keep up with the host's needs.

Getting ready

To step through this recipe, you will need one or more running ESXi Servers, a couple of storage I/O hungry virtual machines, a vCenter Server, working installation of vSphere Client, and a SSH Client (such as Putty). No other prerequisites are required.

How to do it...

To monitor the command queuing in VMkernel you must follow the proceeding steps:

1. Open up the SSH Client and login to the ESXi.
2. Run the `esxtop` command there.
3. On the screen select **D** to monitor the adapter's queue.
4. Check the **KAVG/cmd** column and monitor the value there.

To monitor the queuing at the device level, you have to follow the proceeding steps:

5. Open up the SSH Client and login to the ESXi.
6. Run the `esxtop` command there.
7. On the screen select **U** to monitor the disk device's queue.
8. Check the **ACTV** and **QUED** column and monitor the value there.

How it works...

Here is an example of monitoring the kernel latency value, **KAVG/cmd**. This value is being monitored for the device **vmhba0**. In the first **resxtop** screen, the kernel latency value is 0.02 milliseconds (average per IO command in the monitoring period). This is a good value because it is nearly zero.

In the second **resxtop** screen (type u in the window), where we have the NFS datastore attached to the ESXi host, we can see there are 18 active I/Os (**ACTV**) and 0 I/Os being queued (**QUED**). This means that there are some active I/Os, however queuing is not happening at the VMkernel level.

Queuing happens if there is excessive I/O to the device and the LUN queue depth setting is not sufficient. The default LUN queue depth is 32. However, if there are too many I/Os (more than 32) to handle simultaneously, the device will get bottlenecked to only 32 outstanding I/Os at a time. To resolve this, you would change the queue depth of the device driver.

Also look at what `esxtop` calls DAVG latency, the metrics in vCenter for device latency per I/O command. This is the average delay in milliseconds per I/O from the time an ESXi host sends the command out until the time the host hears back that the array has completed the I/O.

Identifying a severely overloaded storage

When storage is severely overloaded, commands are aborted because the storage subsystem is taking far too long to respond to the commands. The storage subsystem has not responded within an acceptable amount of time, as defined by the guest operating system or application. Aborted commands are a sign that the storage hardware is overloaded and unable to handle the requests in line with the host's expectations.

The number of aborted commands can be monitored by using either vSphere Client or resxtop, as follows:

▸ From the vSphere Client, monitor disk command aborts

▸ From `esxtop`, monitor ABRTS/s

Getting ready

To step through this recipe, you will need one or more running ESXi Servers, a vCenter Server, a working installation of vSphere Client, and a SSH Client (such as Putty). No other prerequisites are required.

How to do it...

To monitor the disk command aborts using vSphere Client you need to follow the proceeding steps:

1. Open up vSphere Client.
2. Log in to the vCenter Server.
3. Navigate to the **Hosts and Clusters** section.
4. Select the host where you want to monitor the disk aborts.
5. Now click on the **Performance** tab at the right-hand side.
6. Select **Advanced** and **Switch to Disk** from the drop-down menu window.
7. Click on **Chart Options** and select the counter **Commands aborted**.
8. Click on **OK** and now you can see the metric in the performance chart.

To monitor the disk command aborts using an SSH client such as Putty you should follow the proceeding steps:

1. Open up SSH client and log in to the ESXi server.
2. Run `esxtop` there.
3. For disk device error, type `U`.
4. Now type `f` to change the settings and type `L` to select **Error Stats**.

Once this is done, you can see the ABRTS/s field there. Monitor this field for the disk command aborts.

This counter tracks the SCSI aborts. Aborts generally occur because the array is taking far too long to respond to commands.

7
Designing vCenter and vCenter Database for Best Performance

In this chapter, we will cover the tasks related to vCenter and vCenter database design for best performance. You will learn the following aspects of vCenter and vCenter database design:

- ▶ vCenter Single Sign-On and its database preparation
- ▶ vCenter Single Sign-On and its deployment
- ▶ Things to bear in mind while designing the vCenter platform
- ▶ Designing vCenter Server for redundancy
- ▶ Designing a highly available vCenter database
- ▶ vCenter database size and location affects performance
- ▶ Considering vCenter Server certificates to minimize security threats
- ▶ Designing vCenter Server for Auto Deploy

Introduction

vCenter Server is evolving into a virtualization platform providing the necessary management framework to deliver the needs of today's virtualization administrators. So, you need to be very careful in taking decisions while designing your vCenter and management platform, which will have performance factors integrated as well. In this chapter we will talk about various decision making factors for vCenter platform, vCenter DB platform and its location, and the effect of this as well. We will also talk about the resilient and secure management framework design using vCenter Heartbeat and Certificates.

We will also touch base with some advanced management features and its effect on vCenter Server designs for your high performing vSphere Infrastructure, such as Auto Deploy and SSO.

vCenter Single Sign-On and its database preparation

For deployment of vSphere SSO, you need to have a database prepared for it. This database can be bundled or can be custom too. If you are considering a bundled SQL Server 2008, then Mixed Mode Authentication is required for that database. So, if you already have a bundled database and are using Windows Authentication mode, then you need to change it to Mixed Mode Authentication.

Now, if you are considering external database (custom) then you do not need ODBC/DSN, rather the SSO installer constructs the JDBC information from the screen input.

The SSO database should be created manually and the scripts to do it are available in InstallerMedia\Single Sign-On\DBScripts\SSOServer\schema. You can find different folders there for different supported databases. The name of the database script located at the above mentioned directory is `rsaIMSLite<database>SetupTablespaces.sql` (Replace `<database>` with Oracle, DB2, or MSSQL).

Only tablespaces need to be created for the `RSA` database, and the SSO installer will run the remaining scripts. You can change the name of the database but cannot change database tablespace names.

If you are using SQL Server, the sysadmin fixed role is required when you do the installation. Two database accounts will be created by the SSO installer and those are `RSA_USER` and `RSA_DBA`. These accounts are required for SSO operation and cannot be changed or removed.

Getting ready

To step through this recipe, you will need vCenter 5.1 installation ISO and a preinstalled database server (we will walk through with SQL Server 2008). No other prerequisites are required.

How to do it...

As we have discussed that the database needs to be prepared before you install SSO, you need to do the following to achieve it:

1. Open up SQL Server management console.

2. Use the following script to prepare the database:

```
USE MASTER
GO
CREATE DATABASE RSA ON PRIMARY(
    NAME='RSA_DATA',
    FILENAME='C:\CHANGE ME\RSA_DATA.mdf',
    SIZE=10MB,
    MAXSIZE=UNLIMITED,
    FILEGROWTH=10%),
FILEGROUP RSA_INDEX(
    NAME='RSA_INDEX',
    FILENAME='C:\CHANGE ME\RSA_INDEX.ndf',
    SIZE=10MB,
    MAXSIZE=UNLIMITED,
    FILEGROWTH=10%)
LOG ON(
    NAME='translog',
    FILENAME='C:\CHANGE ME\translog.ldf',
    SIZE=10MB,
    MAXSIZE=UNLIMITED,
    FILEGROWTH=10% )
GO
EXEC SP_DBOPTION 'RSA', 'autoshrink', true
GO
EXEC SP_DBOPTION 'RSA', 'trunc. log on chkpt.', true
GO
CHECKPOINT
GO
```

> In the preceding code, RSA_INDEX.mdf and RSA_DATA.mdf cannot be changed. However, **RSA** is the name of the DB which can be changed and the areas highlighted in the code can be changed.

3. Here is an example of MS SQL Server. You can see the database files, with an initial size of 10 megabytes and the Autogrow of 10 percent:

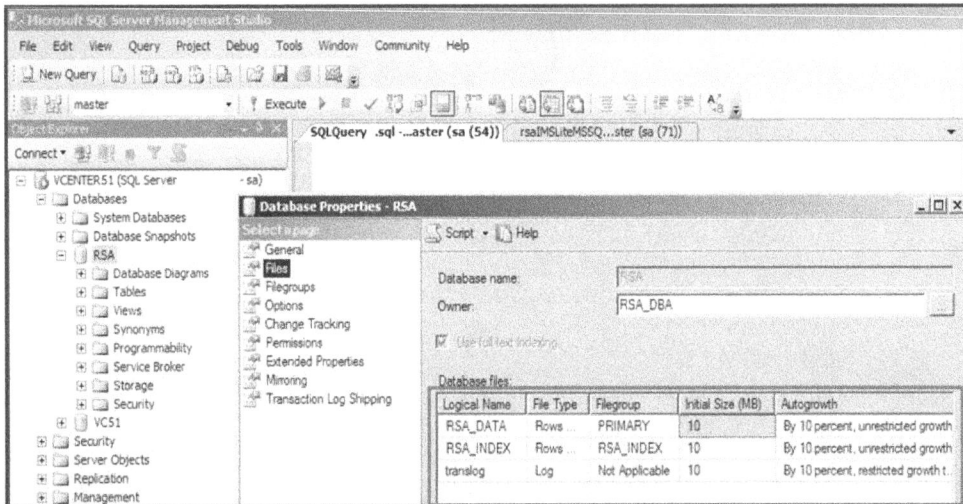

vCenter Single Sign-On and its deployment

1. vSphere 5.1 introduces the vCenter Single Sign On service as a part of the vCenter Server management infrastructure, where Single Sign On simplifies the login process for the Cloud Infrastructure Suite.

2. vSphere Single Sign On provides a Single Sign On method across management apps. It allows you to log in through the vSphere Web Client or API, and perform operations across all components. It is really a better architecture because a single component offers Multifactor Authentication, multisite support, and supports multiple directory service types.

3. Single Sign On supports open industry standards, such as SAML 2.0 and WS-TRUST. SAML 2.0 tokens are used to authenticate user to a different trust domain. It implements the brokered authentication architectural pattern. The main benefits of Single Sign On are:

▶ Allows various vSphere components to communicate with each other

▶ Communication through a token exchange mechanism

▶ No more separate authentication required for each component

4. Now, let me show what the situation today is. The following screenshot shows how the authentication is acquired without Single Sign On:

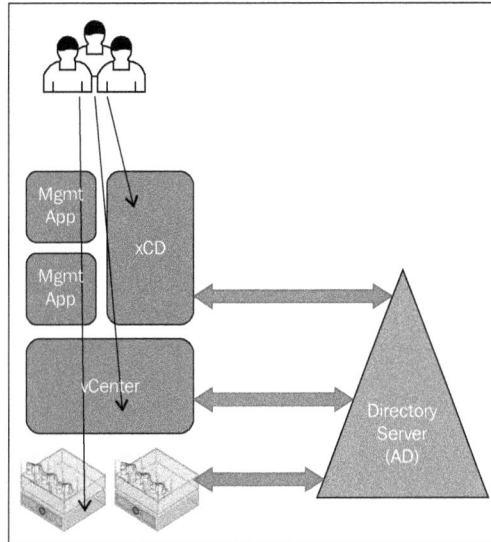

5. However, if you are deploying vSphere Single Sign On, then your authentication method should look like this:

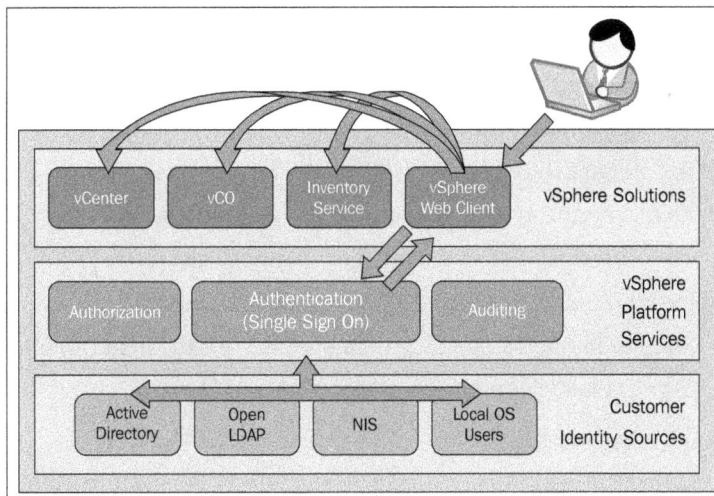

Getting ready

To step through this recipe, you will need vCenter Server 5.1 installer ISO, SQL Server 2008 for vCenter Server and SSO, and a Windows machine, where vCenter and SSO will be installed. We assume that the database is already prepared for vCenter Server and SSO. No other prerequisites are required.

How to do it...

To deploy vSphere SSO, perform the following steps:

1. Login to the windows machine on which you need to install SSO.

   Note: SSO is preinstalled on the vCenter virtual appliance.

2. Now mount the ISO of the vCenter Server installer.

3. If it does not autorun then you need to double-click on the autorun to launch the installer.

   Now, there are two options to deploy SSO. One is using the vCenter Simple Install and another one is using just deploying SSO. This recipe will assume only the SSO installation.

4. Select **vCenter Server Single Sign on** and click on **Install**.

5. Select the desired installation language and click on **OK**.

6. Click on **Next** to start the Single Sign On Installation Wizard.

7. Accept the agreement and click on **Next.**

8. Choose the **Create the primary node for a new vCenter Single Sign On installation**, as this is the first vCenter Single Sign On instant and click on **Next**.

9. Install **Basic vCenter Single Sign On**.

10. Fill the `admin@System-Domain` password then click on **Next**.

11. Choose **Use an existing database**.

12. Fill out the database information.

13. Now fill the fully qualified domain name of your SSO server name and click on **Next**.

14. Choose the SSO installation destination folder and click on **Next**.

15. Confirm the HTTPS port to be used by SSO and click on **Next**.

16. On the **Ready to Install** screen click on **Install** to start the installation.

17. On the SSO installation completion screen click on **Finish**.

There are two modes of installation:

1. vCenter Simple Install

2. Individual Component Install

vCenter Simple installs Single Sign On, Inventory Service, and VMware vCenter Server and it is done in one pass with all components installed on a single server. However, individual component installation requires to follow this order, where each component can be deployed to the same or separate servers:

1. Single Sign On Server

2. Inventory Service

3. VMware vCenter Server

However, for any method of the SSO installation, or for any subsequent installations of vCenter Server in your environment, you do not need to install Single Sign On. One Single Sign On Server can serve your entire vSphere environment. After you install Single Sign On Server once, you can connect all new vCenter Server instances to the same SSO server if you choose to do so. It is also possible to deploy multiple SSO environments. For example; if an organization wants to completely segregate their VDI environment from their Production/Server or Cloud environment, the environments can be built with different SSO servers.

Things to bear in mind while designing the vCenter platform

You need to take certain decisions when you design your vCenter Server. There are two decisions which you need to make and the major one is whether to install vCenter Server on a physical machine or on a virtual machine. Also you need to take another decision which is whether to go for vCenter Server on a Windows System or use the Linux-based vCenter Server Appliance.

Now, one straight forward decision would make your life easy, the moment you choose to go with the Linux-based vCenter Server Appliance. However, SSL certificate installation is more complex in the appliance model. As it is an appliance, it is virtual. But some vendors do make physical appliances (for example, Cisco Nexus 1000V VSM versus Nexus 1010). However, this is not the case with the Windows based installable flavor.

Apart from these two decisions, there are some more you also need to be aware of and those are minimum hardware requirements, with an appropriate level of system redundancy.

Now vCenter Server on a Windows platform runs well on both the physical and virtual platform. However, many organizations put a separate layer for management, thus they are more comfortable in maintaining the management software in different management stack.

One can debate over the fact that putting the vCenter on a virtual platform based on segregation of management software from the same management stack runs a potential risk of failure of that management stack. However, in VMware vSphere you can easily mitigate that risk by putting your vCenter Server on a vSphere HA Cluster. Running vCenter Server on a virtual machine has several benefits as well:

1. It can be easily backed up and restored as a whole unit unlike a physical machine.

2. It can be moved to another ESXi host using vMotion for planned maintenance.

3. It will be load balanced across hosts by using vSphere Distributed Resource Scheduler cluster.

4. It is also protected using vSphere HA.

5. It can be protected more easily for disaster recovery, using SRM or other ways of replicating and failing over to the recovery site.

6. For every other reason you're already using virtual machines over physical machines.

So, considering these benefits of using the vCenter Server on a virtual machine, you can debate over the physical platform, where you need to buy additional softwares, such as vCenter Heartbeat or third party clustering solution. The protection comes in virtual platform easily using vSphere HA. Also, you need to properly size the hardware resource for a physical vCenter Server, wherein you can add CPU/RAM later as required if it is being used in a virtual machine.

An additional benefit is snapshotting a virtual machine whereas for physical machine you need to buy separate software.

How to do it...

If you are choosing a virtual platform for your vCenter Server then you must perform the following items:

1. Create a virtual machine with proper size for installing vCenter Server. Make sure that it guarantees the minimum required hardware for your vCenter Server, which is two 64 bit CPUs or one 64 bit dual core CPU and that has to be 2.0 GHz or faster. Also the memory should be at least 4 gigabytes. Disk size should be 4 gigabytes as well, in addition to the Guest Operating System.

2. For better performance of your vCenter Server, VMware recommends the following numbers. This is effective for vSphere 5.1:

Up to 50 hosts/500 powered-on VMs	2 CPUs	4GB RAM	5GB disk space
Up to 300 hosts/3,000 powered-on VMs	4 CPUs	8GB RAM	10GB disk space
Up to 1,000 hosts/10,000 powered-on VMs	8 CPUs	16GB RAM	10GB disk space

3. If you are using a Linux-based vCenter Server appliance then you should allocate 2 vCPUs, at least 4 gigabytes memory, 4 gigabytes of storage up to a maximum of 80 gigabytes storage.

4. A gigabit connection is recommended for both Linux-based vCenter and Windows based vCenter Installation.

Designing vCenter Server for redundancy

For a better performing vSphere Infrastructure, you need to think about the redundancy of your vCenter Server. So, the question is how would you provide redundancy for your vCenter Server?

Well, this decision can be taken based on certain criteria and those are:

1. How much down time you can tolerate?
2. What is your desired level of failover automation for vCenter Server?
3. What is your budget for maintaining the availability method?

There are a couple of redundancy methods which are available for both your Windows based vCenter Server and Linux based vCenter Server Appliance. However, VMware recommends using HA to protect your vCenter Server Appliance.

If you choose a Windows based vCenter Server then you can choose for third party clustering software such as Microsoft Cluster Service as well to provide redundancy.

> VMware does not certify these third-party solutions. VMware will offer best effort support for any issues encountered with an environment that uses third-party solutions for protecting against VMware VirtualCenter downtime.

You can also choose a manual configuration and manual failover for your vCenter Server system. However, it can take much longer than your automated solution using vSphere HA or vCenter Server Heartbeat or any other third party clustering software. Not only does it take time for the initial configuration of your vCenter Server, but it also takes time to keep these two systems synchronized and failover at the time of service disruption.

How to do it...

Follow the steps to design a redundant vCenter Server:

1. There are couple of ways to provide the redundancy for your vCenter Server. One of the ways is manual configuration and manual failover. You need to do these to maintain the manual redundancy of your vCenter Server:

    ❑ Configuring your vCenter virtual machine and clone it to create a backup vCenter virtual machine

    ❑ Install and configure vCenter Server on a physical machine and use P2V software to create a backup virtual machine

    ❑ Install and configure vCenter Server on a physical machine and using P2P software, image it to another physical machine

2. Make sure that you put this vCenter Server or vCenter Server Appliance on a vSphere HA enabled cluster for automated redundancy. Although vSphere HA does protect against operating system and hardware failures, it does not protect against vCenter Server service failure.

3. For a faster and automated solution of redundant vCenter Server, choose vCenter Server Heartbeat or a third party solution such as Microsoft Cluster Services. One advantage of using vCenter Server Heartbeat is that it monitors for vCenter Server service failure in addition to overall operating system failure.

Other advantages are that vCenter Server Heartbeat can protect the database server, works with either physical or virtual machines, and automatically maintains synchronization between the primary and backup servers.

However, the main disadvantages of these solutions are they need to be purchased and maintained over a period of time.

They are also more difficult to configure than merely running a VM in a vSphere cluster with HA enabled. For many environments, HA provides good enough availability with minimal configuration cost or hassle.

Note: ESXi hosts can do HA restarts even when vCenter Server is down; vCenter is needed to configure HA, but not for it to run. HA will restart even the VM that runs vCenter which manages the HA cluster itself. If this still leaves you uncomfortable, another option is to have a vCenter VM in cluster "A" managing cluster "B", and a VM in cluster "B" managing cluster "A".

Designing a highly available vCenter database

It does not really matter which platform or which flavor of vCenter Server you are using, but you must protect your vCenter Server database. All configuration information about the vSphere inventory objects, such as objects, roles, alarms, performance data, host profiles, and so on are kept in the vCenter Server database.

In a case of failure of database such as lost data or corrupted data, all this information may get lost and should be restored from a backup or the entire inventory should be reconfigured manually. If you do not have a backup copy of your vCenter Server database then at the time of failure you will lose the history of your tasks, events, and performance information apart from those already mentioned previously.

So in a nutshell, you should use any of the available methods to maintain a backup copy of your vCenter Server database. Some options are listed in the next section.

How to do it...

You can choose a number of solutions for maintaining a highly available vCenter Server database:

1. Use any available and supported vendor supplied availability and maintenance solutions.

2. If you are using a vCenter Server database in a virtual machine then protect it using vSphere HA.

3. If you cannot use any vendor specific tools to maintain the availability of the vCenter database then use vCenter Server Heartbeat to protect the database server and it works for both physical and virtual machine. However, it comes with an additional cost.

   For environments that require highly available management components (VDI environments, which constantly deploy new desktops in an automated fashion, or vCloud/self-service/service provider environments) this solution should be investigated.

4. You still need to take regular backup of the vCenter Server database to protect the actual database information.

vCenter database size and location affects performance

For any kind of vCenter platform, you need to have a vCenter database, but the question is how your database size affects your vCenter performance.

If adequate resources are available for your vCenter database then the supported versions of vCenter databases, such as Oracle, SQL, and DB2 perform very well. However, you need to understand that a vCenter Server task retention policy and higher performance statistics collection settings can increase the database size dramatically, which in turn will affect your vCenter Server performance. But, the bundled database of either the vCenter Server system or vCenter Server Appliance is a separate matter. The bundled database is intended only for the evaluation of vSphere software or for supporting small infrastructure of up to five hosts and 50 virtual machines. In this case, the vCenter database is collocated with the vCenter Server instance. Logging level also affects the performance and size of the vCenter database.

Now when this is over, the next question is, should you place the vCenter Server database in the same vCenter Management Server computer or on some other virtual machine.

In everything except a small infrastructure, VMware recommends not to place the vCenter Server database on the same system as vCenter Server.

It is not a matter of whether your vCenter Server is physical or virtual, but removing the database from being collocated removes any possibility of resource contention in between these two except for network latency. If the vCenter Server and database systems are virtual, separation means that either virtual machine can be easily resized to accommodate current performance needs.

VMware bundled with the vCenter database is for supporting small infrastructure. The built-in database is a DB2 Express for vCSA 5.0 GA and postgress database for vCSA 5.0 u1b and vCSA 5.1 (http://kb.vmware.com/kb/2002531).

Microsoft SQL Express is included with the Windows version.

How to do it...

To choose a location and size of the vCenter Server database perform the following:

1. Choose the logging level (this logging level is a vCenter setting and not a database log file setting) carefully so that your vCenter Server database will not grow too much and will not affect the performance in turn.

   Note: Use the following knowledge base article to change the logging level for vCenter Server:

   http://kb.vmware.com/selfservice/microsites/search.
   do?language=en_US&cmd=displayKC&externalId=1004795.

2. Consider the vCenter Server task and event retention policy, which will increase the size of the vCenter Server database.

3. Also choose the performance statistics collection settings carefully, which will also increase the database size and affect your vCenter Server database performance.

4. If you are deploying vCenter for a large environment then do not collocate the vCenter database with the vCenter Server system. It will help you avoid any possibility of CPU and memory resource contention.

5. Preferably, choose a vCenter Server database on a virtual machine if does not already exist in the environment. Having a vCenter Server database on a virtual platform has many benefits as follows:

   1. If needed, it can be easily backed up and can also be recreated.

   2. During planned maintenance, it can be moved to other hosts using vMotion.

   3. It can be load balanced using vSphere DRS across hosts.

   4. You can easily protect it by vSphere HA without extra cost and maintenance. Check with your database vendor for details.

   5. You can take a snapshot of it as well for business continuity and testing.

VMware releases vCenter database sizing calculator, which is based on vCenter Server 4.x and supports SQL Server and Oracle.

VC Database sizing calculator - SQL:

```
http://www.vmware.com/support/vsphere4/doc/vsp_4x_
db_calculator.xls
```

VC Database sizing calculator - Oracle:

```
http://www.vmware.com/support/.../doc/vsp_4x_db_
calculator_oracle.xls
```

Considering vCenter Server Certificates to minimize security threats

Security for vCenter Server is really important. However, it is an organization's security policy and architecture decision, whether to use certificates or not.

If your organization's policy requires a certificate then you must use one. Also, if there is a potential possibility of man-in-the-middle attacks when using management interfaces, such as vSphere Client, then using certificates is a must.

VMware products use standard X.509 Version 3 certificates to encrypt session information sent over Secure Socket Layer (SSL) protocol connections between components. However, by default, vSphere includes self-signed certificates. It is an organization's policy which will decide whether to use self-signed certificates or the internally-signed or externally-signed certificates. You need to purchase externally signed certificates, but that is not the case if you use internally signed certificates or self-signed.

You need to keep a backup of those certificates to protect them from being lost or getting corrupt. Also, you need to consider using certificates when you are going to employ vSphere FT or vCenter in the linked mode.

Always remember that server verification is necessary to prevent a man-in-the-middle attack, where the client is induced to connect to a server that is spoofing or proxying with the server it is supposed to be communicating with.

In addition to being signed by a CA, vCenter certificates should have a distinguished name (DN) field that matches the hostname of the server on which vCenter is installed. Usually this implies that the server is joined to a domain so it has a well-defined and unique hostname and also it implies that you are connecting to it by hostname, not the IP address. If you do intend to connect using the IP address, then the certificate needs, in addition, a subjectAltName field that matches with the host's IP. Once you have created any required certificates and installed them in vCenter, you should verify that vCenter Client is able to connect to the server.

Getting ready

To step through this recipe, you will need one or more vCenter Server, either self-signed certificates or internally or externally signed certificates and a working installation of vSphere Client. No other prerequisites are required.

How to do it...

It is a complex task to implement a CA signed certificate for vCenter Server. There are steps which need to be carried out before you implement a certificate for vCenter:

1. Creating the certificate request.
2. Getting the certificate.
3. Installation and configuration of the certificate in vCenter Server.

If you have the certificate from an internal or external authority then perform the following steps to implement it in on vCenter Server:

1. Log in to vCenter Server as an administrator.
2. If you have not already imported it, double-click on the `c:\certs\Root64.cer` file and import the certificate into the Trusted Root Certificate Authorities | Local Computer Windows certificate store. This ensures that the certificate server is trusted.
3. Take the backup of the certificates for the VMware vCenter Server:

   ❏ For Windows 2008, the following location is typical for vSphere 5.1: `C:\ProgramData\VMware\VMware VirtualCenter\SSL`

   ❏ For Windows 2003, the following location is typical for vSphere 5.1: `C:\Documents and Settings\All Users\Application Data\VMware\VMware VirtualCenter\SSL`

4. Copy the new certificate files into the preceding folder. If you are following this resolution path, the proper certificate is in `c:\Documents and Settings\All Users\Application Data\VMware\VMware VirtualCenter\SSL certs\vCenter`.
5. Open `rui.crt` in a text editor and validate that the first line of the file begins with `-----BEGIN CERTIFICATE-----`. If there is any text prior to this, remove it. The code that validates the certificate may fail in Step 4 if there is an additional text.
6. Go to `https://localhost/mob/?moid=vpxd-securitymanager&vmodl=1` on vCenter Server and load the certificates for the configuration by using the Managed Object browser.
7. Click on **Continue** if you are prompted with a certificate warning.

8. Enter a vCenter Server administrator username and password when prompted.

9. Click on **reloadSslCertificate**.

10. Click on **Invoke Method**. If successful, the window shows this message: **Method Invocation Result: void**.

11. Close both windows.

12. Open a command prompt on vCenter Server and change to the `isregtool` directory. By default, this is `C:\Program Files\VMware\Infrastructure\ VirtualCenter Server\isregtool`.

13. Run the following command to register vCenter Server to the inventory service:

    `register-is.bat [vCenter Server URL] [Inventory Service URL] [SSO Lookup Service URL]`

14. The following URLs are the typical URL (modify if ports are different):

    ❑ vCenter Server URL is `https://<server.domain.com>/sdk`

    ❑ Inventory Service URL is `https://<server.domain.com>:10443/`

    ❑ SSO Lookup Service URL is `https://<server.domain.com>:7444/ lookupservice/sdk`

15. Change to the vCenter Server directory. By default, this is `C:\Program Files\ VMware\Infrastructure\VirtualCenter Server\`.

16. Run the command:

    `vpxd -p`

17. Type the password for the vCenter Server database user to encrypt the password with the new certificate.

18. Restart the VMware VirtualCenter Server service from the service control manager (`services.msc`).

19. Restart the VMware vSphere Profile Driven Storage Service.

20. After the initial restart of the services, wait for five minutes. If the VMware vSphere Profile Driven Storage service stops during this time, restart it.

21. Navigate to `https://vcenterserver.domain.com/` and validate the certificate.

See also

▶ For more information on generating certificate requests and certificates for each of the vCenter Server components, see:

▶ `Creating certificate requests and certificates for the vCenter Server 5.1 components (2037432)`

- ▸ For more information on Replacing Default vCenter 5.1 and ESXi Certificates, see:
- ▸ `http://www.vmware.com/files/pdf/techpaper/vsp_51_vcserver_esxi_ certificates.pdf`
- ▸ For more information on vCenter Certificate Automation Tool, see:
- ▸ `https://my.vmware.com/web/vmware/details?downloadGroup=SSL- TOOL-101&productId=285`
- ▸ For more information on replacing the vCenter SSO certificates, see:
- ▸ `Configuring CA signed SSL certificates for vCenter SSO in vCenter Server 5.1 (2035011)`
- ▸ For more information on replacing the Inventory Service certificates, see:
- ▸ `Configuring CA signed SSL certificates for the Inventory service in vCenter Server 5.1 (2035009)`
- ▸ For more information on replacing the vSphere Web Client certificates, see:
- ▸ `Configuring CA signed SSL certificates for the vSphere Web Client and Log Browser in vCenter Server 5.1 (2035010)`
- ▸ For more information on replacing the vSphere Update Manager Certificates, see:
- ▸ `Configuring CA signed SSL certificates for VMware Update Manager in vSphere 5.1 (2037581)`
- ▸ For more information on replacing the ESXi 5.x host certificates, see:
- ▸ `Configuring CA signed SSL certificates with ESXi 5.x hosts (2015499)`
- ▸ For more information on configuring the CA signed certificate for vCenter Appliance, see:
- ▸ `Configuring certificates signed by a Certificate Authority (CA) for vCenter Server Appliance 5.1 (2036744)`

Designing vCenter Server for Auto Deploy

If you are looking for provisioning 100s of ESXi hosts in your datacenter and don't know how to rapidly provision those then Auto Deploy is your answer. With Auto Deploy, you can specify the image which will be used to provision the ESXi hosts. Also you can specify/configure host profiles which will help you to get those hosts configured if you need those identical and add them to a vCenter Folder or Cluster.

Auto Deploy uses a PXE boot infrastructure in conjunction with vSphere host profiles to provision and customize that host. An ESXi host does not store any state information rather Auto Deploy manages that state information. Auto Deploy stores this state information of each ESXi host in different locations. When a host boots for the first time, the vCenter Server system creates a corresponding host object and stores the information in the database.

However in ESXi 5.1, VMware introduces two different features along with stateless ESXi, those are called Stateless Caching and Stateful Installs.

In stateless caching the host boots from Auto Deploy, but will fall back to the cached image in the event DHCP/TFTP/Auto Deploy server is not available.

In stateful installs the Host does the initial boot from Auto Deploy Server which installs an ESXi image on the local disk. All subsequent boots are from the ESXi image saved on the local disk.

Getting ready

To step through this recipe, you will need one or more ESXi Servers not deployed with Auto Deploy, vCenter Server and Auto Deploy Server installed. No other prerequisites are required.

How to do it...

vCenter is a necessary component in Auto Deploy.

If you configure the hosts provisioned with Auto Deploy with a vSphere Distributed Switch or if you have virtual machines configured with auto start manager then you need to deploy the vCenter Server system and maintain its availability which matches the availability of the auto deploy server. But now the question is how do you do that or what are the approaches you can take to make it happen? Well, there are several approaches which you can choose from:

1. You can deploy your Auto Deploy server on the same machine where your vCenter Server is running.

2. You can choose vCenter Server Heartbeat which delivers high availability by protecting virtual and cloud infrastructure from application, configuration, operating system, or hardware related outages.

3. You can deploy vCenter Server in a virtual machine and then you can put this virtual machine on a vSphere HA protected cluster. Also, you can set the Restart Priority as High for this virtual machine.

4. Do not use any ESXi hosts which are managed or deployed by Auto Deploy for hosting the Auto Deploy or vCenter Server system. Because if there are any outages happened then none of your hosts will be able to boot from Auto Deploy. Take two locally deployed ESXi boxes and create a cluster and put your Auto Deploy components there.

However, this approach is not suitable if you use Auto Start Manager as it is not supported in a cluster enabled for vSphere HA.

8
Virtual Machine and Application Performance Design

In this chapter, we will cover the tasks related with virtual machine and application performance design. You will learn the following aspects of virtual machine and application performance design:

- ▶ Setting the right time in Guest OS
- ▶ vNUMA (Virtual NUMA) considerations
- ▶ Choosing the SCSI controller for storage
- ▶ Impact of VM Swap file placement
- ▶ Using large pages in virtual machines
- ▶ Guest OS networking considerations
- ▶ When you should or should not virtualize an application
- ▶ Measuring the application's performance

Introduction

Proper configuration of the Virtual Machine can reduce the possibility of performance problems from occurring during normal operation.

In this chapter we will discuss the guidelines for creating an optimal virtual machine configuration.

You can maintain and even improve the performance of your applications by ensuring that your virtual machine is optimally configured.

Follow the guidelines when configuring your virtual machine for optimal performance. These guidelines pertain to the guest operating system, VMware Tools, and the virtual hardware resources (CPU, memory, storage, and networking).

Setting the right time in Guest OS

Time measurements within a virtual machine can sometimes be inaccurate due to difficulties with the guest operating system keeping the exact time.

Because virtual machines work by time-sharing host physical hardware, virtual machines cannot exactly duplicate the timing activity of physical machines. Virtual machines use several techniques to minimize and conceal differences in timing performance. However, the differences can still sometimes cause timekeeping inaccuracies and other problems in software running in a virtual machine.

Several things can be done to reduce the problem of timing inaccuracies:

- You should always try to use guest operating systems that require fewer timer interrupts

- Different operating systems and versions have different timer interrupts. For example:
    - Windows systems typically use a base timer interrupt rate of 64 Hz or 100 Hz, which means 100 interrupts per second
    - 2.6 Linux kernels have used a variety of timer interrupt rates (100 Hz, 250 Hz, and 1000 Hz)
    - The most recent 2.6 Linux kernels introduce the NO_HZ kernel configuration option (sometimes called "tickless timer") that uses a variable timer interrupt rate

- You can also use other solutions such as:
    - NTP
    - Windows Time Service
    - Any other time keeping utility

For Linux guests, VMware recommends that NTP be used instead of VMware Tools for time synchronization.

The main reason behind recommending this is sync in VMware Tools will only correct the time that falls behind, so if it ever gets ahead for some reason, it won't fix that, but NTP will and most customers already have Guest OS builds that sync time with NTP or AD anyway (and having Guest OS time synced in two ways could lead to conflicts).

Despite of these potential problems, however, testing has shown that NTP in particular behaves fairly well in a virtual machine when appropriately configured (refer to *Using NTP in Linux and Other Guests*). NTP is prepared for some of its readings to be anomalous because of network delays, scheduling delays on the local host and other factors and is effective at filtering out such readings.

> For further information refer to this white paper.
>
> *Using NTP in Linux and Other Guests*: `http://www.vmware.com/files/pdf/techpaper/Timekeeping-In-VirtualMachines.pdf`

Generally, it is best to use only one clock synchronization service at a time in a given virtual machine to ensure that multiple services do not attempt to make conflicting changes to the clock. So if you are using native synchronization software, we suggest turning VMware Tools periodic clock synchronization off.

If you want to know how to stop the VMware Tools clock synchronization then follow this KB article: `http://kb.vmware.com/kb/1006427`.

If you are using ESXi host with Active Directory Integration then it is of utmost important to synchronize the time between ESXi and Active Directory so that it can serve the Kerberos Security Protocol because if the time skew is greater than 300 seconds then a server may not be able to authenticate to the domain. VMware ESXi supports synchronization of time using an external NTP server also.

Active Directory depends on accurate timekeeping, and the risk you must mitigate is how to prevent clock drift. A successful Active Directory implementation requires planning of time services.

Microsoft uses Kerberos v5 as the authentication protocol and for Kerberos to work properly it requires time synchronization. The time stamped authentication tickets generated by Kerberos are based on the workstation's time. The liveliness of this ticket is only five minutes. If your clock drifts significantly, the authentication tickets will not be issued, become outdated or simply expire. That will result in authentication denial or an inability to log into the domain to access network resources.

So if you are planning for an Active Directory implementation, you should consider the most effective way of providing an accurate time to domain controllers.

The Domain Controller which holds the PDC Emulator role for the forest root domain is the "master" timeserver for the forest. This is the root time server for synchronizing the clocks of all Windows computers in the forest. You can either configure the PDC to use an external source to set its time or by using an internal source. So if you modify the defaults of this domain controller's role to synchronize with an alternative external time source then you can ensure that all other DCs and workstations within the domain are accurate.

> For further information refer to the following two KB articles:
>
> *Timekeeping best practices for Windows, including NTP(1318)*:
> `http://kb.vmware.com/selfservice/microsites/search.`
> `do?language=en_US&cmd=displayKC&externalId=1318`
>
> *Timekeeping best practices for Linux guests(1006427)*: `http://`
> `kb.vmware.com/selfservice/microsites/search.`
> `do?language=en_US&cmd=displayKC&externalId=1006427`

Getting ready

To step through this recipe, you will need a couple of ESXi Servers, a Windows VM running Active Directory Services, an instance of installed vCenter Server, and a working installation of vSphere Client. No other prerequisites are required.

How to do it...

To configure the Windows NTP client you need to follow these steps.

Use the registry editor on the Windows server to make the configuration changes:

1. Enable NTP mode:

   1. Locate at `HKEY_LOCAL_MACHINE\SYSTEM\CurrentControlSet\Services\W32Time\Parameters`.

   2. Set the `Type` value to `NTP`.

2. Enable the NTP Client:

   1. Locate at `HKEY_LOCAL_MACHINE\SYSTEM\CurrentControlSet\Services\W32Time\Config`.

   2. Set the `AnnounceFlags` value to `5`.

3. Specify the upstream NTP servers to sync from:

   1. Locate at `HKEY_LOCAL_MACHINE\SYSTEM\CurrentControlSet\Services\W32Time\TimeProviders`.

   2. Set the `NtpServer` value to a list of at least 3 NTP servers.

> On a Windows 2008 Domain Controller, `NtpServer` is located in `HKEY_LOCAL_MACHINE\SYSTEM\CurrentControlSet\Services\W32Time\Parameters`.

4. Specify a 15-minute update interval:

    1. Locate at `HKEY_LOCAL_MACHINE\SYSTEM\CurrentControlSet\Services\W32Time\TimeProviders\NtpClient`.

    2. Set the `SpecialPollInterval` value to `900`.

5. Restart the W32Time service for the changes to take effect.

When using W32Time or NTP in the guest, disable VMware Tools periodic time synchronization.

To disable VMware Tools periodic time sync, use one of these options:

1. Set `tools.syncTime = 0` in the configuration file (`.vmx` file) of the virtual machine.

2. Or, deselect Time synchronization between the virtual machine and the host operating system in the VMware Tools toolbox GUI of the guest operating system.

3. Or, run the `VMwareService.exe` cmd and `vmx.set_option synctime 1 0` command in the guest operating system. `VMwareService.exe` is typically installed in `C:\Program Files\VMware\VMware Tools`.

These options do not disable one time synchronization done by VMware Tools for events such as tools startup, taking a snapshot, resuming from a snapshot, resuming from suspend, or vMotion.

Now, to configure the ESXi NTP, follow these steps.

Configure ESXi to synchronize the time with the Windows server Active Directory Domain Controller:

1. Connect to the ESXi host or vCenter Server using the vSphere Client.

2. Select the ESXi host in the inventory.

3. Click on the **Configuration** tab.

4. Under the **Software** heading, click on **Time Configuration**.

5. Click on **Properties**.

6.   Ensure that the **NTP Client Enabled** option is selected.

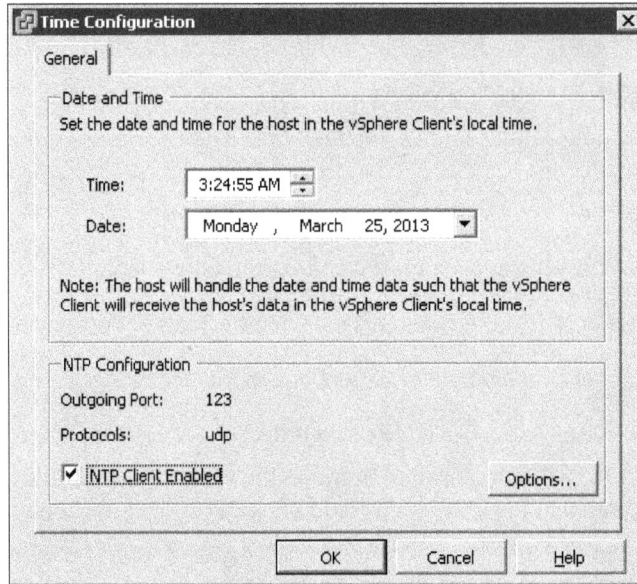

7.   Click on **Options...**.

8.   Click on **NTP Settings**.

9.   Click on **Add...** and specify the fully qualified domain name or IP address of the Windows server Domain Controller(s).

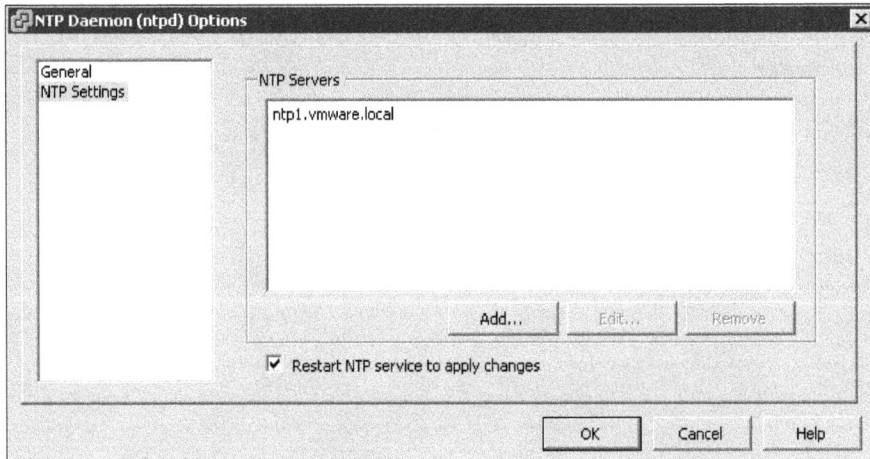

10. Click on **OK**.

11. Click on **OK** to save the changes.

See Also

For complete details, refer to VMware knowledge base article 1006427 at `http://kb.vmware.com/kb/1006427`.

For a detailed discussion on timekeeping, refer to *Timekeeping in VMware Virtual Machines* at `http://www.vmware.com/resources/techresources/238`.

vNUMA (Virtual NUMA) considerations

Non Uniform Memory Access also known as NUMA is designed with memory locality in mind so that pools of adjacent memory are placed in islands called NUMA nodes. Each of today's CPUs has multiple cores but that does not always result in a NUMA node with a given number of cores and RAM. It is the Integrated Memory Controller who decides that. There are multi-core CPU's that are not NUMA aware (original XEON 7300/7400 CPU's, for example), however on a different note, in a Nehalem-EX systems if it has four sockets each with 8 cores for a total of 32 cores and 256GB of RAM total, it would mean that each socket had 64GB of RAM.

What if your VM needs to be bigger than a NUMA node? One of the great new features in vSphere 5 is vNUMA or the ability for NUMA to be presented inside the VM to the guest OS.

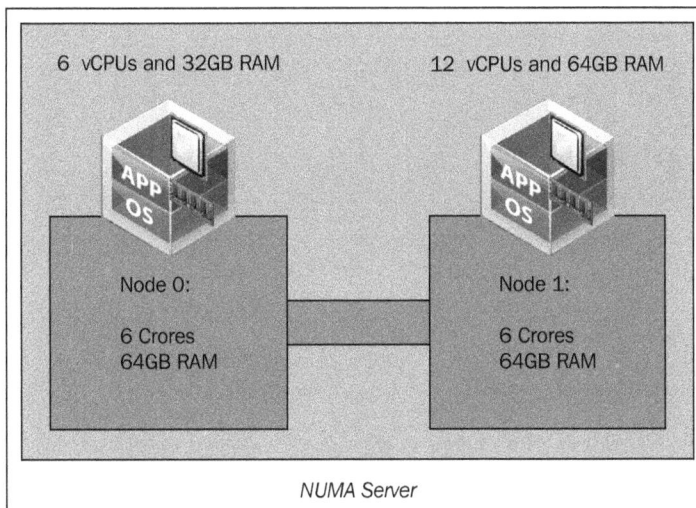

6 vCPUs and 32GB RAM   12 vCPUs and 64GB RAM

Node 0:

6 Crores
64GB RAM

Node 1:

6 Crores
64GB RAM

NUMA Server

vNUMA is designed for modern OS's that are NUMA aware and can make intelligent page management decisions based on locality.

Legacy OS functions in a similar manner by enabling "Node Interleaving" in a Proliant BIOS so that the entire memory pool is seen as contiguous, with no differentiation between nodes. Without vNUMA, the OS and apps are not aware of the NUMA architecture and will just treat the vCPUs and vRAM as one big pool and assign memory and processes.

A characteristic aspect of vNUMA is that it incorporates distributed shared memory (DSM) inside the hypervisor, in contrast to the more traditional approach of providing it in the middleware.

When creating a virtual machine you have the option to specify the number of virtual sockets and the number of cores per virtual socket. If the number of cores per virtual socket on a vNUMA enabled virtual machine is set to any value other than the default of one and that value doesn't align with the underlying physical host topology, performance might be slightly reduced.

Therefore, for best performance, if a virtual machine is to be configured with a non-default number of cores per virtual socket, that number should be an integer multiple or integer divisor of the physical NUMA node size.

Getting ready

To step through this recipe, you will need a couple of ESXi Servers, a couple of working Virtual Machines which have more than eight vCPUs, also some VMs with smaller vCPUs, an instance of installed vCenter Server and a working installation of vSphere Client. No other prerequisites are required.

How to do it...

By default, vNUMA is enabled only for virtual machines with more than eight vCPUs. This feature can be enabled for smaller virtual machines, by adding to the `.vmx` file the following line: `numa.vcpu.maxPerVirtualNode = X (where X is the number of vCPUs per vNUMA node)`.

To make this change with the vSphere Client, perform the following steps:

1. Select the virtual machine that you wish to change, and then click on **Edit virtual machine settings**.
2. Under the **Options** tab, select **General** and then click on **Configuration Parameters**.
3. Look for **numa.vcpu.maxPerVirtualNode**. If it is not present, click on **Add Row** and enter the new variable.
4. Click on the value to be changed and configure it as you wish.

Choosing the SCSI controller for storage

In vSphere 5.1 there are four types of SCSI controller for a VM. Those are:

- ▸ Bus Logic Parallel
- ▸ LSI Logic Parallel
- ▸ LSI Logic SAS
- ▸ PVSCSI

In order to successfully boot a virtual machine, the guest operating system must support the type of SCSI HBA you choose for your virtual machine hardware.

Bus Logic is there for supporting your old Guest OS, an example is Microsoft Windows 2000 Server.

LSI Logic is there for supporting your newer guest operating system. There is not much difference in I/O performance between Bus Logic and LSI Logic, however there is a slight difference in the way the hardware represents itself inside the guest. VMware recommends picking up LSI Logic for your Linux Guests.

LSI Logic SAS has been built to support even newer guest operating system with advanced feature support, for example, clustering support in Windows 2008. As it is a specially built controller, it boosts the I/O performance slightly than your legacy controller. You need to use VM Hardware version 7 and above to get the ability of using it.

PVSCSI controller is VMware's own controller and it is for high performing VMs. It is built to reduce the CPU overhead while still increasing I/O throughput. This driver coalesces interrupts to reduce the amount of CPU processing required.

This controller also requires hardware version 7 and above. As a best practice you can still use a default controller for the OS to come up and for the high I/O load VM, you can use PVSCSI for data disk. In this way operational complexity is reduced.

In some cases, large I/O requests issued by applications in a virtual machine can be split by the guest storage driver. Changing the guest operating system's registry settings to issue larger block sizes can eliminate this splitting, thus enhancing performance.

> For additional information refer to the VMware knowledge base article 9645697 at http://kb.vmware.com/kb/9645697.

Getting ready

To step through this recipe, you will need one or more running ESXi Servers, a fully functioning vCenter Server, and a working installation of vSphere Client. No other prerequisites are required.

How to do it...

SCSI Controller selection can be made at the following times:

1. During the Virtual Machine creation.
2. After creation, by using **Edit Settings**.

The Create Virtual Machine wizard provides a default choice based on the selected operating system choice.

Once a virtual machine has been powered on, the virtual machine must still boot its operating system. A virtual machine does not boot if the guest operating system does not include a driver for the configured virtual SCSI Controller.

The virtual **SCSI Controller** is automatically selected during virtual machine creation, based on the selected guest operating system. The default SCSI Controller selection can be overridden at creation time by using the Create Virtual Machine wizard.

The SCSI Controller selection can also be changed by using the vSphere Client Edit Settings menu item (available by right-clicking on the virtual machine in the inventory panel).

While you are creating a VM, choose the Type of OS you want, and then at the SCSI Controller option screen select the controller you want for this VM. A default choice will be populated though based on your Guest OS selection.

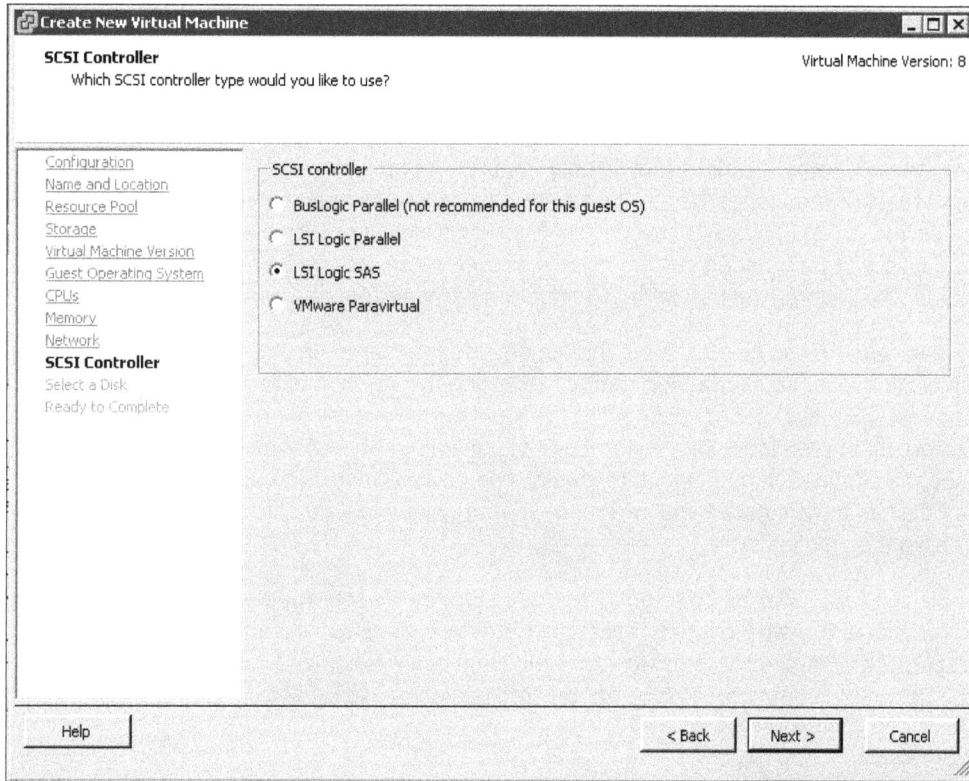

Impact of VM swap file placement

The creation of a virtual machine's swap file is automatic. By default, this file is created in the virtual machine's working directory, but a different location can be set.

Swap file contains swapped memory pages and its size is determined as allocated RAM size—reservation. If performance is important in the design, 100 percent memory reservations should be created, causing no need to swap to disk.

You can optionally configure a special host cache on an SSD (if one is installed) to be used for the swap to host cache feature. This swap cache is shared by all the virtual machines running on the host. In addition, host level swapping of the virtual machines' most active pages benefit from the low latency of SSD. The swap to host cache feature makes the best use of potentially limited SSD space. This feature is also optimized for the large block sizes at which some SSDs work best.

If a host does not use the swap to host cache feature, place the virtual machine swap files on low latency, high bandwidth storage systems. The best choice is usually local SSD. If the host does not have local SSD, the second choice would be remote SSD. Remote SSD would still provide the low latencies of SSD, though with the added latency of remote access.

Other than SSD storage, place the virtual machine's swap file on the fastest available datastore. This datastore might be on a Fiber Channel SAN array or a fast local disk. Do not store swap files on thin provisioned LUNs. Running a virtual machine with a swap file that is stored on a thin provisioned LUN can cause swap file growth to fail if no space on the LUN remains. This failure can lead to the termination of the virtual machine.

Also placing the Swap file has some impact on vMotion operation too. If you place your VM swap file in a local datastore then that will increase the vMotion time for that VM because destination ESXi host cannot connect to the local datastore; the file has to be placed on a datastore that is available for the new ESXi host running the incoming VM. Because of this reason the destination host needs to create a new swap file in its swap file destination. As a new file has to be created and swapped, memory pages potentially need to be copied, it increases the vMotion time.

Also placing your swap file on a replicated datastore increases vMotion time. When moving the contents of a swap file into a replicated datastore, the swap file and its contents need to be replicated to the replica datastore as well, each block is copied from the source datastore to the destination datastore if synchronous replication is used.

Getting ready

To step through this recipe, you will need one or more running ESXi Servers, a couple of datastores attached (Local SSD and Remote SSD) to these ESXi Servers, a vCenter Server, and a working installation of vSphere Client. No other prerequisites are required.

How to do it...

You can define an alternate swap file location at the cluster level and at the virtual machine level.

To define an alternate swap file location at the cluster level:

1. Right-click on the cluster in the inventory and select **Edit Settings**.
2. In the **cluster settings** dialog box, select **Swapfile Location** in the left pane.
3. Choose the option to store the swap file in the datastore specified by the host and click on **OK**.

4. Select the ESXi host in the inventory and click on the **Configuration** tab.

5. In the **Software** panel, click on the **Virtual Machine Swapfile Location** link.

6. Click on the **Edit** link and select the datastore to use as that swap file location. Click on **OK**.

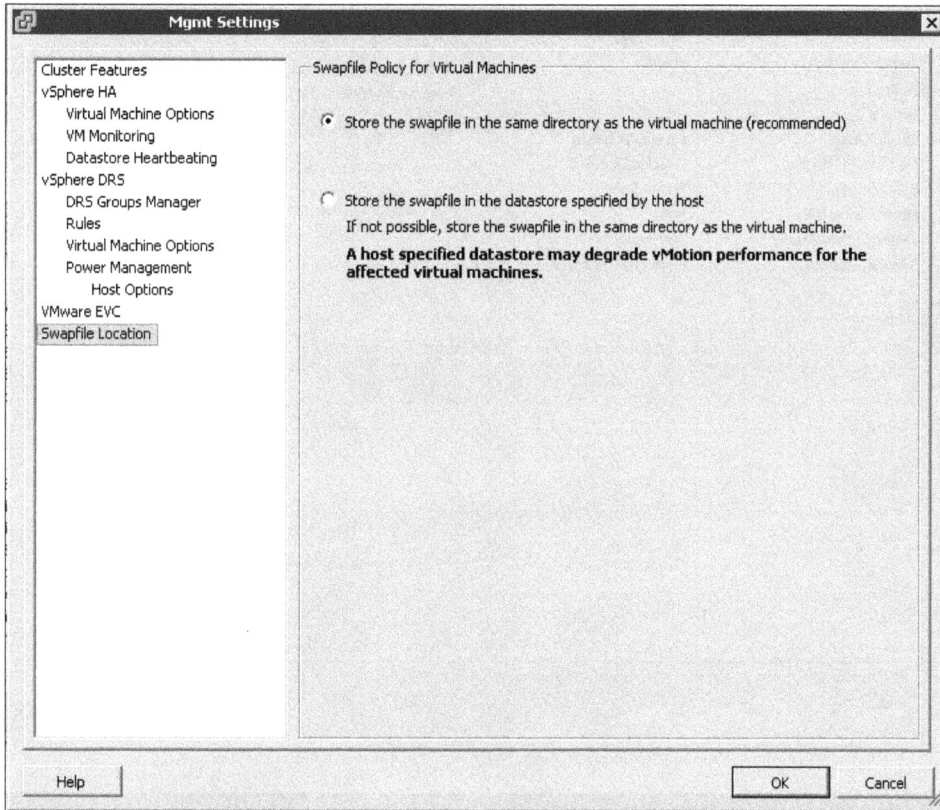

To define an alternate swap file location at the virtual machine level:

1. Right-click on the virtual machine in the inventory and select **Edit Settings**.

2. In the **Virtual Machine Properties** dialog box, click on the **Options** tab.

3. Select **Swapfile Location**.

4. Select **Store in the host's swapfile datastore** and click **OK**.

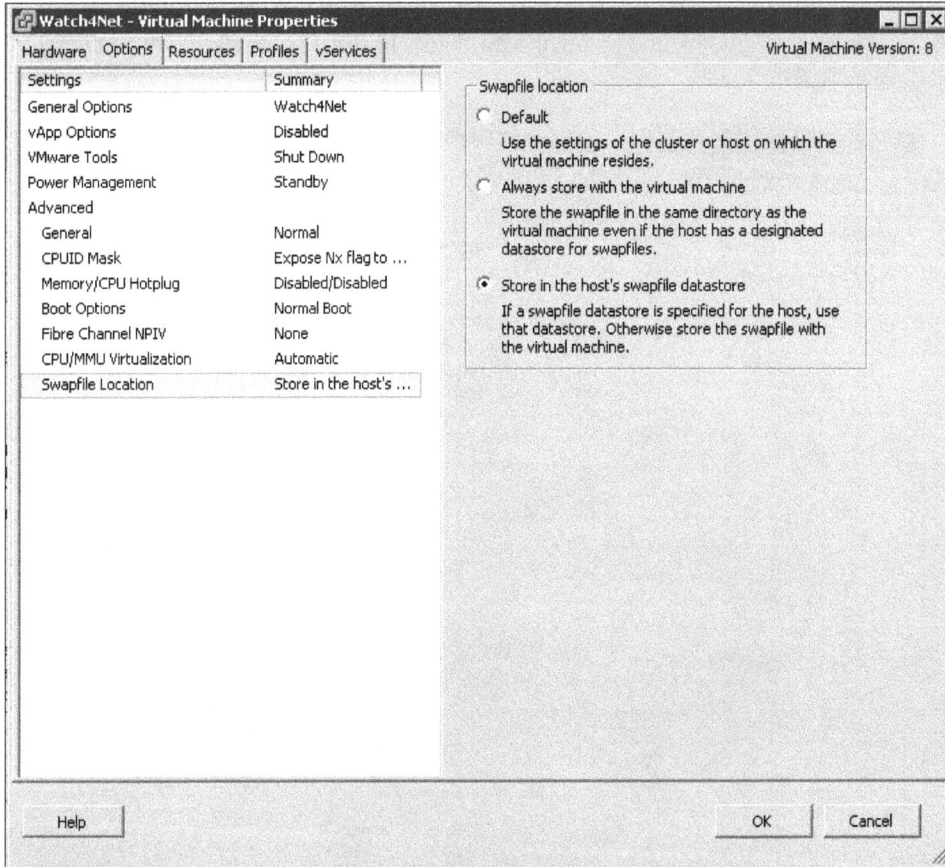

Using large pages in virtual machines

VMware ESXi provides 2MB memory pages, commonly referred to as "large pages" along with usual 4KB memory pages. ESXi will always try to allocate 2M pages for main memory and only on failure try for a 4K or small page. Virtual machines are large pages if 2M sequences of contiguous Memory Page Numbers are available. The idea is to reduce amount of page sharing and also increase the memory footprint of the virtual machines. The biggest benefit is of mitigating TLB-miss (Translation Lookaside Buffer) costs as much as possible for Nested Page Table enabled servers running ESX.

However, allocating memory in 2M chunk may cause the memory allocated to the VM to become fragmented. But as small pages are allocated by a guest and VM, these larger sequences need to be broken up.

So, if defragmentation occurs there could be enough memory to satisfy a large page request even when there is no 2M contiguous Memory Page Number's available. The defragmenter's job is to remap the existing allocated small pages in a 2M region to allow that range to be mapped with a large page.

Transparent Page Sharing runs across a host's VMs periodically (every 60 minutes by default) and reclaims identical 4KB pages. However, this only happens when there are no large pages (2MB pages). If you use large pages (2MB), TPS does not come into picture because of the "cost" of comparing these much larger pages. That is until there is memory contention, at which point the large pages are broken down into 4KB blocks and identical pages are shared.

Large pages offer performance improvements. Reclamation of large pages does not happen if there is not enough physical memory to back all of the VMs memory requests.

Memory savings happens due to TPS kick in when you run lots of VMs with very similar memory usage on a host. You will not see any memory savings until your host thinks it is under pressure which will happen if the large pages don't get shared. The host will wait until it hits 94 percent memory usage (6 percent free), before it deems itself under memory contention and starts to break those large pages into smaller 4KB ones. In a typical environment where you have many similar VMs, you are consistently going to run your host at around 94 percent memory used. All those identical memory pages can still be reclaimed, just as before, and you are gaining a performance gain of large pages.

> More information about large page support can be found in the performance study entitled *Large Page Performance* (available at `http://www.vmware.com/resources/techresources/1039`).

Getting ready

To step through this recipe, you will need one or more running ESXi Servers, a fully functioning vCenter Server, and a working installation of vSphere Client. No other prerequisites are required.

How to do it...

Configuration of large pages in the operating system and the application are outside the scope of this article. See vendor documentation for details on how to adjust these settings. The instructions on where to adjust large page settings for the ESXi 5 host to align with the needs of your guest operating system and applications are as follows:

1. From the vSphere client, open the **Hosts and Clusters** view.
2. Select a host and go to the **Configuration** tab.
3. Under **Software**, click on **Advanced Settings**.

4. Click on **Mem** and adjust the setting.

5. Click on **OK** when complete.

Set the **Mem.AllocGuestLargePage** option to **1** to enable backing of guest large pages with host large pages. Reduces TLB misses and improves performance in server workloads that use guest large pages, `0=disable`.

This configuration is default in vSphere 5.1.

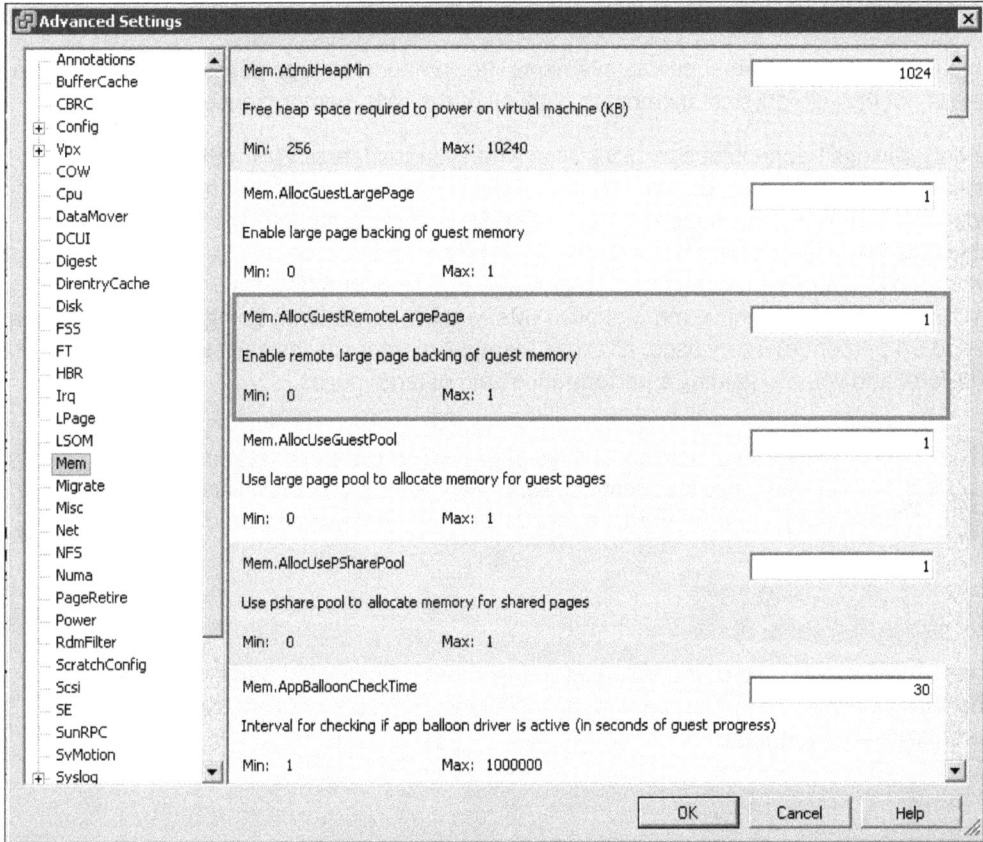

Guest OS networking considerations

Please refer to *Chapter 3, Networking Performance Design*, where the *Selecting the correct virtual network adapter* recipe talks about the tradeoff factors in choosing the correct adapter.

For the best performance, use the vmxnet3 network adapter for operating systems in which it is supported. The virtual machine must use virtual hardware version 7 or later, and VMware Tools must be installed in the guest operating system.

> ▸ If vmxnet3 is not supported in your guest operating system, use enhanced vmxnet (which requires VMware Tools). Both enhanced vmxnet (vmxnet2) and vmxnet3 support jumbo frames for better performance.

> ▸ If vmxnet2 is not supported in your guest operating system, use the flexible device type. This device type automatically converts each vlance adapter to a vmxnet adapter if VMware Tools are installed.

For the best networking performance, use network adapters that support hardware features such as TCP checksum offload, TCP segmentation offload, and jumbo frames.

Ensure that network adapters have the proper speed and duplex settings. Typically, for 10/100 NICs set the speed and duplex. Make sure that the duplex is set to full duplex. For NICS, Gigabit Ethernet or higher, set the speed and duplex to auto negotiate.

You can also choose E1000 which is an emulated version of the Intel 82545EM Gigabit Ethernet NIC. A driver for this NIC is not included with all guest operating systems. Typically Linux versions 2.4.19 and later, Windows XP Professional x64 Edition and later, and Windows Server 2003 (32-bit) and later include the E1000 driver. E1000 does not support jumbo frames prior to ESXi/ESX 4.1.

Refer to this article `http://kb.vmware.com/kb/1001805` as this article contains other known issues related to vNIC selection and OS support.

Getting ready

To step through this recipe, you will need one or more running ESXi Servers, a couple of Virtual Machines attached to the ESXi, a fully functioning vCenter Server, and a working installation of vSphere Client. No other prerequisites are required.

How to do it...

Choosing a Network Adapter based on your performance requirement can be done in two ways. One is when you are creating the Virtual Machine and the other is by using **Edit Settings** of the existing VM.

1. Open up vSphere Client and login to the vCenter Server.

2. In the **Home** screen select any ESXi Server, go to **File**, and select **New Virtual Machine**.

3. Now, after selecting the other entire configuration, go to the **Network** section.

4. Here, select the type of **Network Adapter** you want and choose which **Network Portgroup** you want to connect it to.

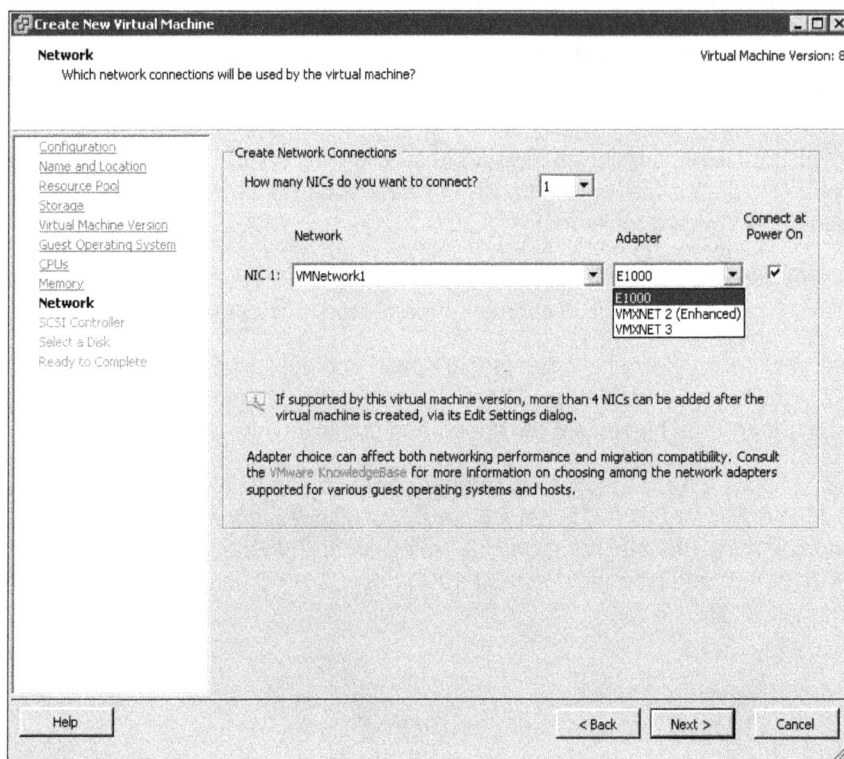

5. Now, finish the other configuration and select **Finish**.

See Also

For other advanced configurations, please refer to these links:

▶ *Configuring Flow Control on ESX and ESXi(1013413)*: `http://kb.vmware.com/selfservice/microsites/search.do?cmd=displayKC&docType=kc&docTypeID=DT_KB_1_1&externalId=1013413`

▶ *Configuring advanced driver module parameters in ESX/ESXi(1017588)*: `http://kb.vmware.com/selfservice/microsites/search.do?cmd=displayKC&docType=kc&docTypeID=DT_KB_1_1&externalId=1017588`

▶ *Modifying the rc.local or sh.local file in ESX/ESXi to execute commands while booting(2043564)*: `http://kb.vmware.com/selfservice/microsites/search.do?cmd=displayKC&docType=kc&docTypeID=DT_KB_1_1&externalId=2043564`

When you should or should not virtualize an application

Applications can be categorized into three basic groups:

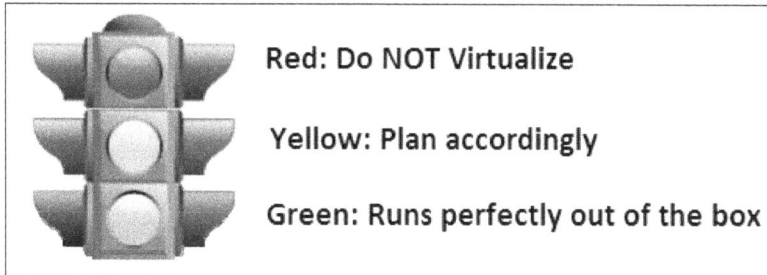

Red: Do NOT Virtualize

Yellow: Plan accordingly

Green: Runs perfectly out of the box

- ▶ **Green**: In this group, applications can be virtualized right out of the box. They have great performance with no tuning required.
- ▶ **Yellow**: In this group, applications have good performance but require some tuning and attention for optimal performance.
- ▶ **Red**: In this group, applications exceed the capabilities of the virtual platform and should not be virtualized.

The vast majority of applications are green, which means that no performance tuning is required. Yellow applications are smaller but still a significant group. There are very few red applications (that is, applications that do not virtualize).

Getting ready

To step through this recipe, you will need one or more running ESXi Servers, more than one datastore attached to the ESXi, a couple of VMs on those datastores, a vCenter Server, and a working installation of vSphere Client. No other prerequisites are required.

How to do it...

To determine which group (green, yellow, or red) your application belongs to, you need to pay attention to CPU, memory, network bandwidth, and storage bandwidth.

1. Regarding your virtual machine configuration, a virtual machine scales to 64 vCPUs. Therefore, if your enterprise application uses more than eight CPUs, or if your application requires more than 1TB of memory, you should not run the application in a virtual machine.

2. A variety of tools provide the information that you need to characterize a native application. For example, the Linux top command gives you CPU usage and the memory size of an application. The iostat and netstat commands give you I/O bandwidth information. On a Windows system, Perfmon provides you with similar counters.

Resource	Application	Category
CPU	CPU Intensive more than 64 CPUs	Green (with latest HW Technology), red
Memory	Memory Intensive greater than 1TB RAM	Green (with latest HW Technology), red
Network Bandwidth	1-27Gb/S greater than 27Gb/S	Yellow, red
Storage Bandwidth	10-250K IOPs (Consider I/O Size) greater than 250K IOPs (consider I/O size)	Yellow, red

Measuring the application's performance

To monitor performance, users look at the application itself. Various tools exist for monitoring application performance. However in this recipe we will use VMware vFabric AppInsight.

Tuning an enterprise application for performance is challenging because, to begin with, the host running the virtual machines in which these applications run might be dealing with workloads of varying characteristics. As a result, the root cause of a performance problem might end up being a combination of problems that are CPU related, memory related, networking related, and storage related.

As a system administrator, you measure performance in terms of resource utilization. From the perspective of the user, the best measurement of performance is the response time of the application itself. In addition to resource utilization metrics, there are two performance measurements that can help an application owner determine whether or not an application's performance is acceptable:

▸ Throughput

▸ Latency

Throughput refers to the number of transactions that can execute in a given amount of time. There are various ways to measure throughput: megabytes per second, IOPS, transactions per second, or instructions per second.

Latency is the measurement of how much time it takes to do a specific job. Examples are instruction completion latency, network latency, disk I/O latency, response time. Throughput and latency are often interrelated.

Application performance issues are not always related to resource utilization problems. Application performance issues can be caused by the application itself, such as malformed queries or lengthy SQL coding. In addition, application performance issues remain the same whether you are using physical hardware or virtual hardware.

VMware vFabric Application Performance Manager is a new breed of application monitoring and management solution that delivers real-time comprehensive visibility of business transactions and down to the code level. In a nutshell it is a proactive application performance management tool.

If you have a scalable cloud application then it closes the loop in response of changing business.

It has various business benefits as well such as:

 ▶ It can reduce the MTTR by correlating the changes in application layer and provides in-depth visibility.

 ▶ It supports monitoring of any application in any cloud based environments.

 ▶ Using native integration using Application Director, it can quickly bring any complex application under the radar.

 ▶ Its open architecture allows extending custom plugins to support a new platform and also allows tracking additional application metrics.

Getting ready

To step through this recipe, you will need one or more running ESXi Servers, a set of applications running within VMs (such as SharePoint, Spring Source, Postgres SQL, Python), a running instance of vFabric AppInsight, a fully functioning vCenter Server, and a working installation of vSphere Client. No other prerequisites are required.

How to do it...

1. Application Performance Manager (APM) is an enabling technology that dynamically identifies and notify on code and configuration changes. It also correlates change impact on application availability and performance and then accelerates troubleshooting or roll back negatively impacting changes.

2. So the question is how vFabric APM does the monitoring. It basically traces the application data and transaction flow and then dynamically identifies complex application traffic flows through its own back end system. vFabric APM provides a topology map which helps you to visualize the logical application structure.

3. It senses the auto scaling applications using complex workflows. This way it can reduce the MTTR (Mean Time To Resolution). Complex workflows executions help you to reduce time-consuming, error prone human interventions in maintaining your critical service levels.

4. It provides a major breakthrough in integration with VMware vCenter Server and VMware vFabric Application Director.

5. Integration with vCenter Server gives you the benefit of visualization of corresponding infrastructure health.

Index

About Packt Publishing

Packt, pronounced 'packed', published its first book "*Mastering phpMyAdmin for Effective MySQL Management*" in April 2004 and subsequently continued to specialize in publishing highly focused books on specific technologies and solutions.

Our books and publications share the experiences of your fellow IT professionals in adapting and customizing today's systems, applications, and frameworks. Our solution-based books give you the knowledge and power to customize the software and technologies you're using to get the job done. Packt books are more specific and less general than the IT books you have seen in the past. Our unique business model allows us to bring you more focused information, giving you more of what you need to know, and less of what you don't.

Packt is a modern, yet unique publishing company, which focuses on producing quality, cutting-edge books for communities of developers, administrators, and newbies alike. For more information, please visit our website: www.PacktPub.com.

About Packt Enterprise

In 2010, Packt launched two new brands, Packt Enterprise and Packt Open Source, in order to continue its focus on specialization. This book is part of the Packt Enterprise brand, home to books published on enterprise software – software created by major vendors, including (but not limited to) IBM, Microsoft and Oracle, often for use in other corporations. Its titles will offer information relevant to a range of users of this software, including administrators, developers, architects, and end users.

Writing for Packt

We welcome all inquiries from people who are interested in authoring. Book proposals should be sent to author@packtpub.com. If your book idea is still at an early stage and you would like to discuss it first before writing a formal book proposal, contact us; one of our commissioning editors will get in touch with you.

We're not just looking for published authors; if you have strong technical skills but no writing experience, our experienced editors can help you develop a writing career, or simply get some additional reward for your expertise.

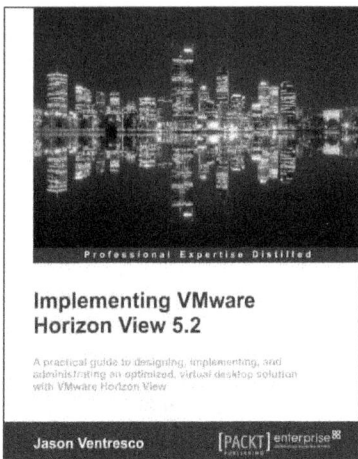

Implementing VMware Horizon View 5.2

ISBN: 978-1-84968-796-6   Paperback: 390 pages

A practical guid to designing, implementing, and administrating an optimized Virtual Desktop solution with VMware Horizon View

1. Detailed description of the deployment and administration of the VMware Horizon View suite

2. Learn how to determine the resources your virtual desktops will require

3. Design your desktop solution to avoid potential problems, and ensure minimal loss of time in the later stages

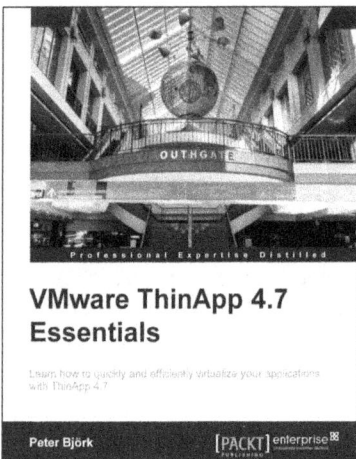

Implementing VMware Horizon View 5.2

A practical guide to designing, implementing, and administrating an optimized, virtual desktop solution with VMware Horizon View

Jason Ventresco   [PACKT] enterprise ⊠

VMware ThinApp 4.7 Essentials

ISBN: 978-1-84968-628-0   Paperback: 256 pages

Learn how to quickly and efficently virtualize your application with ThinApp 4.7

1. Practical book which provides the essentials of application virtualization with ThinApp 4.7

2. Learn the various methods and best practices of application packaging and deployment

3. Save money and time on your projects with this book by learning how to create portable applications

VMware ThinApp 4.7 Essentials

Learn how to quickly and efficiently virtualize your applications with ThinApp 4.7

Peter Björk   [PACKT] enterprise ⊠

Please check **www.PacktPub.com** for information on our titles

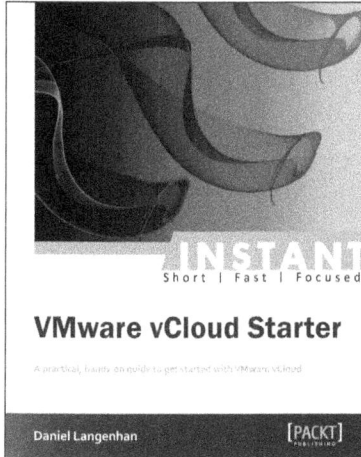

Instant VMware vCloud Starter

ISBN: 978-1-84968-996-0   Paperback: 76 pages

A Practical, hands-on guid to get started with VMware vCloud

1. Learn something new in an Instant! A short, fast, focused guide delivering immediate results.

2. Deploy and operate a VMware vCloud in your own demo kit

3. Understand the basics about the cloud in general and why there is such a hype

4. Build and use templates to quickly deploy complete environments

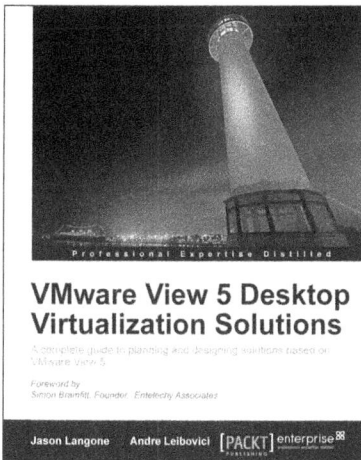

VMware View 5 Desktop Virtualization Solutions

ISBN: 978-1-84968-112-4   Paperback: 288 pages

A complete guid to planning and designing solutions based on VMware View 5

1. Written by VMware experts Jason Langone and Andre Leibovici, this book is a complete guide to planning and designing a solution based on VMware View 5

2. Secure your Visual Desktop Infrastructure (VDI) by having firewalls, antivirus, virtual enclaves, USB redirection and filtering and smart card authentication

3. Analyze the strategies and techniques used to migrate a user population from a physical desktop environment to a virtual desktop solution

Please check **www.PacktPub.com** for information on our titles